# The Bible Speaks Today

*Series Editors:* J. A. Motyer (OT)
John R. W. Stott (NT)

## The Message of the Sermon on the Mount (Matthew 5—7)

Christian Counter-Culture

*[handwritten notes:]* Celebration of discipline · Richard Foster · Masterplan of evangelism · Key Word - Nasb · Bauer-Art-Gingrich

# Titles in this series

# The Message of the Sermon on the Mount (Matthew 5—7)

## Christian Counter-Culture

**John R. W. Stott**

*Rector Emeritus of All Souls' Church, Langham Place, and*
*Director of the London Institute for Contemporary Christianity*

**Inter-Varsity Press**
Leicester, England
Downers Grove, Illinois, U.S.A.

*InterVarsity Press, USA*
*P.O. Box 1400, Downers Grove, IL 60515-1426, USA*
*World Wide Web: www.ivpress.com*
*Email: mail@ivpress.com*

*Inter-Varsity Press, England*
*38 De Montfort Street, Leicester LE1 7GP, England*
*Website: www.ivpbooks.com*
*Email: ivp@ivp-editorial.co.uk*

*InterVarsity Press*®*, USA, is the book-publishing division of InterVarsity Christian Fellowship/USA*®*, a student movement active on campus at hundreds of universities, colleges and schools of nursing in the United States of America, and a member movement of the International Fellowship of Evangelical Students. For information about local and regional activities, write Public Relations Dept., InterVarsity Christian Fellowship/USA, 6400 Schroeder Rd., P.O. Box 7895, Madison, WI 53707-7895, or visit the IVCF website at <www.intervarsity.org>.*

*Inter-Varsity Press, England, is the publishing division of the Universities and Colleges Christian Fellowship (formerly the Inter-Varsity Fellowship), a student movement linking Christian Unions in universities and colleges throughout Great Britain, and a member movement of the International Fellowship of Evangelical Students. For information about local and national activities write to UCCF, 38 De Montfort Street, Leicester LE1 7GP, email us at email@uccf.org.uk, or visit the UCCF website at www.uccf.org.uk.*

USA  *ISBN-10: 0-87784-296-5 (paperback)*
        *ISBN-13: 978-0-87784-296-5*
Series set  *ISBN-10: 0-87784-925-0*
              *ISBN-13: 978-0-87784-925-4*
   UK  *ISBN-10: 0-85111-732-5*
         *ISBN-13: 978-0-85111-732-4*

*Printed in the United States of America*

**Library of Congress Cataloging-in-Publication Data**

*Stott, John R. W.*
  *The message of the Sermon on the mount.*

  *(The Bible speaks today)*
  *Rev. ed. of: Christian counter-culture. 1978.*
  *Includes bibliographical references.*
  *1. Sermon on the Mount.  I. Christian*
*counter-culture.  II. Title.  III. Series.*
*BT380.2.S86    1985        226'.9077        84-27763*

**British Library Cataloguing in Publication Data**

*A catalogue record for this book is available from the British Library.*

| P | 39 | 38 | 37 | 36 | 35 | 34 | 33 | 32 | |
|---|----|----|----|----|----|----|----|----|---|
| Y | 20 | 19 | 18 | 17 | 16 | 15 | 14 | 13 | 12 |

# General preface

*The Bible Speaks Today* describes a series of both Old Testament and New Testament expositions, which are characterized by a threefold ideal: to expound the biblical text with accuracy, to relate it to contemporary life, and to be readable.

These books are, therefore, not 'commentaries', for the commentary seeks rather to eludicate the text than to apply it, and tends to be a work rather of reference than of literature. Nor, on the other hand, do they contain the kinds of 'sermons' which attempt to be contemporary and readable, without taking Scripture seriously enough.

The contributors to this series are all united in their convictions that God still speaks through what he has spoken, and that nothing is more necessary for the life, health and growth of Christians than that they should hear what the Spirit is saying to them through his ancient—yet ever modern—Word.

J. A. MOTYER
J. R. W. STOTT
*Series Editors*

# Contents

# Author's preface

The Sermon on the Mount has a unique fascination. It seems to present the quintessence of the teaching of Jesus. It makes goodness attractive. It shames our shabby performance. It engenders dreams of a better world.

As John Donne put it in a sermon preached during Lent 1629, not without a little pardonable hyperbole: 'All the articles of our religion, all the canons of our church, all the injunctions of our princes, all the homilies of our fathers, all the body of divinity, is in these three chapters, in this one Sermon on the Mount.'[1]

I have to confess that I have myself fallen under its spell, or rather under the spell of him who preached it. For the last seven years at least I have been constantly pondering it. In consequence, I have found my mind wrestling with its problems and my heart set on fire by the nobility of its ideals. During this period I have tried to share my thoughts and my excitement with students of Cambridge University, with other student groups in the United States and Canada, with the congregation of All Souls, Langham Place and with those thousands of eager pilgrims who came from all over the world to the 1972 Keswick Convention.

Of course commentaries by the hundred have been written on the Sermon on the Mount. I have been able to study about twenty-five of them, and my debt to the commentators will be apparent to the reader. Indeed, my text is liberally sprinkled with quotations from them, for I think we should value tradition more highly than we often do, and sit more humbly at the feet of the masters.

My aim for this exposition, in keeping with the whole *Bible speaks today* series, has been to listen carefully to the text. I have wanted above all to let it speak, or better to let Christ speak it again, and speak it to the contemporary world. So I have sought

[1] Quoted by McArthur, p. 12.

to face with integrity the dilemmas which the Sermon raises for modern Christians, and not to dodge them. For Jesus did not give us an academic treatise calculated merely to stimulate the mind. I believe he meant his Sermon on the Mount to be obeyed. Indeed, if the church realistically accepted his standards and values as here set forth, and lived by them, it would be the alternative society he always intended it to be, and would offer to the world an authentic Christian counter-culture.

I am extremely grateful to John Maile, New Testament lecturer at Spurgeon's College, London, for reading the manuscript and making some helpful suggestions, and to both Frances Whitehead and Vivienne Curry for typing it.

JOHN R. W. STOTT

# Chief abbreviations

AG
: *A Greek–English lexicon of the New Testament and other early Christian literature* by William F. Arndt and F. Wilbur Gingrich (University of Chicago Press and Cambridge University Press, 1957).

Allen
: *A critical and exegetical commentary on the Gospel according to St Matthew* by W. C. Allen (*International critical commentary*, 1907: T. and T. Clark, 3rd edition, 1912).

*Antiquities*
: *The antiquities of the Jews* in *The works of Flavius Josephus, c. AD* 75-95, translated by William Whiston (London, n.d.).

Augustine
: *Our Lord's Sermon on the Mount*, an exposition by Augustine of Hippo. Early fifth century AD. Translated by William Findlay, in the Library of Nicene and Post-Nicene Fathers, vol. VI, edited by Philip Schaff, 1887. (Eerdmans, 1974.)

AV
: The Authorized (King James') Version of the Bible, 1611.

Bonhoeffer
: *The cost of discipleship* by Dietrich Bonhoeffer (1937: 6th and complete English edition, SCM, 1959).

Bruce
: *Commentary on the synoptic Gospels* by A. B. Bruce, in *The expositor's Greek Testament*, edited by W. Robertson Nicholl (Hodder, 1897).

Calvin
: *Commentary on a harmony of the evangelists, Matthew, Mark and Luke*, I, by John Calvin (1558: translated by William Pringle, 1845: Eerdmans, n.d.).

Chrysostom
: *Homilies on the Gospel of St Matthew*, Part I, by John Chrysostom (n.d.: translated by George Prevost, Oxford, 1843).

Daube      *The New Testament and rabbinic Judaism* by David Daube (University of London, Athlone Press, 1956).

Davies      *The setting of the Sermon on the Mount* by W. D. Davies (Cambridge University Press, 1964).

Glover      *A teacher's commentary on the Gospel of St Matthew* by Richard Glover (Marshall, Morgan and Scott, 1956).

GNB      The Good News Bible (Today's English Version), (NT 1966, 4th edition 1976; OT 1976: The Bible Societies and Collins).

*Homilies*      *The second book of homilies* (1571) in *Homilies and canons* (SPCK, 1914).

Hunter      *Design for life: an exposition of the Sermon on the Mount* by A. M. Hunter (SCM, 1953; revised edition 1965).

JB      The Jerusalem Bible (Darton, Longman and Todd, 1966).

JBP      *The New Testament in Modern English* by J. B. Phillips (Collins, 1958).

Jeremias      *The Sermon on the Mount* by Joachim Jeremias (the Ethel M. Wood Lecture delivered before the University of London on 7 March 1961: University of London, Athlone Press, 1961).

Lenski      *The interpretation of St Matthew's Gospel* by R. C. H. Lenski (1943: Augsburg, 1964).

Lloyd-Jones      *Studies in the Sermon on the Mount* by D. Martyn Lloyd-Jones (IVP: vol. I, 1959, vol. II, 1960. References are to the combined edition, 1977).

Luther      *The Sermon on the Mount* by Martin Luther (1521: translated by Jaroslav Pelikan: in vol. 21 of *Luther's works*, Concordia, 1956).

McArthur      *Understanding the Sermon on the Mount* by Harvey McArthur (Harper, 1960; Epworth, 1961).

McNeile      *The Gospel according to St Matthew: the Greek text with introduction, notes and indexes* by A. H. McNeile (1915: Macmillan, 1965).

NEB      The New English Bible (NT 1961, 2nd edition 1970; OT 1970).

NIV      New International Version (NT: Hodder, 1974).

Plummer      *An exegetical commentary on the Gospel according to St Matthew* by Alfred Plummer (Elliot Stock, 1910).

RSV            The Revised Standard Version of the Bible (NT
               1946, 2nd edition 1971; OT 1952).

Ryle           *Expository thoughts on the Gospels* by J. C. Ryle
               (1856: anniversary edition of *Matthew and Mark*,
               Zondervan).

Spurgeon       *The Gospel of the kingdom* by C. H. Spurgeon
               (Passmore and Alabaster, 1893).

Stier          *The words of the Lord Jesus*, I, by Rudolf Stier,
               translated by William B. Pope, 1855 (T. and T.
               Clark, 1874).

Stonehouse     *The witness of Matthew and Mark to Christ* by N. B.
               Stonehouse (Tyndale Press, 1944; 2nd edition
               1958).

Tasker         *The Gospel according to St Matthew* by R. V. G.
               Tasker (*Tyndale New Testament Commentary*; IVP,
               1961).

Thielicke      *Life can begin again: sermons on the Sermon on the
               Mount* by Helmut Thielicke (1956: translated by
               John W. Doberstein, Fortress, 1963).

Tolstoy        *A confession, The gospel in brief* and *What I believe* by
               Leo Tolstoy (1882–1884: translated by Aylmer
               Maude in the World's Classics series, no. 229;
               Oxford University Press, new edition 1940).

*War*          *The Jewish war* in *The works of Flavius Josephus*,
               c. AD 75–95, translated by William Whiston
               (London, n.d.).

Windisch       *The meaning of the Sermon on the Mount* by Hans
               Windisch (1929: 2nd edition 1937: English trans-
               lation, Westminster, 1941).

# Matthew 5:1, 2
## Introduction: what is this sermon?

The Sermon on the Mount is probably the best-known part of the teaching of Jesus, though arguably it is the least understood, and certainly it is the least obeyed. It is the nearest thing to a manifesto that he ever uttered, for it is his own description of what he wanted his followers to be and to do. To my mind no two words sum up its intention better, or indicate more clearly its challenge to the modern world, than the expression 'Christian counterculture'. Let me tell you why.

The years which followed the end of the second world war in 1945 were marked by innocent idealism. The ghastly nightmare was over. 'Reconstruction' was the universal goal. Six years of destruction and devastation belonged to the past; the task now was to build a new world of co-operation and peace. But idealism's twin sister is disillusion—disillusion with those who do not share the ideal or (worse) who oppose it or (worse still) who betray it. And disillusion with what *is* keeps feeding the idealism of what *could be*.

We seem to have been passing through decades of disillusion. Each rising generation is disaffected with the world it has inherited. Sometimes the reaction has been naive, though that is not to say it has been insincere. The horrors of Vietnam were not brought to an end by those who gave out flowers and chalked up their slogan 'Make love not war', yet their protest did not pass unnoticed. Others today are repudiating the greedy affluence of the west which seems to grow ever fatter either by the spoliation of the natural environment or by the exploitation of developing nations or by both at once; and they register the completeness of their rejection by living simply, dressing casually, going barefoot and avoiding waste. Instead of the shams of bourgeois socializing they hunger for the authentic relationships of love. They despise the superficiality of both irreligious materialism and religious conformism, for they sense that there is an awesome 'reality' far bigger than these trivialities, and they seek this elusive 'transcendental' dimension through meditation, drugs or sex. They abominate the very concept of the rat race, and consider it more honourable to drop out than to participate. All this is symptomatic of the inability of the younger generation to accommodate themselves to the status quo or acclimatize themselves to the prevailing culture. They are not at home. They are alienated.

And in their quest for an alternative, 'counter-culture' is the word they use. It expresses a wide range of ideas and ideals, experiments and goals. Good documentations are given by Theodore Roszak in *The making of a counter-culture* (1969), by Os Guinness in *The dust of death* (1973) and by Kenneth Leech in *Youthquake* (1973).

In a way Christians find this search for a cultural alternative one of the most hopeful, even exciting, signs of the times. For we recognize in it the activity of that Spirit who before he is the comforter is the disturber, and we know to whom their quest will lead them if it is ever to find fulfilment. Indeed, it is significant that when Theodore Roszak is fumbling for words to express the reality for which contemporary youth is seeking, alienated as it is by the scientist's insistence on 'objectivity', he feels obliged to resort to the words of Jesus: 'What does it profit a man that he should gain the whole world but lose his soul?'[1]

Yet alongside the hope which this mood of protest and quest inspires in Christians, there is also (or should be) a sense of shame. For if today's young people are looking for the right things (meaning, peace, love, reality), they are looking for them in the wrong places. The first place to which they should be able to turn is the one place which they normally ignore, namely the church. For too often what they see in the church is not counter-culture but conformism, not a new society which embodies their ideals but another version of the old society which they have renounced, not life but death. They would readily endorse today what Jesus said of a church in the first century: 'You have the name of being alive, and you are dead.'[2]

---

[1] *The making of a counter-culture* (Anchor Books, Doubleday, 1969), p. 233.
[2] Rev. 3:1.

It is urgent that we not only see but feel the greatness of this tragedy. For insofar as the church is conformed to the world, and the two communities appear to the onlooker to be merely two versions of the same thing, the church is contradicting its true identity. No comment could be more hurtful to the Christian than the words, 'But you are no different from anybody else.'

For the essential theme of the whole Bible from beginning to end is that God's historical purpose is to call out a people for himself; that this people is a 'holy' people, set apart from the world to belong to him and to obey him; and that its vocation is to be true to its identity, that is, to be 'holy' or 'different' in all its outlook and behaviour.

This is how God put it to the people of Israel soon after he had rescued them from their Egyptian slavery and made them his special people by covenant: 'I am the Lord your God. You shall not do as they do in the land of Egypt, where you dwelt, and you shall not do as they do in the land of Canaan, to which I am bringing you. You shall not walk in their statutes. You shall do my ordinances and keep my statutes and walk in them. I am the Lord your God.'[1] This appeal of God to his people, it will be noted, began and ended with the statement that he was the Lord their God. It was because he was their covenant God, and because they were his special people, that they were to be different from everybody else. They were to follow his commandments and not take their lead from the standards of those around them.

Throughout the centuries which followed, the people of Israel kept forgetting their uniqueness as the people of God. Although in Balaam's words they were 'a people dwelling alone, and not reckoning itself among the nations', yet in practice they kept becoming assimilated to the people around them: 'They mingled with the nations and learned to do as they did.'[2] So they demanded a king to govern them 'like all the nations', and when Samuel remonstrated with them on the ground that God was their king, they were stubborn in their insistence: 'No! but we will have a king over us, that we also may be like all the nations.'[3] Worse even than the inauguration of the monarchy was their idolatry. 'Let us be like the nations,' they said to themselves, '... and worship wood and stone.'[4] So God kept sending his prophets to them to remind them who they were and to plead

[1] Lv. 18:1–4.    [2] Nu. 23:9; Ps. 106:35.
[3] 1 Sa. 8:5, 19, 20.    [4] Ezk. 20:32.

17

with them to follow his way. 'Learn not the way of the nations,' he said to them through Jeremiah, and through Ezekiel, 'Do not defile yourselves with the idols of Egypt; I am the Lord your God.'[1] But God's people would not listen to his voice, and the specific reason given why his judgment fell first upon Israel and then nearly 150 years later upon Judah was the same: 'The people of Israel had sinned against the Lord their God . . . and had . . . walked in the customs of the nations. . . . Judah also did not keep the commandments of the Lord their God, but walked in the customs which Israel had introduced.'[2]

All this is an essential background to any understanding of the Sermon on the Mount. The Sermon is found in Matthew's Gospel towards the beginning of Jesus' public ministry. Immediately after his baptism and temptation he had begun to announce the good news that the kingdom of God, long promised in the Old Testament era, was now on the threshold. He himself had come to inaugurate it. With him the new age had dawned, and the rule of God had broken into history. 'Repent,' he cried, 'for the kingdom of heaven is at hand.'[3] Indeed, 'He went about all Galilee, teaching in their synagogues and preaching the gospel of the kingdom' (23). The Sermon on the Mount, then, is to be seen in this context. It portrays the repentance (*metanoia*, the complete change of mind) and the righteousness which belong to the kingdom. That is, it describes what human life and human community look like when they come under the gracious rule of God.

And what do they look like? Different! Jesus emphasized that his true followers, the citizens of God's kingdom, were to be entirely different from others. They were not to take their cue from the people around them, but from him, and so prove to be genuine children of their heavenly Father. To me the key text of the Sermon on the Mount is 6:8: 'Do not be like them.' It is immediately reminiscent of God's word to Israel in olden days: 'You shall not do as they do.'[4] It is the same call to be different. And right through the Sermon on the Mount this theme is elaborated. Their character was to be completely distinct from that admired by the world (the beatitudes). They were to shine

---

[1] Je. 10:1, 2; Ezk. 20:7.
[2] 2 Ki. 17:7, 8, 19; *cf.* Ezk. 5:7; 11:12.
[3] Mt. 4:17.
[4] Lv. 18:3.

like lights in the prevailing darkness. Their righteousness was to exceed that of the scribes and Pharisees, both in ethical behaviour and in religious devotion, while their love was to be greater and their ambition nobler than those of their pagan neighbours.

There is no single paragraph of the Sermon on the Mount in which this contrast between Christian and non-Christian standards is not drawn. It is the underlying and uniting theme of the Sermon; everything else is a variation of it. Sometimes it is the Gentiles or pagan nations with whom Jesus contrasts his followers. Thus pagans love and salute each other, but Christians are to love their enemies (5:44–47); pagans pray after a fashion, 'heaping up empty phrases', but Christians are to pray with the humble thoughtfulness of children to their Father in heaven (6:7–13); pagans are preoccupied with their own material necessities, but Christians are to seek first God's rule and righteousness (6:32, 33).

At other times Jesus contrasts his disciples not with Gentiles but with Jews, not (that is) with heathen people but with religious people, in particular with the 'scribes and Pharisees'. Professor Jeremias is no doubt right to distinguish between these as 'two quite different groups' in that 'the scribes are the theological teachers who have had some years of education, the Pharisees on the other hand are not theologians, but rather groups of pious laymen from every part of the community'.[1] Certainly Jesus sets Christian morals over against the ethical casuistry of the scribes (5:21–48) and Christian devotion over against the hypocritical piety of the Pharisees (6:1–18).

Thus the followers of Jesus are to be different—different from both the nominal church and the secular world, different from both the religious and the irreligious. The Sermon on the Mount is the most complete delineation anywhere in the New Testament of the Christian counter-culture. Here is a Christian value-system, ethical standard, religious devotion, attitude to money, ambition, life-style and network of relationships—all of which are totally at variance with those of the non-Christian world. And this Christian counter-culture is the life of the kingdom of God, a fully human life indeed but lived out under the divine rule.

We come now to Matthew's editorial introduction to the

[1] P. 23.

Sermon, which is brief but impressive; it indicates the importance which he attached to it.

*Seeing the crowds, he went up on the mountain, and when he sat down his disciples came to him. And he opened his mouth and taught them (5:1, 2).*

There can be little doubt that Jesus' main purpose in going up a hill or mountain to teach was to withdraw from the 'great crowds . . . from Galilee and the Decapolis and Jerusalem and Judea and from beyond the Jordan'[1] who had been following him. He had spent the early months of his public ministry wandering throughout Galilee, 'teaching in their synagogues and preaching the gospel of the kingdom and healing every disease and every infirmity among the people'. As a result, 'his fame spread throughout all Syria', and people came in large numbers bringing their sick to be healed.[2] So he had to escape, not just to secure for himself the opportunity to be quiet and to pray, but also to give more concentrated instruction to his disciples.

Further, it seems likely (as many commentators ancient and modern have suggested) that he deliberately *went up on the mountain* to teach, in order to draw a parallel between Moses who received the law at Mount Sinai and himself who explained its implications to his disciples on the so-called 'Mount of the Beatitudes', the traditional site of the Sermon on the northern shores of the Lake of Galilee. For, although Jesus was greater than Moses and although his message was more gospel than law, yet he did choose twelve apostles as the nucleus of a new Israel to correspond to the twelve patriarchs and tribes of the old. He also claimed to be both teacher and lord, gave his own authoritative interpretation of Moses' law, issued commandments and expected obedience. He even later invited his disciples to assume his 'yoke' or submit to his teaching, as they had previously borne the yoke of Torah.[3]

Some scholars have constructed very elaborate schemes to demonstrate this parallel. B. W. Bacon in 1918, for example, argued that Matthew deliberately structured his Gospel in five sections, each ending with the formula 'when Jesus had finished. . . .'

[1] 4:25.
[2] 4:23, 24.
[3] Mt. 11:29, 30.

(7:28; 11:1; 13:53; 19:1; 26:1), in order that the 'five books of Matthew' might correspond to the 'five books of Moses' and so be a kind of New Testament Pentateuch.[1]

A different parallelism was suggested by Austin Farrer, namely that Matthew 5–7 was modelled on Exodus 20–24, the eight beatitudes corresponding to the ten commandments, with the rest of the Sermon expounding and applying them as the commandments were also expounded and applied.[2]

These ingenious attempts to find parallels are understandable because in many passages of the New Testament the saving work of Jesus is pictured as a new exodus,[3] and the Christian life as a joyful celebration of it: 'For Christ, our paschal lamb, has been sacrificed. Let us, therefore, celebrate the festival.'[4] Yet Matthew does not explicitly liken Jesus to Moses, and we cannot legitimately claim more than that in the Sermon 'the *substance* of the New Law, the New Sinai, the New Moses are present.'[5]

At all events, Jesus *sat down*, assuming the posture of a rabbi or legislator, and *his disciples came to him*, to listen to his teaching. Then *he opened his mouth* (an expression indicating the solemnity of his utterance) *and taught them*.

Three basic questions immediately form in the mind of a modern reader who studies the Sermon on the Mount. He is not likely to be receptive to its teaching unless he is given satisfactory answers to these questions. First, is the Sermon on the Mount an authentic utterance of Jesus? Did he really preach it? Secondly, are its contents relevant to the contemporary world, or are they hopelessly out of date? Thirdly, are its standards attainable, or must we dismiss them as a largely unpractical ideal?

### 1. Is the Sermon authentic?

The Sermon on the Mount occurs only in the first Gospel (Matthew's). In the third Gospel (Luke's) there is a similar sermon, sometimes called 'the Sermon on the Plain'.[6] Luke says it was delivered 'on a level place' to which Jesus 'came down' after

---

[1] B. W. Bacon's theory is summarized and criticized by W. D. Davies, pp. 15–25.

[2] Austin Farrer's theory is criticized by W.D. Davies on pp. 9–13.

[3] *Cf.* Mt. 2:15.

[4] 1 Cor. 5:7, 8.

[5] Davies, p. 108.

[6] Lk. 6:17–49.

MATTHEW 5:1, 2

having gone 'into the hills' to pray.[1] But the apparent difference
of location need not detain us, for the 'level place' may well have
been not a plain or valley but a plateau in the hills.

✷ A comparison of the contents of the two sermons reveals at
once that they are not identical. Luke's is considerably shorter,
consisting of only 30 verses in contrast to Matthew's 107, and
each includes material absent from the other. Nevertheless, there
are also obvious similarities between them. Both sermons begin
with 'beatitudes', end with the parable of the two housebuilders,
and in between contain the golden rule, the commands to love
our enemies and to turn the other cheek, the prohibition against
judging people, and the vivid illustrations of the log or speck in
the eye and of the tree and its fruit. This common material, with a
common beginning and ending, suggests that the two are versions of the same sermon. What, however, is the relation between
the two? How are we to explain the combination of similarities
and variations?

✷ Many have denied that the Sermon on the Mount was ever in
any meaningful sense a 'sermon' preached by Jesus on a particular
occasion. It is a well-known feature of the first evangelist's
editorial practice to bring together into a collection some of the
related teachings of Jesus. The best example is his series of seven
of our Lord's parables.[2] Some have argued, therefore, that
Matthew 5 to 7 represent an accumulation of the sayings of Jesus,
skilfully woven into the form of a sermon by the evangelist, or by
an early Christian community from which he took it. Even
Calvin believed this: 'The design of both Evangelists was to
collect into one place the leading points of the doctrine of Christ
which related to a devout and holy life.'[3] As a result, the Sermon
is 'a brief summary . . . collected out of his many and various
discourses'.[4]

Some modern commentators have been more outspoken. One
example may be sufficient. W. D. Davies calls the Sermon 'merely
a collection of unrelated sayings of diverse origins, a patchwork',
and after a rehearsal of source criticism, form criticism and liturgical criticism, he concludes: 'Thus the impact of recent criticism
in all its forms is to cast doubt on the propriety of seeking to
understand this section . . . as an interrelated totality derived
from the actual teaching of Jesus.'[5] He later concedes that the

[1] Lk. 6:12, 17.    [2] Mt. 13.
[3] P. 258.    [4] P. 259.    [5] Pp. 1, 5.

tide has turned towards so-called redaction criticism, which at least credits the evangelists themselves with being real authors who shaped the tradition they preserve. Nevertheless, he remains sceptical as to how much original teaching of Jesus is contained in the Sermon on the Mount.

How one reacts to this kind of literary criticism depends on one's fundamental theological presuppositions about God himself, the nature and purpose of his revelation in Christ, the work of the Holy Spirit and the evangelist's sense of truth. Personally, I find it hard to accept any view of the Sermon which attributes its contents rather to the early church than to Jesus, or even regards it as an amalgam of his sayings drawn from various occasions. The main reason is that both Matthew and Luke present their material as a sermon of Christ, and appear to intend their readers to understand it as such. Both give it a precise historical and geographical context, ascribing it to his early ministry in Galilee and stating that he delivered it 'on the mountain' or 'on a level place' in the hills. Matthew records the astonished reaction of the crowds when he had finished, especially because of the authority with which he had spoken.[1] And both say that, when it was over, 'he entered Capernaum'.[2]

This does not mean, however, that both evangelists give us the *ipsissima verba* of the whole sermon. Clearly they do not, for in any case Jesus spoke in Aramaic, and both Gospels provide a Greek translation. Besides, as we have seen, their versions differ from each other. There are several possible ways of explaining this. Either both give their individual selections and translations, whether from a common source or from independent sources. Or Luke gives a briefer summary, omitting a good deal, while Matthew records more if not most of it. Or Matthew elaborates an originally shorter sermon, enlarging it by adding from other contexts authentic and appropriate utterances of Jesus. We could still assert that the Holy Spirit directed the selection and arrangement.

For myself I prefer a suggestion which Professor A. B. Bruce made in his commentary of 1897. He believed that the material contained in Matthew 5 to 7 represents the instruction 'not of a single hour or day, but of a period of retirement'.[3] He conjectured

[1] 7:28, 29.
[2] Mt. 8:5; Lk. 7:1.
[3] P. 94.

that Jesus might have had his disciples with him on the mountain for a kind of 'holiday Summer School'. So he referred to these chapters not as 'our Lord's Sermon on the Mount' (an expression first used by Augustine) but as 'the Teaching on the Hill'.[1] Moreover, the Sermon as recorded in Matthew would have lasted only about ten minutes, so presumably what the evangelists give us is their own condensed summaries.

## 2. Is the Sermon relevant?

Whether the Sermon is relevant to modern life or not can be judged only by a detailed examination of its contents. What is immediately striking is that, however it came to be composed, it forms a wonderfully coherent whole. It depicts the behaviour which Jesus expected of each of his disciples, who is also thereby a citizen of God's kingdom. We see him as he is in himself, in his heart, motives and thoughts, and in the secret place with his Father. We also see him in the arena of public life, in his relations with his fellow men, showing mercy, making peace, being persecuted, acting like salt, letting his light shine, loving and serving others (even his enemies), and devoting himself above all to the extension of God's kingdom and righteousness in the world. Perhaps a brief analysis of the Sermon will help to demonstrate its relevance to ourselves in the twentieth century.

### a. A Christian's character (5:3–12)
The beatitudes emphasize eight principal marks of Christian character and conduct, especially in relation to God and to men, and the divine blessing which rests on those who exhibit these marks.

### b. A Christian's influence (5:13–16)
The two metaphors of salt and light indicate the influence for good which Christians will exert in the community if (and only if) they maintain their distinctive character as portrayed in the beatitudes.

### c. A Christian's righteousness (5:17–48)
What is to be a Christian's attitude to the moral law of God? Is the very category of law abolished in the Christian life, as the

[1] P. 95.

advocates of the 'new morality' and of the 'not under law' school strangely assert? No. Jesus had not come to abolish the law and the prophets, he said, but to fulfil them. He went on to state both that greatness in God's kingdom was determined by conformity to their moral teaching, and even that entry into the kingdom was impossible without a righteousness greater than that of the scribes and Pharisees (5:17-20). Of this greater Christian righteousness he then gave six illustrations (5:21-48), relating to murder, adultery, divorce, swearing, revenge and love. In each antithesis ('You have heard that it was said . . . but I say to you . . .') he rejected the easy-going tradition of the scribes, reaffirmed the authority of Old Testament Scripture and drew out the full and exacting implications of God's moral law.

### d. A Christian's piety (6:1-18)
In their 'piety' or religious devotion Christians are to resemble neither the hypocritical display of the Pharisees nor the mechanical formalism of pagans. Christian piety is to be marked above all by reality, by the sincerity of God's children who live in their heavenly Father's presence.

### e. A Christian's ambition (6:19-34)
The 'worldliness' which Christians are to avoid can take either a religious or a secular shape. So we are to differ from non-Christians not only in our devotions, but also in our ambitions. In particular, Christ changes our attitude to material wealth and possessions. It is impossible to worship both God and money; we have to choose between them. Secular people are preoccupied with the quest for food, drink and clothing. Christians are to be free of these self-centred material anxieties and instead to give themselves to the spread of God's rule and God's righteousness. That is to say, our supreme ambition is to be the glory of God, and neither our own glory nor even our own material well-being. It is a question of what we 'seek first'.

### f. A Christian's relationships (7:1-20)
Christians are caught up in a complex network of relationships, each of which arises from our relation to Christ. Once we are properly related to him, our other relationships are all affected. New relationships are created; old relationships are changed. Thus, we are not to judge our brother but to serve him (1-5). We

are also to avoid offering the gospel to those who have decisively rejected it (6), to keep praying to our heavenly Father (7–12) and to beware of false prophets who hinder people from finding the narrow gate and the hard way (13–20).

### g. *A Christian's commitment* (7:21–27)

The ultimate issue posed by the whole Sermon concerns the authority of the preacher. It is not enough either to call him 'Lord' (21–23) or to listen to his teaching (24–27). The basic question is whether we *mean* what we say and *do* what we hear. On this commitment hangs our eternal destiny. Only the man who obeys Christ as Lord is wise. For only he is building his house on a foundation of rock, which the storms neither of adversity nor of judgment will be able to undermine.

The crowds were astonished by the authority with which Jesus taught (28, 29). It is an authority to which the followers of Jesus in every generation must submit. The issue of the lordship of Christ is as relevant today, both in principle and in detailed application, as when he originally preached his Sermon on the Mount.

### 3. Is the Sermon practical?

This third question is that of the pragmatist. It is one thing to be convinced of the Sermon's relevance in theory, but quite another to be sure that it will work in practice. Are its standards attainable? Or must we rest content with admiring them wistfully from afar?

⁜ Perhaps a majority of readers and commentators, looking the reality of human perversity in the face, have declared the standards of the Sermon on the Mount to be unattainable. Its ideals are noble but unpractical, they say, attractive to imagine but impossible to fulfil. They know something of man's self-assertive egoism; how then can he be meek? They know his imperious sexual passion; how then can he refrain from lustful looks and thoughts? They know his absorption in the cares of the world; how then can he be forbidden to worry? They know his proneness to anger and his thirst for revenge; how then can he be expected to love his enemies? More than this. Is not the requirement to turn the other cheek to an assailant as dangerous to the health of society as it is beyond the attainment of the individual?

To invite further violence in this way not only leaves it unchecked, but actively encourages it. No. The Sermon on the Mount is of no practical value to either individuals or communities. At best, it represents the unpractical idealism of a visionary. It is a dream which could never come true.

A modification of this view, first expressed by Johannes Weiss in 1892 and later popularized by Albert Schweitzer, is that Jesus was making exceptional demands for an exceptional situation. Because they believed that Jesus was expecting the end of history to arrive almost immediately, they argued that he was giving his disciples an 'interim ethic', which required them to make total sacrifices like leaving their possessions and loving their enemies—sacrifices appropriate only for that moment of crisis. In this case the Sermon on the Mount becomes a kind of 'martial law',[1] which only a major emergency could justify. It is emphatically not an ethic for every day.

And there have been many other attempts to accommodate the Sermon on the Mount to the low levels of our moral attainment. In the fourth and fifth chapters of his book *Understanding the Sermon on the Mount*, Harvey McArthur first surveys and then evaluates no fewer than twelve different ways of interpreting the Sermon.[2] He says he might well have subtitled this section 'Versions and Evasions of the Sermon on the Mount', for all but one of the twelve interpretations offer prudential qualifications of its apparently absolute demands.

At the opposite extreme are those superficial souls who glibly assert that the Sermon on the Mount expresses ethical standards which are self-evidently true, common to all religions and easy to follow. 'I live by the Sermon on the Mount,' they say. The most charitable reaction to such people is to assume that they have never read the Sermon which they so confidently dismiss as commonplace. Quite different (although he too believed the Sermon had been preached in order to be obeyed) was Leo Tolstoy. True, he knew himself to be an abysmal failure, but he retained a belief that the precepts of Jesus could be practised, and he put his conviction into the lips of Prince Nekhlyudov, the hero of his last great novel *Resurrection*, which was published in 1899–1900.

---

[1] The expression is that of Jeremias (p. 14).
[2] Pp. 105–148.

Tolstoy's prince is generally recognized as a portrait of himself, and a thinly disguised one at that. At the end of the novel Nekhlyudov re-read the Gospel of Matthew. He saw in the Sermon on the Mount 'not beautiful abstract thoughts, presenting for the most part exaggerated and impossible demands, but simple, clear, practical commandments, which if obeyed (and this was quite feasible) would establish a completely new order of human society, in which the violence that filled Nekhlyudov with such indignation would not only cease of itself, but the greatest blessing man can hope for—the kingdom of heaven on earth—would be attained'.

Nekhlyudov sat staring at the light of the lamp that burned low, and his heart stopped beating. Recalling all the monstrous confusion of the life we lead, he pictured to himself what this life might be like if people were taught to obey these commandments, and his soul was swept by an ecstasy such as he had not felt for many a day. It was as though, after long pining and suffering, he had suddenly found peace and liberation.

He did not sleep that night, and as happens to vast numbers who read the Gospels, he understood for the first time the full meaning of words read and passed over innumerable times in the past. Like a sponge soaking up water he drank in all the vital, important and joyous news which the book revealed to him. And everything he read seemed familiar to him, confirming and making real what he had long known but had never fully understood nor really believed. But now he understood and believed . . .

He said to himself: 'Seek ye first the kingdom of God, and his righteousness; and all these things shall be added unto you. But we seek all these things and obviously fail to attain them.

'This, then, must be my life's work. One task is completed and another is ready to my hand.'

That night an entirely new life began for Nekhlyudov, not so much because he had entered into new conditions of life but because everything that happened to him from that time on was endowed with an entirely different meaning for him. How this new chapter of his life will end, the future will show.[1]

Tolstoy embodied in himself the tension between the ideal and

[1] Penguin Classics, 1966, pp. 566-568.

the reality. For on the one hand he was convinced that to obey the Sermon on the Mount was 'quite feasible', while on the other hand his own mediocre performance told him that it was not. The truth lies in neither extreme position. For the standards of the Sermon are neither readily attainable by every man, nor totally unattainable by any man. To put them beyond anybody's reach is to ignore the purpose of Christ's Sermon; to put them within everybody's is to ignore the reality of man's sin. They are attainable all right, but only by those who have experienced the new birth which Jesus told Nicodemus was the indispensable condition of seeing and entering God's kingdom. For the righteousness he described in the Sermon is an inner righteousness. Although it manifests itself outwardly and visibly in words, deeds and relationships, yet it remains essentially a righteousness of the heart. It is what a man thinks in his heart and where he fixes his heart[1] which really matter. It is here too that the problem lies. For men are in their nature 'evil'.[2] It is out of their heart that evil things come[3] and out of their heart that their mouth speaks, just as it is the tree which determines its fruit. So there is but one solution: 'Make the tree good, and its fruit good'.[4] A new birth is essential.

Only a belief in the necessity and the possibility of a new birth can keep us from reading the Sermon on the Mount with either foolish optimism or hopeless despair. Jesus spoke the Sermon to those who were already his disciples and thereby also the citizens of God's kingdom and the children of God's family.[5] The high standards he set are appropriate only to such. We do not, indeed could not, achieve this privileged status by attaining Christ's standards. Rather by attaining his standards, or at least approximating to them, we give evidence of what by God's free grace and gift we already are.

[1] Cf. Mt. 5:28; 6:21.
[2] Mt. 7:11.
[3] Cf. Mk. 7:21–23.
[4] Mt. 7:16–20; 12:33–37.
[5] E.g. 5:16, 48; 6:9, 32, 33; 7:11.

# Matthew 5:3-12

# A Christian's character: the beatitudes

[3] *Blessed are the poor in spirit, for theirs is the kingdom of heaven.*
[4] *Blessed are those who mourn, for they shall be comforted.*
[5] *Blessed are the meek, for they shall inherit the earth.*
[6] *Blessed are those who hunger and thirst for righteousness, for they shall be satisfied.*
[7] *Blessed are the merciful, for they shall obtain mercy.*
[8] *Blessed are the pure in heart, for they shall see God.*
[9] *Blessed are the peacemakers, for they shall be called sons of God.*
[10] *Blessed are those who are persecuted for righteousness' sake, for theirs is the kingdom of heaven.*
[11] *Blessed are you when men revile you and persecute you and utter all kinds of evil against you falsely on my account.* [12] *Rejoice and be glad, for your reward is great in heaven, for so men persecuted the prophets who were before you.*

Everybody who has ever heard of Jesus of Nazareth, and knows anything at all of his teaching, must surely be familiar with the beatitudes with which the Sermon on the Mount begins. Their simplicity of word and profundity of thought have attracted each fresh generation of Christians, and many others besides. The more we explore their implications, the more seems to remain unexplored. Their wealth is inexhaustible. We cannot plumb their depths. Truly, 'We are near heaven here.'[1]

Before we are ready to consider each beatitude separately, there are three general questions about them which need to be asked. These concern the people described, the qualities commended and the blessings promised.

[1] Bruce, p. 95.

## a. The people described

The beatitudes set forth the balanced and variegated character of Christian people. These are not eight separate and distinct groups of disciples, some of whom are meek, while others are merciful and yet others are called upon to endure persecution. They are rather eight qualities of the same group who at one and the same time are meek and merciful, poor in spirit and pure in heart, mourning and hungry, peacemakers and persecuted.

Further, the group exhibiting these marks is not an élitist set, a small spiritual aristocracy remote from the common run of Christians. On the contrary, the beatitudes are Christ's own specification of what every Christian ought to be. All these qualities are to characterize all his followers. Just as the ninefold fruit of the Spirit which Paul lists is to ripen in every Christian character, so the eight beatitudes which Christ speaks describe his ideal for every citizen of God's kingdom. Unlike the gifts of the Spirit which he distributes to different members of Christ's body in order to equip them for different kinds of service, the same Spirit is concerned to work all these Christian graces in us all. There is no escape from our responsibility to covet them all.

## b. The qualities commended

It is well known that there is at least a verbal discrepancy between the beatitudes in Matthew's Gospel and those in Luke's. Thus, Luke writes 'Blessed are you poor', while Matthew has 'Blessed are the poor in spirit'. Again, Luke's 'Blessed are you who hunger now' is recorded by Matthew as 'Blessed are those who hunger and thirst for righteousness'.

In consequence of this, some have argued that Luke's version is the true one; that Jesus was making a social or sociological judgment about the poor and the hungry; that he was promising the undernourished food and the proletariat riches in the kingdom of God; and that Matthew spiritualized what were originally material pledges.

But this is an impossible interpretation, unless we are prepared to believe either that Jesus contradicted himself or that the evangelists were clumsy enough to make him appear to do so. For in the Judean desert, in the temptations which Matthew narrates in the previous chapter, Jesus had refused to turn stones into bread, and had repudiated the idea of establishing a material kingdom. Consistently throughout his ministry he rejected the same temptation. When the feeding of the five thousand prompted the crowd 'to come and take him by force to make him king', Jesus immediately withdrew into the hills by himself.[1] And when Pilate asked him if there was any substance in the Jewish leaders' charges against him and whether in fact he had any political ambitions, his reply was unambiguous: 'My kingship is not of this world.'[2] That is, it has a different origin and therefore a different character.

To say this is not to suggest that Jesus was indifferent to physical poverty and hunger. On the contrary, he had compassion on the needy and fed the hungry, and he told his followers to do the same. Yet the blessing of his kingdom was not primarily one of economic advantage.

Further, if he was not offering physical relief immediately, neither was he promising it in a future heaven and meanwhile pronouncing the poor and the hungry 'blessed'. To be sure, in some circumstances God can use poverty as a means to spiritual blessing, just as wealth can be a hindrance to it. But this does not make poverty in itself a desirable condition which Jesus blesses. The church has always been wrong whenever it has used the first beatitude either to condone the poverty of the masses, or to commend the voluntary poverty of monks and others who have taken a vow to renounce possessions. Christ may indeed still call some to a life of poverty, but his call cannot justly be heard through this beatitude.

No. The poverty and hunger to which Jesus refers in the beatitudes are spiritual states. It is 'the poor *in spirit*' and 'those who hunger and thirst *for righteousness*' whom he declares blessed. And it is safe to deduce from this that the other qualities he mentions are spiritual also. It is true that the Aramaic word Jesus used may have been simply 'poor', as in Luke's version. But then 'the poor', God's poor, were already a clearly defined group in the Old Testament, and Matthew will have been correct to translate 'poor in spirit'. For 'the poor' were not so much the poverty stricken as the pious who—partly because they were needy, downtrodden, oppressed or in other ways afflicted—had put their faith and hope in God.

[1] Jn. 6:15.
[2] Jn. 18:36.

*c. The blessings promised*

Each quality is commended, inasmuch as each person who exhibits it is pronounced 'blessed'. The Greek word *makarios* can and does mean 'happy'. So JBP translates the opening words of each beatitude, 'How happy are... !' And several commentators have explained them as Jesus' prescription for human happiness. The most ingenious attempt I know was made by Ernest M. Ligon of the Department of Psychology, Union College, Schenectady, New York, in his book *The psychology of Christian personality*.[1] Acknowledging his debt to Harry Emerson Fosdick, he sets out to interpret the Sermon on the Mount 'from the point of view of mental health' (p. vii). 'The most significant mistake that men have made in interpreting these verses of Jesus (*sc.* the beatitudes)', he writes, 'is the failure to note the first word in each of them, *happy*.'[2] In his view they 'constitute Jesus' theory of happiness'.[3] They are not so much ethical duties as 'a series of eight fundamental emotional attitudes. If a man reacts to his environment in the spirit of them, his life will be a happy one,'[4] for he will have discovered the basic 'formula for mental health'.[5] In particular, according to Dr Ligon, the Sermon emphasizes the 'forces' of faith and love, 'experimental faith' and 'fatherly love'. These two principles are indispensable for the development of 'strong and healthy personalities'.[6] Not only may the chaos of fear be overcome by faith and destructive anger by love, but also 'the inferiority complex and its many byproducts' by the Golden Rule.[7]

There is no need to dismiss this interpretation as entirely fallacious. For nobody knows better than our Creator how we may become truly human beings. He made us. He knows how we work best. It is through obeying his own moral laws that we find and fulfil ourselves. And all Christians can testify from experience that there is a close connection between holiness and happiness.

Nevertheless, it is seriously misleading to render *makarios* 'happy'. For happiness is a subjective state, whereas Jesus is making an objective judgment about these people. He is declaring not what they may feel like ('happy'), but what God thinks of them and what on that account they are: they are 'blessed'.

What is this blessing? The second half of each beatitude elucidates it. They possess the kingdom of heaven and they inherit the

---

[1] Macmillan, 1935; paperback, 1961.
[2] P. 89.   [3] P. 24.   [4] P. 27.
[5] P. 91.   [6] P. 18.   [7] Pp. 332 f.

earth. The mourners are comforted and the hungry are satisfied. They receive mercy, they see God, they are called the sons of God. Their heavenly reward is great. And all these blessings belong together. Just as the eight qualities describe every Christian (at least in the ideal), so the eight blessings are given to every Christian. True, the particular blessing promised in each case is appropriate to the particular quality mentioned. At the same time it is surely not possible to inherit the kingdom of heaven without inheriting the earth, to be comforted without being satisfied or to see God without receiving his mercy and being called his children. The eight qualities together constitute the responsibilities, and the eight blessings the privileges, of being a citizen of God's kingdom. This is what the enjoyment of God's rule means.

✗ Are these blessings present or future? Personally, I think the only possible answer is 'both'. Some commentators, however, have insisted that they are future, and have emphasized the 'eschatological' nature of the beatitudes. Certainly the second part of the last beatitude promises the persecuted a great reward in heaven, and this must be future (11). Certainly too it is only in the first and eighth beatitudes that the blessing is expressed in the present tense, 'theirs is the kingdom of heaven' (3, 10); and even then this verb was probably not there when Jesus spoke in Aramaic. The other six beatitudes contain a verb in the simple future tense ('they shall'). Nevertheless, it is plain from the rest of Jesus' teaching that the kingdom of God is a present reality which we can 'receive', 'inherit' or 'enter' now. Similarly, we can obtain mercy and comfort now, can become God's children now, and in this life can have our hunger satisfied and our thirst quenched. Jesus promised all these blessings to his followers in the here and now. The promise that we 'shall see God' may sound like a reference to the final 'beatific vision',[1] and no doubt includes it. But we already begin to see God in this life both in the person of his Christ[2] and with spiritual vision.[3] We even begin to 'inherit the earth' in this life since if we are Christ's all things are already ours, 'whether . . . the world or life or death or the present or the future'.[4]

So then the promises of Jesus in the beatitudes have both a

[1] *Cf.* 1 Cor. 13:12; Heb. 12:14; 1 Jn. 3:2; Rev. 22:4.
[2] Jn. 14:9.
[3] 1 Jn. 3:6; 3 Jn. 11.
[4] 1 Cor. 3:22, 23.

present and a future fulfilment. We enjoy the firstfruits now; the full harvest is yet to come. And, as Professor Tasker rightly points out, 'The future tense . . . emphasizes their certainty and not merely their futurity. The mourners will *indeed* be comforted, etc.'[1]

This brings us to a further question about the 'blessings' Jesus promised. It is a problem we cannot avoid. Do not the beatitudes teach a doctrine of salvation by human merit and good works, which is incompatible with the gospel? Does not Jesus state clearly, for example, that the merciful will obtain mercy and the pure in heart will see God? And does not this imply that it is by showing mercy that we win mercy and by becoming pure in heart that we attain the vision of God?

Some interpreters have boldly argued this very thesis. They have tried to represent the Sermon on the Mount as nothing but a thinly Christianized form of the Old Testament law and of the ethics of Judaism. Here is Jesus the Rabbi, Jesus the lawgiver, they say, issuing commandments, expecting obedience and promising salvation to those who respond. Probably the most forthright exponent of this view has been Hans Windisch in his *The meaning of the Sermon on the Mount* (1929). He puts his emphasis on 'historical exegesis' and rejects what he calls 'Paulinizing exegesis', by which he means trying to interpret the Sermon in a way which harmonizes with Paul's gospel of grace. In his view this cannot be done: 'From the standpoint of Paul, Luther and Calvin the soteriology of the Sermon on the Mount is irredeemably heretical.'[2] In other words, it preaches the law not the gospel, and offers righteousness by works not by faith. So 'there is a gulf here between Jesus and Paul that no art of theological exegesis can bridge'.[3] H. Windisch goes even further. He speculates that Paul's emphasis on free salvation had led many to regard good works as superfluous, and that Matthew deliberately composed the Sermon on the Mount as a kind of anti-Pauline tract![4]

It is this same fear that the promises of the Sermon on the Mount depend for their fulfilment on human merit that led J. N. Darby to relegate them to the future 'kingdom age'. His

[1] P. 61.
[2] P. 6.
[3] P. 107.
[4] *E.g.* Windisch, p. 96. W. D. Davies examines and dismisses this reconstruction; pp. 316–341.

dispensationalism was popularized by the Scofield Reference Bible (1909) which, commenting on 5:2, calls the Sermon 'pure law', although conceding that its principles have 'a beautiful moral application to the Christian'.

But both the speculations of H. Windisch and the fears of the dispensationalists are groundless. Indeed, the very first beatitude proclaims salvation by grace not works, for it pledges the kingdom of God to 'the poor in spirit', that is, to people who are so spiritually poverty-stricken that they have nothing in the way of merit to offer. The reader can guess with what hot indignation Luther repudiated the suggestion made by some in his day that the Sermon on the Mount teaches salvation by merit! He added to his exposition a long ten-page Postscript in order to counter this monstrous idea. In it he castigated 'those silly false preachers' who 'have drawn the conclusion that we enter the kingdom of heaven and are saved by our own works and actions'.[1] This 'abomination of the sophists' so turns the gospel upside down, he declares, that it 'amounts to throwing the roof to the ground, upsetting the foundation, building salvation on mere water, hurling Christ from his throne completely and putting our works in his place'.[2]

How, then, can we explain the expressions which Jesus used in the beatitudes, indeed his whole emphasis in the Sermon on righteousness? The correct answer seems to be that the Sermon on the Mount as a kind of 'new law', like the old law, has two divine purposes, both of which Luther himself clearly understood. First, it shows the non-Christian that he cannot please God by himself (because he cannot obey the law) and so directs him to Christ to be justified. Secondly, it shows the Christian who has been to Christ for justification how to live so as to please God. More simply, as both the Reformers and the Puritans used to summarize it, the law sends us to Christ to be justified, and Christ sends us back to the law to be sanctified.

There can be no doubt that the Sermon on the Mount has on many people the first effect just noted. As they read it, it drives them to despair. They see in it an unattainable ideal. How can they develop this heart-righteousness, turn the other cheek, love their enemies? It is impossible. Exactly! In this sense, the Sermon is 'Mosissimus Moses' (Luther's expression); 'It is Moses quad-

[1] P. 285.
[2] P. 288.

rupled, Moses multiplied to the highest degree',[1] because it is a law of inward righteousness which no child of Adam can possibly obey. It can therefore only condemn us and make the forgiveness of Christ indispensable. May we not say that this was a part of the Sermon's purpose? It is true that Jesus does not explicitly say so, unless it be in the first beatitude as already mentioned. But the implication is there throughout the new law just as much as it is in the old.

Luther is even more clear about the second purpose of the Sermon: 'Christ is saying nothing in this Sermon about how we become Christians, but only about the works and fruit that no one can do unless he already is a Christian and in a state of grace.'[2] The whole Sermon in fact presupposes an acceptance of the gospel (as Chrysostom and Augustine had understood), an experience of conversion and new birth, and the indwelling of the Holy Spirit. It describes the kind of people reborn Christians are (or should be). So the beatitudes set forth the blessings which God bestows (not as a reward for merit but as a gift of grace) upon those in whom he is working such a character.

Professor Jeremias, who refers to the first explanation ('the theory of the impossible ideal') as 'Lutheran orthodoxy'[3] and does not mention that Luther himself also gave this second explanation, suggests that the Sermon was used as 'an early Christian catechism' and therefore presupposes that the hearers were Christians already: 'It was preceded by the proclamation of the Gospel; and it was preceded by conversion, by being overpowered by the Good News.'[4] Thus the Sermon 'is spoken to men who have already received forgiveness, who have found the pearl of great price, who have been invited to the wedding, who through their faith in Jesus belong to the new creation, to the new world of God'.[5] In this sense, then, 'the Sermon on the Mount is not Law, but Gospel'. To make the difference between the two clear, he continues, one should avoid terms like 'Christian morality' and speak instead of 'lived faith', for 'then it is clearly stated that the gift of God precedes his demands'.[6]

Professor A. M. Hunter helpfully sets this matter in the context of the whole New Testament: 'The New Testament makes it clear that the early Church's message always . . . had two aspects—one theological, the other ethical: (i) the Gospel which

---

[1] Jeremias, p. 12  [2] P. 291.  [3] P. 11.
[4] P. 24.  [5] P. 30.  [6] P. 32.

the apostles preached; and (ii) the Commandment, growing out of the Gospel, which they taught to those who accepted the Gospel. The Gospel was a declaration of what God, in his grace, had done for men through Christ; the Commandment was a statement of what God required from men who had become the objects of his gracious action.'[1] The apostle Paul commonly divided his letters in this way, with first a doctrinal, then a practical section. 'But in this', A. M. Hunter continues, 'Paul was only doing what his Lord had done before him. Jesus not only proclaimed that the kingdom of God had come with himself and his work; he also set before his disciples the moral ideal of that kingdom . . . It is the ideal adumbrated in the Sermon on the Mount.'[2]

To sum up these three introductory points relating to the beatitudes, we may say that the people described are the generality of Christian disciples, at least in the ideal; that the qualities commended are spiritual qualities; and that the blessing promised (as an unearned free gift) is the gloriously comprehensive blessing of God's rule, tasted now and consummated later, including the inheritance of both earth and heaven, comfort, satisfaction and mercy, the vision and the sonship of God.

We are ready now to look at the beatitudes in detail. Various classifications have been attempted. They are certainly not a random catalogue but, in Chrysostom's words, 'a sort of golden chain'.[3] Perhaps the simplest division is to see the first four as describing the Christian's relation to God, and the second four his relations and duties to his fellow men.

## 1. The poor in spirit (3)

It has already been mentioned that the Old Testament supplies the necessary background against which to interpret this beatitude. At first to be 'poor' meant to be in literal, material need. But gradually, because the needy had no refuge but God,[4] 'poverty' came to have spiritual overtones and to be identified with humble dependence on God. Thus the psalmist designated himself 'this poor man' who cried out to God in his need, 'and the Lord heard him, and saved him out of all his troubles'.[5] The 'poor man' in the Old Testament is one who is both afflicted and unable to

[1] P. 110.  [2] Pp. 110, 111.
[3] P. 209.  [4] Zeph. 3:12.  [5] Ps. 34:6.

save himself, and who therefore looks to God for salvation, while recognizing that he has no claim upon him. This kind of spiritual poverty is specially commended in Isaiah. It is 'the poor and needy', who 'seek water and there is none, and their tongue is parched with thirst', for whom God promises to 'open rivers on the bare heights, and fountains in the midst of the valleys', and to 'make the wilderness a pool of water, and the dry land springs of water'.[1] The 'poor' are also described as people with 'a contrite and humble spirit'; to them God looks and with them (though he is 'the high and lofty One who inhabits eternity, whose name is Holy') he is pleased to dwell.[2] It is to such that the Lord's anointed would proclaim good tidings of salvation, a prophecy which Jesus consciously fulfilled in the Nazareth synagogue: 'The Spirit of the Lord is upon me, because he has anointed me to preach good news to the poor.'[3] Further, the rich tended to compromise with surrounding heathenism; it was the poor who remained faithful to God. So wealth and worldliness, poverty and godliness went together.

Thus, to be 'poor in spirit' is to acknowledge our spiritual poverty, indeed our spiritual bankruptcy, before God. For we are sinners, under the holy wrath of God, and deserving nothing but the judgment of God. We have nothing to offer, nothing to plead, nothing with which to buy the favour of heaven.

> Nothing in my hand I bring,
> Simply to thy cross I cling;
> Naked, come to thee for dress;
> Helpless, look to thee for grace;
> Foul, I to the fountain fly;
> Wash me, Saviour, or I die.

This is the language of the poor in spirit. We do not belong anywhere except alongside the publican in Jesus' parable, crying out with downcast eyes, 'God, be merciful to me a sinner!' As Calvin wrote: 'He only who is reduced to nothing in himself, and relies on the mercy of God, is *poor in spirit*.'[4]

To such, and only to such, the kingdom of God is given. For God's rule which brings salvation is a gift as absolutely free as it

[1] Is. 41:17, 18.
[2] Is. 57:15; 66:1, 2.
[3] Is. 61:1; Lk. 4:18; cf. Mt. 11:5.
[4] P. 261.

is utterly undeserved. It has to be received with the dependent humility of a little child. Thus, right at the beginning of his Sermon on the Mount, Jesus contradicted all human judgments and all nationalistic expectations of the kingdom of God. The kingdom is given to the poor, not the rich; the feeble, not the mighty; to little children humble enough to accept it, not to soldiers who boast that they can obtain it by their own prowess. In our Lord's own day it was not the Pharisees who entered the kingdom, who thought they were rich, so rich in merit that they thanked God for their attainments; nor the Zealots who dreamed of establishing the kingdom by blood and sword; but publicans and prostitutes, the rejects of human society, who knew they were so poor they could offer nothing and achieve nothing. All they could do was to cry to God for mercy; and he heard their cry.

Perhaps the best later example of the same truth is the nominal church of Laodicea to whom John was directed to send a letter from the glorified Christ. He quoted their complacent words, and added his own assessment of them: 'You say, I am rich, I have prospered, and I need nothing; not knowing that you are wretched, pitiable, poor, blind, and naked.'[1] This visible church, for all its Christian profession, was not truly Christian at all. Self-satisfied and superficial, it was composed (according to Jesus) of blind and naked beggars. But the tragedy was they would not admit it. They were rich, not poor, in spirit.

Still today the indispensable condition of receiving the kingdom of God is to acknowledge our spiritual poverty. God still sends the rich away empty.[2] As C. H. Spurgeon expressed it, 'The way to rise in the kingdom is to sink in ourselves.'[3]

## 2. Those who mourn (4)

One might almost translate this second beatitude 'Happy are the unhappy' in order to draw attention to the startling paradox it contains. What kind of sorrow can it be which brings the joy of Christ's blessing to those who feel it? It is plain from the context that those here promised comfort are not primarily those who mourn the loss of a loved one, but those who mourn the loss of their innocence, their righteousness, their self-respect. It is not

[1] Rev. 3:17.    [2] Lk. 1:53.    [3] P. 21.

the sorrow of bereavement to which Christ refers, but the sorrow of repentance.

This is the second stage of spiritual blessing. It is one thing to be spiritually poor and acknowledge it; it is another to grieve and to mourn over it. Or, in more theological language, confession is one thing, contrition is another.

We need, then, to observe that the Christian life, according to Jesus, is not all joy and laughter. Some Christians seem to imagine that, especially if they are filled with the Spirit, they must wear a perpetual grin on their face and be continuously boisterous and bubbly. How unbiblical can one become? No. In Luke's version of the Sermon Jesus added to this beatitude a solemn woe: 'Woe to you that laugh now.'[1] The truth is that there are such things as Christian tears, and too few of us ever weep them.

Jesus wept over the sins of others, over their bitter consequences in judgment and death, and over the impenitent city which would not receive him. We too should weep more over the evil in the world, as did the godly men of biblical times. 'My eyes shed streams of tears,' the psalmist could say to God, 'because men do not keep thy law.'[2] Ezekiel heard God's faithful people described as those 'who sigh and groan over all the abominations that are committed in (Jerusalem)'.[3] And Paul wrote of the false teachers troubling the churches of his day: 'Many, of whom I . . . now tell you even with tears, live as enemies of the cross of Christ.'[4]

It is not only the sins of others, however, which should cause us tears; for we have our own sins to weep over as well. Have they never caused us any grief? Was Cranmer exaggerating when in his 1662 Holy Communion service he put into the lips of church people the words, 'We acknowledge *and bewail* our manifold sins and wickedness'? Was Ezra mistaken to pray and make confession, 'weeping and casting himself down before the house of God'?[5] Was Paul wrong to groan, 'Wretched man that I am! Who will deliver me from this body of death?', and to write to the sinful church of Corinth: 'Ought you not rather to mourn?'[6]

[1] Lk. 6:25.
[2] Ps. 119:136.
[3] Ezk. 9:4.
[4] Phil. 3:18.
[5] Ezr. 10:1.
[6] Rom. 7:24; 1 Cor. 5:2; *cf.* 2 Cor. 12:21.

I think not. I fear that we evangelical Christians, by making much of grace, sometimes thereby make light of sin. There is not enough sorrow for sin among us. We should experience more 'godly grief' of Christian penitence,[1] like that sensitive and Christ-like eighteenth-century missionary to the American Indians David Brainerd, who wrote in his journal on 18 October 1740: 'In my morning devotions my soul was exceedingly melted, and bitterly mourned over my exceeding sinfulness and vileness.' Tears like this are the holy water which God is said to store in his bottle.[2]

Such mourners, who bewail their own sinfulness, will be comforted by the only comfort which can relieve their distress, namely the free forgiveness of God. 'The greatest of all comfort is the absolution pronounced upon every contrite mourning sinner.'[3] 'Consolation' according to the Old Testament prophets was to be one of the offices of the Messiah. He was to be 'the Comforter' who would 'bind up the brokenhearted'.[4] That is why godly men like Simeon were said to be looking and longing 'for the consolation of Israel'.[5] And Christ does pour oil into our wounds and speak peace to our sore, scarred consciences. Yet still we mourn over the havoc of suffering and death which sin spreads throughout the world. For only in the final state of glory will Christ's comfort be complete, for only then will sin be no more and 'God will wipe away every tear from their eyes'.[6]

## 3. The meek (5)

The Greek adjective *praüs* means 'gentle', 'humble', 'considerate', 'courteous', and therefore exercising the self-control without which these qualities would be impossible. Although we rightly recoil from the image of our Lord as 'gentle Jesus, meek and mild', because it conjures up a picture of him as weak and effeminate, yet he described himself as 'gentle (*praüs*) and lowly in heart' and Paul referred to his 'meekness and gentleness'.[7] So, linguistically speaking, the NEB is quite correct to refer in this beatitude to

[1] 2 Cor. 7:10.
[2] Ps. 56:8.
[3] Lenski, p. 187.
[4] Is. 61:1; *cf.* 40:1.
[5] Lk. 2:25.
[6] Rev. 7:17.
[7] Mt. 11:29; 2 Cor. 10:1; *cf.* Zc. 9:9.

'those of a gentle spirit'. But what sort of gentleness is it, on account of which those who have it are pronounced blessed?

It seems important to note that in the beatitudes 'the meek' come between those who mourn over sin and those who hunger and thirst after righteousness. The particular form of meekness which Christ requires in his disciples will surely have something to do with this sequence. I believe Dr Lloyd-Jones is right to emphasize that this meekness denotes a humble and gentle attitude to others which is determined by a true estimate of ourselves. He points out that it is comparatively easy to be honest with ourselves before God and acknowledge ourselves to be sinners in his sight. He goes on: 'But how much more difficult it is to allow *other people* to say things like that about me! I instinctively resent it. We all of us prefer to condemn ourselves than to allow somebody else to condemn us.'[1]

For example, if I may apply this principle to everyday ecclesiastical practice: I myself am quite happy to recite the General Confession in church and call myself a 'miserable sinner'. It causes me no great problem. I can take it in my stride. But let somebody else come up to me after church and call me a miserable sinner, and I want to punch him on the nose! In other words, I am not prepared to allow other people to think or speak of me what I have just acknowledged before God that I am. There is a basic hypocrisy here; there always is when meekness is absent.

Dr Lloyd-Jones sums it up admirably: 'Meekness is essentially a true view of oneself, expressing itself in attitude and conduct with respect to others . . . The man who is truly meek is the one who is truly amazed that God and man can think of him as well as they do and treat him as well as they do.'[2] This makes him gentle, humble, sensitive, patient in all his dealings with others.

These 'meek' people, Jesus added, 'shall inherit the earth'. One would have expected the opposite. One would think that 'meek' people get nowhere because everybody ignores them or else rides roughshod over them and tramples them underfoot. It is the tough, the overbearing who succeed in the struggle for existence; weaklings go to the wall. Even the children of Israel had to fight for their inheritance, although the Lord their God gave them the promised land. But the condition on which we enter our spiritual

[1] P. 65.
[2] Pp. 68, 69.

inheritance in Christ is not might but meekness, for, as we have already seen, everything is ours if we are Christ's.[1]

Such was the confidence of holy and humble men of God in Old Testament days when the wicked seemed to triumph. It was never expressed more aptly than in Psalm 37, which Jesus seems to have been quoting in the beatitudes: 'Fret not yourself because of the wicked . . . The meek shall possess the land . . . Those blessed by the Lord shall possess the land . . . Wait for the Lord, and keep to his way, and he will exalt you to possess the land; you will look on the destruction of the wicked.'[2] The same principle operates today. The godless may boast and throw their weight about, yet real possession eludes their grasp. The meek, on the other hand, although they may be deprived and disenfranchised by men, yet because they know what it is to live and reign with Christ, can enjoy and even 'possess' the earth, which belongs to Christ. Then on the day of 'the regeneration' there will be 'new heavens and a new earth' for them to inherit.[3] Thus the way of Christ is different from the way of the world, and every Christian even if he is like Paul in 'having nothing' can yet describe himself as 'possessing everything'.[4] As Rudolf Stier put it, 'Self-renunciation is the way to world-dominion.'[5]

## 4. Those who hunger and thirst for righteousness (6)

Already in the Virgin Mary's song, the Magnificat, the spiritually poor and the spiritually hungry have been associated, and both have been declared blessed. For God 'has filled the *hungry* with good things, and the *rich* he has sent empty away'.[6] This general principle is here particularized. The hungry and thirsty whom God satisfies are those who 'hunger and thirst for righteousness'. Such spiritual hunger is a characteristic of all God's people, whose supreme ambition is not material but spiritual. Christians are not like pagans, engrossed in the pursuit of possessions; what they have set themselves to 'seek first' is God's kingdom and righteousness.[7]

[1] 1 Cor. 3:22.
[2] Ps. 37:1, 11, 22, 34; *cf.* Is. 57:13; 60:21.
[3] Mt. 19:28, literally; 2 Pet. 3:13; Rev. 21:1.
[4] 2 Cor. 6:10.
[5] P. 105.
[6] Lk. 1:53.
[7] Mt. 6:33.

Righteousness in the Bible has at least three aspects: legal, moral and social.

Legal righteousness is justification, a right relationship with God. The Jews 'pursued righteousness', Paul wrote later, but failed to attain it because they pursued it in the wrong way. They sought 'to establish their own' righteousness and 'did not submit to God's righteousness', which is Christ himself.[1] Some commentators have seen such a reference here, but this is scarcely possible since Jesus is addressing those who already belong to him.

Moral righteousness is that righteousness of character and conduct which pleases God. Jesus goes on after the beatitudes to contrast this Christian righteousness with pharisaic righteousness (20). The latter was an external conformity to rules; the former is an inner righteousness of heart, mind and motive. For this we should hunger and thirst.

It would be a mistake to suppose, however, that the biblical word 'righteousness' means only a right relationship with God on the one hand and a moral righteousness of character and conduct on the other. For biblical righteousness is more than a private and personal affair; it includes social righteousness as well. And social righteousness, as we learn from the law and the prophets, is concerned with seeking man's liberation from oppression, together with the promotion of civil rights, justice in the law courts, integrity in business dealings and honour in home and family affairs. Thus Christians are committed to hunger for righteousness in the whole human community as something pleasing to a righteous God.

Luther expressed this concept with his customary vigour: 'The command to you is not to crawl into a corner or into the desert, but to run out, if that is where you have been, and to offer your hands and your feet and your whole body, and to wager everything you have and can do.' What is required, he goes on, is 'a hunger and thirst for righteousness that can never be curbed or stopped or sated, one that looks for nothing and cares for nothing except the accomplishment and maintenance of the right, despising everything that hinders this end. If you cannot make the world completely pious, then do what you can.'[2]

There is perhaps no greater secret of progress in Christian

[1] *Cf.* Rom. 9:30-10:4.
[2] P. 27.

living than a healthy, hearty spiritual appetite. Again and again
Scripture addresses its promises to the hungry. God 'satisfies
him who is thirsty, and the hungry he fills with good things'.[1] If
we are conscious of slow growth, is the reason that we have a
jaded appetite? It is not enough to mourn over past sin; we must
also hunger for future righteousness.

Yet in this life our hunger will never be fully satisfied, nor our
thirst fully quenched. True, we receive the satisfaction which the
beatitude promises. But our hunger is satisfied only to break out
again. Even the promise of Jesus that whoever drinks of the
water he gives 'will never thirst' is fulfilled only if we keep
drinking.[2] Beware of those who claim to have attained, and who
look to past experience rather than to future development! Like
all the qualities included in the beatitudes, hunger and thirst are
perpetual characteristics of the disciples of Jesus, as perpetual as
poverty of spirit, meekness and mourning. Not till we reach
heaven will we 'hunger no more, neither thirst any more', for
only then will Christ our Shepherd lead us 'to springs of living
water'.[3]

More than this, God has promised a day of judgment, in which
right will triumph and wrong be overthrown, and after which
there will be 'new heavens and a new earth in which righteousness dwells'.[4] For this final vindication of the right we also long,
and we shall not be disappointed.

Looking back, we can see that the first four beatitudes reveal a
spiritual progression of relentless logic. Each step leads to the
next and presupposes the one that has gone before. To begin
with, we are to be 'poor in spirit', acknowledging our complete
and utter spiritual bankruptcy before God. Next we are to
'mourn' over the cause of it, our sins, yes, and our sin too—the
corruption of our fallen nature, and the reign of sin and death
in the world. Thirdly, we are to be 'meek', humble and gentle
towards others, allowing our spiritual poverty (admitted and
bewailed) to condition our behaviour to them as well as to God.
And fourthly we are to 'hunger and thirst for righteousness'. For
what is the use of confessing and lamenting our sin, of acknowledging the truth about ourselves to both God and men, if we
leave it there? Confession of sin must lead to hunger for righteousness.

[1] Ps. 107:9.  [2] Jn. 4:13, 14; 7:37.
[3] Rev. 7:16, 17.  [4] 2 Pet. 3:13.

In the second half of the beatitudes (the last four) we seem to turn even more from our attitude to God to our attitude to our fellow human beings. Certainly the 'merciful' show mercy to men, and 'peacemakers' seek to reconcile men to each other, and those who are 'persecuted' are persecuted by men. It seems likely therefore that the sincerity denoted by being 'pure in heart' also concerns our attitude and relation to our fellow human beings.

## 5. The merciful (7)

'Mercy' is compassion for people in need. Richard Lenski helpfully distinguishes it from 'grace': 'The noun *eleos* (mercy) . . . always deals with what we see of pain, misery and distress, these results of sin; and *charis* (grace) always deals with the sin and guilt itself. The one extends relief, the other pardon; the one cures, heals, helps, the other cleanses and reinstates.'[1]

Jesus does not specify the categories of people he has in mind to whom his disciples are to show mercy. He gives no indication whether he is thinking primarily of those overcome by disaster, like the traveller from Jerusalem to Jericho whom robbers assaulted and to whom the good Samaritan 'showed mercy', or of the hungry, the sick and the outcast on whom he himself regularly took pity, or of those who wrong us so that justice cries out for punishment but mercy for forgiveness. There was no need for Jesus to elaborate. Our God is a merciful God and shows mercy continuously; the citizens of his kingdom must show mercy too.

Of course the world (at least when it is true to its own nature) is unmerciful, as indeed also the church in its worldliness has often been. The world prefers to insulate itself against the pains and calamities of men. It finds revenge delicious, and forgiveness, by comparison, tame. But those who show mercy find it. 'How blest are those who show mercy; mercy shall be shown to them' (NEB). The same truth is echoed in the next chapter: 'If you forgive men their trespasses, your heavenly Father also will forgive you.'[2] This is not because we can merit mercy by mercy or forgiveness by forgiveness, but because we cannot receive the mercy and forgiveness of God unless we repent, and we cannot claim to have repented of *our* sins if we are unmerciful towards the sins of *others*. Nothing moves us to forgive like the wondering know-

[1] P. 191.
[2] 6:14.

ledge that we have ourselves been forgiven. Nothing proves more clearly that we have been forgiven than our own readiness to forgive. To forgive and to be forgiven, to show mercy and to receive mercy: these belong indissolubly together, as Jesus illustrated in his parable of the unmerciful servant.[1] Or, interpreted in the context of the beatitudes, it is 'the meek' who are also 'the merciful'. For to be meek is to acknowledge to others that *we* are sinners; to be merciful is to have compassion on others, for *they* are sinners too.

## 6. The pure in heart (8)

It is immediately obvious that the words 'in heart' indicate the kind of purity to which Jesus is alluding, as the words 'in spirit' indicated the kind of poverty he meant. The 'poor in spirit' are the spiritually poor as distinct from those whose poverty is only material. From whom, then, are 'the pure in heart' being distinguished?

The popular interpretation is to regard purity of heart as an expression for inward purity, for the quality of those who have been cleansed from moral—as opposed to ceremonial—defilement. And there is good biblical precedent for this, especially in the Psalms. It was recognized that no-one could ascend the Lord's hill or stand in his holy place unless he had 'clean hands and a pure heart'. So David, conscious that his Lord desired 'truth in the inward being', could pray, 'Teach me wisdom in my secret heart,' and, 'Create in me a clean heart, O God.'[2] Jesus took up this theme in his controversy with the Pharisees and complained about their obsession with external, ceremonial purity. 'You Pharisees cleanse the outside of the cup and of the dish, but inside you are full of extortion and wickedness.' They were 'like whitewashed tombs, which outwardly appear beautiful, but within they are full of dead men's bones and all uncleanness'.[3]

Luther gave this distinction between inward and outward purity a characteristically earthy turn. For he contrasted purity of heart not only with ceremonial defilement, but also with actual physical dirt. 'Christ . . . wants to have the heart pure, though

[1] Mt. 18:21-35.
[2] Ps. 24:3, 4; 51:6, 10; *cf.* Ps. 73:1; Acts 15:9; 1 Tim. 1:5.
[3] Lk. 11:39; Mt. 23:25-28.

outwardly the person may be a drudge in the kitchen, black, sooty, and grimy, doing all sorts of dirty work.'[1] Again, 'Though a common labourer, a shoemaker or a blacksmith may be dirty and sooty or may smell because he is covered with dirt and pitch, . . . and though he stinks outwardly, inwardly he is pure incense before God' because he ponders the word of God in his heart and obeys it.[2]

This emphasis on the inward and moral, whether contrasted with the outward and ceremonial or the outward and physical, is certainly consistent with the whole Sermon on the Mount which requires heart-rightcousness rather than mere rule-righteousness. Nevertheless, in the context of the other beatitudes, 'purity of heart' seems to refer in some sense to our relationships. Professor Tasker defines the pure in heart as 'the single-minded, who are free from the tyranny of a divided self'.[3] In this case the pure heart is the single heart and prepares the way for the 'single eye' which Jesus mentions in the next chapter.[4]

More precisely, the primary reference is to sincerity. Already in the verses of Psalm 24 quoted above, the person with 'clean hands and a pure heart' is one 'who does not lift up his soul to what is false (sc. an idol), and does not swear deceitfully' (4). That is, in his relations with both God and man he is free from falsehood. So the pure in heart are 'the utterly sincere' (JBP). Their whole life, public and private, is transparent before God and men. Their very heart—including their thoughts and motives—is pure, unmixed with anything devious, ulterior or base. Hypocrisy and deceit are abhorrent to them; they are without guile.

Yet how few of us live one life and live it in the open! We are tempted to wear a different mask and play a different role according to each occasion. This is not reality but play-acting, which is the essence of hypocrisy. Some people weave round themselves such a tissue of lies that they can no longer tell which part of them is real and which is make-believe. Alone among men Jesus Christ was absolutely pure in heart, being entirely guileless.

Only the pure in heart will see God, see him now with the eye of faith and see his glory in the hereafter, for only the utterly sincere can bear the dazzling vision in whose light the darkness of deceit must vanish and by whose fire all shams are burned up.

[1] P. 33.   [2] P. 34.
[3] P. 62; cf. Ps. 86:11, 12.   [4] 6:22, AV.

## 7. The peacemakers (9)

The sequence of thought from purity of heart to peacemaking is natural, because one of the most frequent causes of conflict is intrigue, while openness and sincerity are essential to all true reconciliation.

Every Christian, according to this beatitude, is meant to be a peacemaker both in the community and in the church. True, Jesus was to say later that he had 'not come to bring peace, but a sword', for he had come 'to set a man against his father, and a daughter against her mother, and a daughter-in-law against her mother-in-law', so that a man's enemies would be 'those of his own household'.[1] And what he meant by this was that conflict would be the inevitable result of his coming, even in one's own family, and that, if we are to be worthy of him, we must love him best and put him first, above even our nearest and dearest relatives.[2] It is clear beyond question throughout the teaching of Jesus and his apostles, however, that we should never ourselves seek conflict or be responsible for it. On the contrary, we are called to peace, we are actively to 'pursue' peace, we are to 'strive for peace with all men', and so far as it depends on us, we are to 'live peaceably with all'.[3]

Now peacemaking is a divine work. For peace means reconciliation, and God is the author of peace and of reconciliation. Indeed, the very same verb which is used in this beatitude of us is applied by the apostle Paul to what God has done through Christ. Through Christ God was pleased 'to reconcile to himself all things, . . . *making peace* by the blood of his cross'. And Christ's purpose was to 'create in himself one new man in place of the two (*sc.* Jew and Gentile), so *making peace*'.[4] It is hardly surprising, therefore, that the particular blessing which attaches to peacemakers is that 'they shall be called sons of God'. For they are seeking to do what their Father has done, loving people with his love, as Jesus is soon to make explicit.[5] It is the devil who is a troublemaker; it is God who loves reconciliation and who now through his children, as formerly through his only begotten Son, is bent on making peace.

[1] Mt. 10:34–36.
[2] Mt. 10:37.
[3] 1 Cor. 7:15; 1 Pet. 3:11; Heb. 12:14; Rom. 12:18.
[4] Col. 1:20; Eph. 2:15.
[5] 5:44, 45.

This will remind us that the words 'peace' and 'appeasement' are not synonyms. For the peace of God is not peace at any price. He made peace with us at immense cost, even at the price of the life-blood of his only Son. We too—though in our lesser ways—will find peacemaking a costly enterprise. Dietrich Bonhoeffer has made us familiar with the concept of 'cheap grace';[1] there is such a thing as 'cheap peace' also. To proclaim 'Peace, peace,' when there is no peace, is the work of the false prophet, not the Christian witness. Many examples could be given of peace through pain. When we are ourselves involved in a quarrel, there will be either the pain of apologizing to the person we have injured or the pain of rebuking the person who has injured us. Sometimes there is the nagging pain of having to refuse to forgive the guilty party until he repents. Of course a cheap peace can be bought by cheap forgiveness. But true peace and true forgiveness are costly treasures. God forgives us only when we repent. Jesus told us to do the same: 'If your brother sins, rebuke him, and if he repents, forgive him.'[2] How can we forgive an injury when it is neither admitted nor regretted?

Or again, we may not be personally involved in a dispute, but may find ourselves struggling to reconcile to each other two people or groups who are estranged and at variance with each other. In this case there will be the pain of listening, of ridding ourselves of prejudice, of striving sympathetically to understand both the opposing points of view, and of risking misunderstanding, ingratitude or failure.

Other examples of peacemaking are the work of reunion and the work of evangelism, that is, seeking on the one hand to unite churches and on the other to bring sinners to Christ. In both these, true reconciliation can be degraded into cheap peace. The visible unity of the church is a proper Christian quest, but only if unity is not sought at the expense of doctrine. Jesus prayed for the oneness of his people. He also prayed that they might be kept from evil and in truth. We have no mandate from Christ to seek unity without purity, purity of both doctrine and conduct. If there is such a thing as 'cheap reunion', there is 'cheap evangelism' also, namely the proclamation of the gospel without the cost of discipleship, the demand for faith without repentance. These

[1] Pp. 35 ff.
[2] Lk. 17:3.

are forbidden short cuts. They turn the evangelist into a fraud. They cheapen the gospel and damage the cause of Christ.

## 8. Those who are persecuted for righteousness' sake (10–12)

It may seem strange that Jesus should pass from peacemaking to persecution, from the work of reconciliation to the experience of hostility. Yet however hard we may try to make peace with some people, they refuse to live at peace with us. Not all attempts at reconciliation succeed. Indeed, some take the initiative to oppose us, and in particular to 'revile' or slander us. This is not because of our foibles or idiosyncracies, but 'for righteousness' sake' (10) and 'on my account' (11), that is, because they find distasteful the righteousness for which we hunger and thirst (6), and because they have rejected the Christ we seek to follow. Persecution is simply the clash between two irreconcilable value-systems.

How did Jesus expect his disciples to react under persecution? Verse 12: *Rejoice and be glad!* We are not to retaliate like an unbeliever, nor to sulk like a child, nor to lick our wounds in self-pity like a dog, nor just to grin and bear it like a Stoic, still less to pretend we enjoy it like a masochist. What then? We are to rejoice as a Christian should rejoice and even to 'leap for joy'.[1] Why so? Partly because, Jesus added, *your reward is great in heaven* (12a). We may lose everything on earth, but we shall inherit everything in heaven—not as a reward for merit, however, because 'the promise of the reward is free'.[2] Partly because persecution is a token of genuineness, a certificate of Christian authenticity, *for so men persecuted the prophets who were before you* (12b). If we are persecuted today, we belong to a noble succession. But the major reason why we should rejoice is because we are suffering, he said, *on my account* (11), on account of our loyalty to him and to his standards of truth and righteousness. Certainly the apostles learnt this lesson well for, having been beaten and threatened by the Sanhedrin, 'they left the presence of the council, rejoicing that they were counted worthy to suffer dishonour for the name'.[3] They knew, as we should, that 'wounds and hurts are medals of honour'.[4]

It is important to notice that this reference to persecution is a

[1] Lk. 6:23.  [2] Calvin, p. 267.
[3] Acts 5:41.  [4] Lenski, p. 197.

beatitude like the rest. Indeed, it has the distinction of being a double beatitude, for Jesus first stated it in the third person like the other seven (*Blessed are those who are persecuted for righteousness' sake*, 10) and then repeated it in the direct speech of the second person (*Blessed are you when men revile you and persecute you* ..., 11). Since all the beatitudes describe what every Christian disciple is intended to be, we conclude that the condition of being despised and rejected, slandered and persecuted, is as much a normal mark of Christian discipleship as being pure in heart or merciful. Every Christian is to be a peacemaker, and every Christian is to expect opposition. Those who hunger for righteousness will suffer for the righteousness they crave. Jesus said so both here and elsewhere. So did his apostles Peter and Paul.[1] It has been so in every age. We should not be surprised if anti-Christian hostility increases, but rather be surprised if it does not. We need to remember the complementary woe which Luke records: 'Woe to you, when all men speak well of you.'[2] Universal popularity was as much the lot of the false prophets as persecution was of the true.

Few men of this century have understood better the inevitability of suffering than Dietrich Bonhoeffer. He seems never to have wavered in his Christian antagonism to the Nazi regime, although it meant for him imprisonment, the threat of torture, danger to his own family and finally death. He was executed by the direct order of Heinrich Himmler in April 1945 in the Flossenburg concentration camp, only a few days before it was liberated. It was the fulfilment of what he had always believed and taught: 'Suffering, then, is the badge of true discipleship. The disciple is not above his master. Following Christ means *passio passiva*, suffering because we have to suffer. That is why Luther reckoned suffering among the marks of the true Church, and one of the memoranda drawn up in preparation for the Augsburg Confession similarly defines the Church as the community of those "who are persecuted and martyred for the gospel's sake" ... Discipleship means allegiance to the suffering Christ, and it is therefore not at all surprising that Christians should be called upon to suffer. In fact, it is a joy and a token of his grace.'[3]

[1] *E.g.* Jn. 15:18-25; 1 Pet. 4:13, 14; Acts 14:22; 2 Tim. 3:12.
[2] Lk. 6:26.
[3] Bonhoeffer, pp. 80, 81.

The beatitudes paint a comprehensive portrait of a Christian disciple. We see him first alone on his knees before God, acknowledging his spiritual poverty and mourning over it. This makes him meek or gentle in all his relationships, since honesty compels him to allow others to think of him what before God he confesses himself to be. Yet he is far from acquiescing in his sinfulness, for he hungers and thirsts after righteousness, longing to grow in grace and in goodness.

We see him next with others, out in the human community. His relationship with God does not cause him to withdraw from society, nor is he insulated from the world's pain. On the contrary, he is in the thick of it, showing mercy to those battered by adversity and sin. He is transparently sincere in all his dealings and seeks to play a constructive role as a peacemaker. Yet he is not thanked for his efforts, but rather opposed, slandered, insulted and persecuted on account of the righteousness for which he stands and the Christ with whom he is identified.

Such is the man or woman who is 'blessed', that is, who has the approval of God and finds self-fulfilment as a human being.

Yet in all this the values and standards of Jesus are in direct conflict with the commonly accepted values and standards of the world. The world judges the rich to be blessed, not the poor, whether in the material or in the spiritual sphere; the happy-go-lucky and carefree, not those who take evil so seriously that they mourn over it; the strong and brash, not the meek and gentle; the full not the hungry; those who mind their own business, not those who meddle in other men's matters and occupy their time in do-goodery like 'showing mercy' and 'making peace'; those who attain their ends even if necessary by devious means, not the pure in heart who refuse to compromise their integrity; those who are secure and popular, and live at ease, not those who have to suffer persecution.

Probably nobody has hated the 'softness' of the Sermon on the Mount more than Friedrich Nietzsche. Although the son and the grandson of Lutheran pastors, he rejected Christianity during his student days. His book *The anti-Christ*[1] (a title he had dared to apply to himself in his autobiographical sketch *Ecce homo*) is his most violent anti-Christian polemic and was written in 1888, the year before he went mad. In it he defines what is 'good' as 'all that heightens the feeling of power, the will to power, power itself in

[1] First published 1895; Penguin Classics 1968.

man', and what is 'bad' as 'all that proceeds from weakness'.[1] Consequently, in answer to his own question, 'What is more harmful than any vice?', he replies, 'Active sympathy for the ill-constituted and weak—Christianity.'[2] He sees Christianity as a religion of pity instead of a religion of power; so 'nothing in our unhealthy modernity is more unhealthy than Christian pity.'[3] He despises 'the Christian conception of God—God as God of the sick, God as spider, God as spirit'—a conception from which 'everything strong, brave, masterful, proud' has been eliminated.[4] 'In the entire New Testament there is only *one* solitary figure one is obliged to respect,' he affirms, and that is Pontius Pilate, the Roman governor.[5] Jesus, by contrast, he disdains as 'God on the cross', and Christianity as 'mankind's greatest misfortune.'[6] The cause of his venom is plain. The ideal that Jesus commended is the little child. He lent no support whatever to Nietzsche's commendation of the 'superman'. So Nietzsche repudiated the whole value-system of Jesus. 'I *condemn* Christianity,' he wrote. 'The Christian church has left nothing untouched by its depravity, it has made of every value a disvalue.'[7] Instead (in the last words of his book) he called for a 'revaluation of all values'.[8]

But Jesus will not compromise his standards to accommodate Nietzsche, or his followers, or any of us who may unconsciously have imbibed bits and pieces of Nietzsche's power-philosophy. In the beatitudes Jesus throws out a fundamental challenge to the non-Christian world and its outlook, and requires his disciples to adopt his altogether different set of values. As Thielicke puts it, 'Anybody who enters into fellowship with Jesus must undergo a transvaluation of values.'[9]

This is what Bonhoeffer (who incidentally was brought up in the same Lutheran tradition as Nietzsche) termed the 'extraordinariness' of the Christian life. 'With every beatitude', he wrote, 'the gulf is widened between the disciples and the people, and their call to come forth from the people becomes increasingly manifest.' It is particularly obvious in the blessing on mourners. Jesus 'means refusing to be in tune with the world or to accommodate oneself to its standards. Such men mourn for the world, for its guilt, its fate and its fortune. While the world keeps holiday they stand aside, and while the world sings "Gather ye rose-buds

---

[1] P. 15.   [2] P. 116.   [3] Pp. 118-119.
[4] Pp. 127-128.   [5] P. 162.   [6] Pp. 168 f.
[7] P. 186.   [8] P. 187.   [9] P. 77.

while ye may", they mourn. They see that for all the jollity on board, the ship is beginning to sink. The world dreams of progress, of power and of the future, but the disciples meditate on the end, the last judgment and the coming of the kingdom. To such heights the world cannot rise. And so the disciples are strangers in the world, unwelcome guests and disturbers of the peace. No wonder the world rejects them!'[1]

Such a reversal of human values is basic to biblical religion. The ways of the God of Scripture appear topsy-turvy to men. For God exalts the humble and abases the proud, calls the first last and the last first, ascribes greatness to the servant, sends the rich away empty-handed and declares the meek to be his heirs. The culture of the world and the counter-culture of Christ are at loggerheads with each other. In brief, Jesus congratulates those whom the world most pities, and calls the world's rejects 'blessed'.

[1] Pp. 93, 98.

# Matthew 5:13–16
## A Christian's influence: salt and light

*You are the salt of the earth; but if salt has lost its taste, how shall its saltness be restored? It is no longer good for anything except to be thrown out and trodden under foot by men.*
*[14]You are the light of the world. A city set on a hill cannot be hid. [15]Nor do men light a lamp and put it under a bushel, but on a stand, and it gives light to all in the house. [16]Let your light so shine before men, that they may see your good works and give glory to your Father who is in heaven.*

If the beatitudes describe the essential character of the disciples of Jesus, the salt and light metaphors indicate their influence for good in the world.

Yet the very notion that Christians can exert a healthy influence in the world should bring us up with a start. What possible influence could the people described in the beatitudes exert in this hard, tough world? What lasting good can the poor and the meek do, the mourners and the merciful, and those who try to make peace not war? Would they not simply be overwhelmed by the floodtide of evil? What can they accomplish whose only passion is an appetite for righteousness, and whose only weapon is purity of heart? Are not such people too feeble to achieve anything, especially if they are a small minority in the world?

It is evident that Jesus did not share this scepticism. Rather the reverse. The world will undoubtedly persecute the church (10–12); yet it is the church's calling to serve this persecuting world (13–16). 'This must be your only retaliation,' Rudolf Stier expressed it, '—love and truth for hatred and lies.'[1] Incredible

[1] P. 121.

as it may sound, Jesus referred to that handful of Palestinian peasants as the salt of *the earth* and the light of *the world*, so far-reaching was their influence to be. It is also a remarkable providence of God that in this most Jewish of the four Gospels there should be such an allusion to the whole earth, to the world-wide power for good of Christ's followers.

In order to define the nature of their influence, Jesus resorted to two domestic metaphors. Every home, however poor, used and still uses both salt and light. During his own boyhood Jesus must often have watched his mother use salt in the kitchen and light the lamps when the sun went down. Salt and light are indispensable household commodities. Several commentators quote Pliny's dictum that nothing is more useful than 'salt and sunshine' (*sale et sole*).[1] The need for light is obvious. Salt, on the other hand, had a variety of uses. It was both a condiment and a preservative. It seems to have been recognized from time immemorial as an essential component of human diet and as a seasoning or relish to food: 'Can that which is tasteless be eaten without salt?'[2] In particular, however, in the centuries before refrigeration had been invented, it was used to keep meat wholesome and to prevent decay. Indeed it still is. H. V. Morton has described the making of 'biltong', the dried meat of South Africa: 'The meat, having been cut and trimmed to the required size, is well rubbed with coarse salt . . . If properly cured, it will keep indefinitely.'[3]

The basic truth which lies behind these metaphors and is common to them both is that the church and the world are distinct communities. On the one hand there is 'the earth'; on the other there is 'you' who are the earth's salt. On the one hand there is 'the world'; on the other there is 'you' who are the world's light. True, the two communities ('they' and 'you') are related to each other, but their relatedness depends on their distinctness. It is important to assert this clearly in our day in which it is theologically fashionable to blur the distinction between the church and the world, and to refer to all mankind indiscriminately as 'the people of God'.

Further, the metaphors tell us something about both communities. The world is evidently a dark place, with little or no light of

[1] *Natural history*, xxxi, 102.
[2] Jb. 6:6.
[3] *In search of South Africa* (Hodder, 1948), pp. 292 f.

its own, since an external source of light is needed to illumine it. True, it is 'always talking about its enlightenment',[1] but much of its boasted light is in reality darkness. The world also manifests a constant tendency to deteriorate. The notion is not that the world is tasteless and that Christians can make it less insipid ('The thought of making the world palatable to God is quite impossible'[2]), but that it is putrefying. It cannot stop itself from going bad. Only salt introduced from outside can do this. The church, on the other hand, is set in the world with a double role, as salt to arrest—or at least to hinder—the process of social decay, and as light to dispel the darkness.

When we look at the two metaphors more closely, we see that they are deliberately phrased in order to be parallel to each other. In each case Jesus first makes an affirmation ('You are the salt of the earth,' 'You are the light of the world'). Then he adds a rider, the condition on which the affirmation depends (the salt must retain its saltness, the light must be allowed to shine). Salt is good for nothing if its saltness is lost; light is good for nothing if it is concealed.

## 1. The salt of the earth (13)

The affirmation is straightforward: 'You are salt to the world' (NEB). This means that, when each community is itself and is true to itself, the world decays like rotten fish or meat, while the church can hinder its decay.

Of course God has set other restraining influences in the community. He has himself established certain institutions in his common grace, which curb man's selfish tendencies and prevent society from slipping into anarchy. Chief among these are the state (with its authority to frame and enforce laws) and the home (including marriage and family life). These exert a wholesome influence in the community. Nevertheless, God intends the most powerful of all restraints within sinful society to be his own redeemed, regenerate and righteous people. As R. V. G. Tasker puts it, the disciples are 'to be a moral disinfectant in a world where moral standards are low, constantly changing, or non-existent'.[3]

The effectiveness of salt, however, is conditional: it must retain

[1] Lloyd-Jones, p. 164.    [2] Lenski, p. 199.
[3] P. 63.

its saltness. Now, strictly speaking, salt can never lose its saltness. I am given to understand that sodium chloride is a very stable chemical compound, which is resistant to nearly every attack. Nevertheless, it can become contaminated by mixture with impurities, and then it becomes useless, even dangerous.[1] Desalted salt is unfit even for manure, *i.e.* the compost heap. Dr David Turk has suggested to me that what was then popularly called 'salt' was in fact a white powder (perhaps from around the Dead Sea) which, while containing sodium chloride, also contained much else, since, in those days, there were no refineries. Of this dust the sodium chloride was probably the most soluble component and so the most easily washed out. The residue of white powder still looked like salt, and was doubtless still called salt, but it neither tasted nor acted like salt. It was just road dust.

So too a Christian. 'Have salt in yourselves,' Jesus said on another occasion.[2] Christian saltiness is Christian character as depicted in the beatitudes, committed Christian discipleship exemplified in both deed and word.[3] For effectiveness the Christian must retain his Christlikeness, as salt must retain its saltness. If Christians become assimilated to non-Christians and contaminated by the impurities of the world, they lose their influence. The influence of Christians in and on society depends on their being distinct, not identical. Dr Lloyd-Jones emphasizes this: 'The glory of the gospel is that when the Church is absolutely different from the world, she invariably attracts it. It is then that the world is made to listen to her message, though it may hate it at first.'[4] Otherwise, if we Christians are indistinguishable from non-Christians, we are useless. We might as well be discarded like saltless salt, 'thrown out and trodden under foot by men'. 'But what a downcome,' comments A. B. Bruce, 'from being saviours of society to supplying materials for footpaths!'[5]

[1] I am indebted to Mr G. J. Hobson, a chemist in Carnforth, Lancashire, for writing to me in August 1972 about this, in order to correct an earlier blunder of mine and to supply a lack in my scientific knowledge.

[2] Mk. 9:50.

[3] Lk. 14:34, 35; Col. 4:6.

[4] P. 41.

[5] P. 102.

## 2. The light of the world (14–16)

Jesus introduces his second metaphor with a similar affirmation: *you are the light of the world.* True, he was later to say, 'I am the light of the world.'[1] But by derivation we are too, shining with the light of Christ, shining in the world like stars in the night sky.[2] I sometimes think how splendid it would be if non-Christians, curious to discover the secret and source of our light, were to come up to us and enquire:

> Twinkle, twinkle, little star,
> How I wonder what you are!

What this light is Jesus clarifies as our 'good works'. Let men once *see your good works,* he said, and they will *give glory to your Father who is in heaven,* for it is by such good works that our light is to shine. It seems that 'good works' is a general expression to cover everything a Christian says and does because he is a Christian, every outward and visible manifestation of his Christian faith. Since light is a common biblical symbol of truth, a Christian's shining light must surely include his spoken testimony. Thus, the Old Testament prophecy that God's Servant would be 'a light to the nations' is said to have been fulfilled not only in Christ himself, the light of the world, but also by Christians who bear witness to Christ.[3] Evangelism must be counted as one of the 'good works' by which our light shines and our Father is glorified.

Luther was right to emphasize this but wrong (I think) to make it the exclusive reference. 'Matthew does not have in mind the ordinary works that people should do for one another out of love . . . Rather he is thinking principally about the distinctly Christian work of teaching correctly, of stressing faith, and of showing how to strengthen and preserve it; this is how we testify that we really are Christians.' He went on in his commentary to draw a distinction between the first and second tables of the decalogue, that is, the ten commandments expressing our duty to God and to our neighbour. 'The works we are talking about now deal with the first three great commandments, which

---

[1] Jn. 8:12; 9:5.
[2] *Cf.* Phil. 2:15.
[3] Is. 42:6; 49:6; Lk. 2:32; Acts 26:23; 13:47.

pertain to God's honour, name and Word.'[1] It is healthy to be reminded that believing, confessing and teaching the truth are also 'good works' which give evidence of our regeneration by the Holy Spirit.[2] We must not limit them to these, however. 'Good works' are works of love as well as of faith. They express not only our loyalty to God, but our care for our fellows as well. Indeed, the primary meaning of 'works' must be practical, visible deeds of compassion. It is when people see these, Jesus said, that they will glorify God, for they embody the good news of his love which we proclaim. Without them our gospel loses its credibility and our God his honour.

As with the salt, so with the light, the affirmation is followed by a condition: *Let your light . . . shine before men.* If salt can lose its saltness, the light in us can become darkness.[3] But we are to allow the light of Christ within us to shine out from us, so that people may see it. We are not to be like a town or village nestling in a valley whose lights are concealed from view, but like *a city set on a hill* which *cannot be hid* and whose lights are clearly seen for miles around. Again, we are to be like a lighted lamp, 'a burning and shining lamp' as John the Baptist was,[4] which is set on a lampstand in a prominent position in the house so that *it gives light to all in the house*, and is not stuck 'under the meal-tub' (NEB) or 'under a bucket' (JBP), where it can do no good.

That is, as the disciples of Jesus, we are not to conceal the truth we know or the truth of what we are. We are not to pretend to be other than we are, but be willing for our Christianity to be visible to all. 'Flight into the invisible is a denial of the call. A community of Jesus which seeks to hide itself has ceased to follow him.'[5] Rather are we to be ourselves, our true Christian selves, openly living the life described in the beatitudes, and not ashamed of Christ. Then people will see us and our good works, and seeing us will glorify God. For they will inevitably recognize that it is by the grace of God we are what we are, that *our* light is *his* light, and that our works are his works done in us and through us. So it is the light they will praise, not the lamp which bears it; it is our Father in heaven whom they will glorify, not the children he has

[1] P. 66.
[2] *Cf.* Jn. 6:28, 29; 1 Cor. 12:3; 1 Jn. 3:23, 24; 5:1.
[3] 6:23.
[4] Jn. 5:35.
[5] Bonhoeffer, p. 106.

begotten and who exhibit a certain family likeness. Even those who revile us may not be able to help glorifying God for the very righteousness on account of which they persecute us (10–12).

## 3. Lessons to learn

The salt and light metaphors which Jesus used have much to teach us about our Christian responsibilities in the world. Three lessons are prominent.

*a. There is a fundamental difference between Christians and non-Christians, between the church and the world*
True, some non-Christians adopt a deceptive veneer of Christian culture. Some professing Christians, on the other hand, seem indistinguishable from non-Christians and so deny their Christian name by their non-Christian behaviour. Yet the essential difference remains. We might say that they are as different as chalk from cheese. Jesus said they are as different as light from darkness, as different as salt from decay and disease. We serve neither God, nor ourselves, nor the world by attempting to obliterate or even minimize this difference.

This theme is basic to the Sermon on the Mount. The Sermon is built on the assumption that Christians *are* different, and it issues a call to us to *be* different. Probably the greatest tragedy of the church throughout its long and chequered history has been its constant tendency to conform to the prevailing culture instead of developing a Christian counter-culture.

*b. We must accept the responsibility which this distinction puts upon us*
It is when in each metaphor we bring the affirmation and the condition together that our responsibility stands out. Each affirmation begins in the Greek sentence with the emphatic pronoun 'you', as much as to say 'you and only you' are the earth's salt and the world's light. And *therefore*—the condition follows with inexorable logic—you simply must not fail the world you are called to serve. You must be what you are. You are salt, and so you must retain your saltness and not lose your Christian tang. You are light, and so you must let your light shine and not conceal it in any way, whether by sin or by compromise, by laziness or by fear.

This call to assume our Christian responsibility, because of what God has made us and where he has put us, is particularly relevant to young people who feel frustrated in the modern world. The problems of the human community are so great, and they feel so small, so feeble, so ineffective. 'Alienation'—a term popularized by Marx—is the word commonly used today to describe these frustration feelings.

What message do we have, then, for such people who feel themselves strangled by 'the system', crushed by the machine of modern technocracy, overwhelmed by political, social and economic forces which control them and over which they have no control? They feel themselves victims of a situation they are powerless to change. What can they do? It is in the soil of this frustration that revolutionaries are being bred, dedicated to the violent overthrow of the system. It is from the very same soil that revolutionaries of Jesus can arise, equally dedicated activists— even more so—but committed rather to spread his revolution of love, joy and peace. And this peaceful revolution is more radical than any programme of violence, both because its standards are incorruptible and because it changes people as well as structures. Have we lost our confidence in the power of the gospel of Christ? Then listen to Luther: 'With his single word I can be more defiant and boastful than they with all their power, swords and guns.'[1]

So we are not helpless and powerless after all! For we have Jesus Christ, his gospel, ideals and power, and Jesus Christ is all the salt and light this dark and rotten world needs. But we must have salt in ourselves, and we must let our light shine.

*c. We must see our Christian responsibility as twofold.*
'Salt and light have one thing in common: they give and expend themselves—and thus are the opposite of any and every kind of self-centred religiosity.'[2]

Nevertheless, the kind of service each renders is different. In fact, their effects are complementary. The function of salt is largely negative: it prevents decay. The function of light is positive: it illumines the darkness.

So Jesus calls his disciples to exert a double influence on the secular community, a negative influence by arresting its decay and a positive influence by bringing light into its darkness. For it is

[1] P. 55.
[2] Thielicke, p. 33.

one thing to stop the spread of evil; it is another to promote the spread of truth, beauty and goodness.

Putting the two metaphors together, it seems legitimate to discern in them the proper relation between evangelism and social action in the total mission of Christ in the world—a relation which perplexes many believers today. We are called to be both salt and light to the secular community.

Take first our vocation to be salt. The apostle Paul paints a grim picture at the end of the first chapter of his Roman letter of what happens when society suppresses (out of love for evil) the truth it knows by nature. It deteriorates. Its values and standards steadily decline until it becomes utterly corrupt. When men reject what they know of God, God gives them up to their own distorted notions and perverted passions, until society stinks in the nostrils of God and of all good people.

Now Christians are set in secular society by God to hinder this process. God intends us to penetrate the world. Christian salt has no business to remain snugly in elegant little ecclesiastical salt cellars; our place is to be rubbed into the secular community, as salt is rubbed into meat, to stop it going bad. And when society does go bad, we Christians tend to throw up our hands in pious horror and reproach the non-Christian world; but should we not rather reproach ourselves? One can hardly blame unsalted meat for going bad. It cannot do anything else. The real question to ask is: where is the salt?

Jesus was teaching somewhere near the sea of Galilee. Less than a hundred miles to the south the River Jordan flows into another sea, the Salt Sea, so salty that it is dead. And on its western side there lived at that time a Dead Sea Community, whose library of scrolls caused such a sensation when it was accidentally discovered a few years ago. They were a monastic community of Essenes who had withdrawn from the wicked world. They called themselves 'the sons of light', but they took no steps to let their light shine, and in their ghetto their salt was as useless as the deposits on the shores of the nearby sea. Is it possible that Jesus was thinking of them? W. D. Davies thinks he made 'a side-glance' in their direction.[1] It is an attractive conjecture.

What does it mean in practice to be the salt of the earth? To begin with, we Christian people should be more courageous,

[1] P. 250.

more outspoken in condemning evil. Condemnation is negative, to be sure, but the action of salt is negative. Sometimes standards slip and slide in a community for want of a clear Christian protest. Luther makes much of this, emphasizing that denunciation and proclamation go hand in hand when the gospel is truly preached: 'Salting has to bite. Although they criticize us as biters, we know that this is how it has to be and that Christ has commanded the salt to be sharp and continually caustic . . . If you want to preach the Gospel and help people, you must be sharp and rub salt into their wounds, showing the reverse side and denouncing what is not right. . . . The real salt is the true exposition of Scripture, which denounces the whole world and lets nothing stand but the simple faith in Christ.'[1]

Helmut Thielicke takes up this same theme of the necessarily sharp or 'biting' quality of true Christian witness. To look at some Christians, he says, 'one would think that their ambition is to be the honeypot of the world. They sweeten and sugar the bitterness of life with an all too easy conception of a loving God . . . But Jesus, of course, did not say, "You are the honey of the world." He said, "You are the salt of the earth." Salt bites, and the unadulterated message of the judgment and grace of God has always been a biting thing.'[2]

And alongside this condemnation of what is false and evil, we should take our stand boldly for what is true, good and decent whether in our neighbourhood, in our college, profession or business, or in the wider sphere of national life, including the mass media.

Christian salt takes effect by deeds as well as words. We have already seen that God has created both the state and the family as social structures to restrain evil and encourage goodness. And Christians have a responsibility to see that these structures are not only preserved but are also operated with justice. Too often evangelical Christians have interpreted their social responsibility in terms only of helping the casualties of a sick society, and have done nothing to change the structures which cause the casualties. Just as doctors are concerned not only with the treatment of patients but also with preventive medicine and public health, so we should concern ourselves with what might be called preventive social medicine and higher standards of moral hygiene.

[1] Pp. 55, 56, 59.
[2] P. 28.

However small our part may be, we cannot opt out of seeking to create better social structures, which guarantee justice in legislation and law enforcement, the freedom and dignity of the individual, civil rights for minorities and the abolition of social and racial discrimination. We should neither despise these things nor avoid our responsibility for them. They are part of God's purpose for his people. Whenever Christians are conscientious citizens, they are acting like salt in the community. As Sir Frederick Catherwood put it in his contribution to the symposium *Is revolution change?* 'To try to improve society is not worldliness but love. To wash your hands of society is not love but worldliness.'[1]

But fallen human beings need more than barricades to stop them becoming as bad as they could be. They need regeneration, new life through the gospel. Hence our second vocation to be 'the light of the world'. For the truth of the gospel is the light, contained indeed in fragile earthenware lamps, yet shining through our very earthenness with the more conspicuous brightness. We are called both to spread the gospel and to frame our manner of life in a way that is worthy of the gospel.[2]

So then, we should never put our two vocations to be salt and light, our Christian social and evangelistic responsibilities, over against each other as if we had to choose between them. We should not exaggerate either, nor disparage either, at the expense of the other. Neither can be a substitute for the other. The world needs both. It is bad and needs salt; it is dark and needs light. Our Christian vocation is to be both. Jesus Christ said so, and that should be enough.

In the United States one of the ministries which has been described as being on the edge of the so-called 'Jesus movement' is known as the 'Jesus Christ Light and Power House'. It is a Christian commune in Westwood, administered by Hal Lindsey and Bill Counts, who give biblical teaching to the residents. 'Light and power' are a fine combination, and both are to be found in Jesus Christ. But when will somebody in America establish a 'Jesus Christ Salt and Light Company Inc.'?

In the United Kingdom there has arisen in recent years an almost spontaneous movement known as the 'Festival of Light'. I thank God for the courageous and exuberant witness of the young people (as they mostly are) who belong to it. It seeks to

[1] Edited by Brian Griffiths (IVP, 1972), p. 35.
[2] *Cf.* Phil. 1:27.

combine a protest against pornography and a campaign for the moral law of God in public life with a clear testimony to Jesus Christ. Perhaps it should become even more self-consciously a 'Festival of Salt and Light'.

At all events, we must not be shy of our vocation to be salt as well as light, or we shall be guilty of separating what Jesus has united.

A Christian's character as described in the beatitudes and a Christian's influence as defined in the salt and light metaphors are organically related to one another. Our influence depends on our character. But the beatitudes set an extremely high and exacting standard. It may be helpful, therefore, as a conclusion to this chapter, to look back over both paragraphs and note the incentives to righteousness which Jesus gives.

First, this is the way we ourselves will be blessed. The beatitudes identify those whom God declares to be 'blessed', those who please him and who themselves find fulfilment. True blessedness is found in goodness, and nowhere else.

Secondly, this is the way the world will best be served. Jesus offers his followers the immense privileges of being the world's salt and light if only they will live by the beatitudes.

Thirdly, this is the way God will be glorified. Here towards the beginning of his ministry Jesus tells his disciples that if they let their light shine so that their good works are seen, their Father in heaven will be glorified. At the end of his ministry, in the upper room, he will express the same truth in similar words: 'By this my Father is glorified, that you bear much fruit, and so prove to be my disciples.'[1]

This, then, is the great desirability of the good and Christlike life, and so of the Christian counter-culture. It brings blessing to ourselves, salvation to others and ultimately glory to God.

[1] Jn. 15:8.

# Matthew 5:17-20

## A Christian's righteousness: Christ, the Christian and the law

*Think not that I have come to abolish the law and the prophets; I have come not to abolish them but to fulfil them.* [18] *For truly, I say to you, till heaven and earth pass away, not an iota, not a dot, will pass from the law until all is accomplished.* [19] *Whoever then relaxes one of the least of these commandments and teaches men so, shall be called least in the kingdom of heaven; but he who does them and teaches them shall be called great in the kingdom of heaven.* [20] *For I tell you, unless your righteousness exceeds that of the scribes and Pharisees, you will never enter the kingdom of heaven.*

So far Jesus has spoken of a Christian's character, and of the influence he will have in the world if he exhibits this character and if his character bears fruit in 'good works'. He now proceeds to define further this character and these good works in terms of righteousness. He explains that the righteousness he has already mentioned twice as that for which his disciples hunger (6) and on account of which they suffer (10) is a conformity to God's moral law and yet surpasses the righteousness of the scribes and Pharisees (20). The 'good works' are works of obedience. He began his Sermon with beatitudes in the third person ('Blessed are the poor in spirit'); he continued in the second person ('You are the salt of the earth'); and now he changes to the authoritative first person and uses for the first time his distinctive and dogmatic formula *I say to you* (18) or *I tell you* (20).

This paragraph is of great importance not only for its definition of Christian righteousness but also for the light it throws on the relation between the New Testament and the Old Testament, between the gospel and the law. It divides itself into two parts, first Christ and the law (17, 18) and secondly the Christian and the law (19, 20).

## 1. Christ and the law (17, 18)

He begins by telling them not for one moment to imagine that he had come *to abolish the law and the prophets, i.e.* the whole Old Testament or any part of it.[1] The way in which Jesus phrases this negative statement suggests that some had indeed been thinking the very thought which he now contradicts. Although his public ministry had so recently begun, already his contemporaries were deeply disturbed by his supposed attitude to the Old Testament. Perhaps the sabbath controversy had flared up thus early, for Mark puts both the sabbath plucking of corn and the sabbath healing of a man's withered hand before even the appointment of the twelve.[2] Certainly from the very beginning of his ministry, people had been struck by his authority. 'What is this?' they asked. 'A new teaching! With authority he commands even the unclean spirits, and they obey him' (Mk. 1:27). It was natural therefore that many were asking what the relation was between *his* authority and the authority of the law of Moses. It was clear to them that the scribes were submissive to it, for they were 'teachers of the law'. They devoted themselves to its interpretation and claimed for themselves no authority apart from the authorities they quoted. But it was not so clear with Jesus. Jesus spoke with his own authority. He loved to use a formula no ancient prophet or modern scribe had ever used. He would introduce some of his most impressive utterances with 'Truly I say to you', speaking in his own name and with his own authority. What was this authority of his? Was he setting himself up as an authority over against the sacred law, the word of God? So it seemed to some. Hence their question, spoken or unspoken, which Jesus now answered unequivocally: *Think not that I have come to abolish the law and the prophets.*

People are still asking today, though in different ways, about the relation between Jesus and Moses, the New Testament and the Old. Since Jesus grasped the nettle and declared himself plainly on the issue, we should not be shy of following suit. He had come (notice in passing his awareness that he had come into the world on a mission) neither to *abolish* the law and the prophets, setting them aside or abrogating them, nor even just

---

[1] *Cf.* 7:12.
[2] Mk. 2:23–3:6.

to endorse them in a dead and literalistic way, but to *fulfil* them.

The verb translated 'to fulfil' (*plērōsai*) means literally 'to fill' and indicates, as Chrysostom expressed it, that 'his (*sc.* Christ's) sayings were no repeal of the former, but a drawing out and filling up of them'.[1] In order to grasp the far-reaching implications of this, we need to recall that 'the law and the prophets', namely the Old Testament, contain various kinds of teaching. The relation of Jesus Christ to these differs, but the word 'fulfilment' covers them all.

✱ First, the Old Testament contains *doctrinal teaching*. 'Torah', usually translated 'law', really means 'revealed instruction'; and the Old Testament does indeed instruct us about God and man and salvation, *etc*. All the great biblical doctrines are there. Yet it was only a partial revelation. Jesus 'fulfilled' it all in the sense of bringing it to completion by his person, his teaching and his work.[2] Bishop Ryle summed it up like this: 'The Old Testament is the Gospel in the bud, the New Testament is the Gospel in full flower. The Old Testament is the Gospel in the blade; the New Testament is the Gospel in full ear.'[3]

✱ Second, the Old Testament contains *predictive prophecy*. Much of it looks forward to the days of the Messiah, and either foretells him in word or foreshadows him in type. Yet this was only anticipation. Jesus 'fulfilled' it all in the sense that what was predicted came to pass in him. The first statement of his public ministry was, 'Fulfilled is the time . . .' (Mk. 1:14). His very words here, *I have come*, imply the same truth. Again and again he claimed that the Scriptures bore witness to him, and Matthew emphasizes this more than any other evangelist by his repeated formula, 'All this took place to fulfil what the Lord had spoken by the prophet . . .'[4] The climax was his death on the cross in which the whole ceremonial system of the Old Testament, both priesthood and sacrifice, found its perfect fulfilment. Then the ceremonies ceased. Yet, as Calvin rightly comments, 'It was only the use of them that was abolished, for their meaning was more fully confirmed.'[5]

[1] P. 229.
[2] *Cf.* Heb. 1:1, 2.
[3] P. 38.
[4] 1:22; *cf.* 2:23; 3:3; 4:14, *etc. Cf.* 11:13 where it is said that the law as well as the prophets 'prophesied until John'. Both pointed forward to Christ, and both were fulfilled in him.
[5] P. 278; *cf.* Lk. 22:16.

They were but a 'shadow' of what was to come; the 'substance' belonged to Christ.[1]

Third, the Old Testament contains *ethical precepts*, or the moral law of God. Yet they were often misunderstood and even more often disobeyed. Jesus 'fulfilled' them in the first instance by obeying them, for he was 'born under law' and was determined (as he had already told John the Baptist) 'to fulfil all righteousness'.[2] 'He has in fact nothing to add to the commandments of God,' wrote Bonhoeffer, 'except this, that he keeps them.'[3] He does more than obey them himself; he explains what obedience will involve for his disciples. He rejects the superficial interpretation of the law given by the scribes; he himself supplies the true interpretation. His purpose is not to change the law, still less to annul it, but 'to reveal the full depth of meaning that it was intended to hold'.[4] So then he 'fulfils it by declaring the radical demands of the righteousness of God'.[5] This is what he stresses in the rest of Matthew 5 by giving examples, as we shall see.

In every generation of the Christian era there have been those who could not accommodate themselves to Christ's attitude to the law. The famous second-century heretic Marcion, who rewrote the New Testament by eliminating its references to the Old, naturally erased this passage.[6] Some of his followers went further. They dared even to reverse its meaning by exchanging the verbs so that the sentence then read: 'I have come not to fulfil the law and the prophets, but to abolish them'! Their counterparts today seem to be those who have embraced the so-called 'new morality', for they declare that the very category of law is abolished for the Christian (though Christ said he had not come to abolish it), that no law any longer binds Christian people except the law of love, and in fact that the command to love is the only absolute there is. I shall have more to say about them later. For the moment it is enough to emphasize that according to this verse (17) the attitude of Jesus to the Old Testament was not one of destruction and of discontinuity, but rather of a constructive, organic continuity. He

---

[1] Col. 2:17.
[2] Gal. 4:4; Mt. 3:15.
[3] P. 111.
[4] McNeile, p. 58.
[5] Stonehouse, p. 209.
[6] See Tertullian's *Against Marcion*, iv. 7.

summed up his position in a single word, not 'abolition' but 'fulfilment'.

The apostle Paul taught very clearly the same truth.[1] His statement that 'Christ is the end of the law'[2] does not mean that we are now free to disobey it, for the opposite is the case.[3] It means rather that acceptance with God is not through obedience to the law but through faith in Christ, and indeed that the law itself bears witness to this good news.[4]

Having stated that his purpose in coming was to fulfil the law, Jesus went on to give the cause and the consequence of this. The cause is the permanence of the law until it is fulfilled (18), and the consequence is the obedience to the law which the citizens of God's kingdom must give (19, 20).

This is what Jesus has to say about the law he has come to fulfil: *Truly I say to you, till heaven and earth pass away, not an iota* (which is Greek for *yod*, the smallest letter of the Hebrew alphabet, almost as small as a comma), *not a dot* (*keraia*, a horn, referring probably to one of the tiny hooks or projections which distinguish some Hebrew letters from others), *will pass from the law until all is accomplished*. His reference now was only to 'the law' rather than to 'the law and the prophets' as in the previous verse, but we have no reason to suppose that he was deliberately omitting the prophets; 'the law' was a comprehensive term for the total divine revelation of the Old Testament. None of it will pass away or be discarded, he says, not a single letter or part of a letter, until it has all been fulfilled. And this fulfilment will not be complete until the heaven and the earth themselves pass away. For one day they will pass away in a mighty rebirth of the universe.[5] Then time as we know it will cease, and the written words of God's law will be needed no longer, for all things in them will have been fulfilled. Thus the law is as enduring as the universe. The final fulfilment of the one and the new birth of the other will coincide. Both will 'pass away' together (*parelthē* is repeated). Jesus could not have stated more clearly than this his own view of Old Testament Scripture.[6]

[1] *E.g.* Acts 26:22, 23.
[2] Rom. 10:4.
[3] Rom. 8:4.
[4] Rom. 3:21.
[5] Mt. 24:35; *cf.* 19:28.
[6] *Cf.* Lk. 16:16, 17.

## 2. The Christian and the law (19, 20)

The word 'therefore' introduces the deduction which Jesus now draws for his disciples from the enduring validity of the law and his own attitude with respect to it. It reveals a vital connection between the law of God and the kingdom of God. Because he has come not to abolish but to fulfil, and because not an iota or dot will pass from the law until all has been fulfilled, *therefore* greatness in the kingdom of God will be measured by conformity to it. Nor is personal obedience enough; Christian disciples must also teach to others the permanently binding nature of the law's commandments. True, not all the commandments are equally 'weighty'.[1] Yet even *one of the least of these commandments*, precisely because it is a commandment of God the King, is important. To relax it—*i.e.* to loosen its hold on our conscience and its authority in our life—is an offence to God whose law it is. To disregard a 'least' commandment in the law (in either obedience or instruction) is to demote oneself into a 'least' subject in the kingdom; greatness in the kingdom belongs to those who are faithful in doing and teaching the whole moral law. 'The peerage of Christ's kingdom', wrote Spurgeon, 'is ordered according to obedience.'[2]

Jesus now goes further still. Not only is greatness in the kingdom assessed by a righteousness which conforms to the law, but entry into the kingdom is impossible without a conformity better (much better: the Greek expression is very emphatic) than that of the scribes and Pharisees, for God's kingdom is a kingdom of righteousness. But surely, someone will protest, the scribes and Pharisees were famous for their righteousness? Was not obedience to God's law the master-passion of their lives? Did they not calculate that the law contains 248 commandments and 365 prohibitions, and did they not aspire to keeping them all? How then can Christian righteousness actually *exceed* pharisaic righteousness, and how can this superior Christian righteousness be made a condition of entering God's kingdom? Does this not teach a doctrine of salvation by good works and so contradict the first beatitude which says the kingdom belongs to 'the poor in spirit' who have nothing, not even righteousness, to plead?

Our Lord's statement must certainly have astonished his first hearers as it astonishes us today. But the answer to these ques-

[1] *Cf.* 23:23.
[2] P. 25.

tions is not far to seek.* Christian righteousness far surpasses pharisaic righteousness in kind rather than in degree. It is not so much, shall we say, that Christians succeed in keeping some 240 commandments when the best Pharisees may only have scored 230. No. Christian righteousness is greater than pharisaic righteousness because it is deeper, being a righteousness of the heart. There has been much talk since Freud of 'depth-psychology'; the concern of Jesus was for a 'depth-morality'. Pharisees were content with an external and formal obedience, a rigid conformity to the letter of the law; Jesus teaches us that God's demands are far more radical than this. The righteousness which is pleasing to him is an inward righteousness of mind and motive. For 'The Lord looks on the heart'.[1]

It was a new heart-righteousness which the prophets foresaw as one of the blessings of the Messianic age. 'I will put my law within them, and I will write it upon their hearts,' God promised through Jeremiah (31:33). How would he do it? He told Ezekiel: 'I will put my Spirit within you, and cause you to walk in my statutes' (36:27). Thus God's two promises to put his law within us and to put his Spirit within us coincide. We must not imagine (as some do today) that when we have the Spirit we can dispense with the law, for what the Spirit does in our hearts is, precisely, to write God's law there. So 'Spirit', 'law', 'righteousness' and 'heart' all belong together. The Pharisees thought an external conformity to the law would be righteousness enough. The 'Teacher of Righteousness' who figures in the Dead Sea scrolls was stricter, for he 'defined the demands of the Law more exhaustively and more stringently than did even the Pharisees, and urged upon the Sect (sc. the Essenes of Qumran) radical obedience to them all'. Yet Jesus was more radical still, for if the Essenes asked for 'more and more obedience', he asked for 'deeper and deeper obedience'.[2] Now it is this deep obedience which is a righteousness of the heart and is possible only in those whom the Holy Spirit has regenerated and now indwells. This is why entry into God's kingdom is impossible without a righteousness greater (i.e., deeper) than that of the Pharisees. It is because such a righteousness is evidence of the new birth, and no-one enters the kingdom without being born again.[3]

[1] 1 Sa. 16:7; cf. Lk. 16:15.
[2] Davies, p. 216.
[3] Jn. 3:3, 5.

The rest of Matthew 5 contains examples of this greater, or rather deeper, righteousness. It consists of six parallel paragraphs which illustrate the principle Jesus has just propounded in verses 17 to 20 of the perpetuity of the moral law, of his coming to fulfil it and of his disciples' responsibility to obey it more completely than the scribes and Pharisees were doing. Each paragraph contains a contrast or 'antithesis' introduced by the same formula (with minor variations): *You have heard that it was said to the men of old . . . But I say to you . . .* (21, 22).

What is this antithesis? It is clear who the authoritative *egō* is. But with whom is Jesus contrasting himself? It is essential to consider this question now before, in the next three chapters, we look in greater detail at the six antitheses themselves. Many commentators have maintained that in these paragraphs Jesus is setting himself against Moses; that he is here deliberately inaugurating a new morality, and is contradicting and repudiating the old; and that his introductory formula could be paraphrased 'you know what the Old Testament taught . . . But I teach something quite different.' Popular as this interpretation is, I do not hesitate to say that it is mistaken. It is more than mistaken; it is untenable. What Jesus is contradicting is not the law itself, but certain perversions of the law of which the scribes and Pharisees were guilty. Far from contradicting the law, Jesus endorses it, insists on its authority and supplies its true interpretation. Four arguments will be sufficient to prove that this is so.

First, there is the substance of the antitheses themselves. At first sight in each instance what Jesus quotes appears to come from the Mosaic law. All six examples either consist of or include some echo of it, *e.g., You shall not kill* (21), *You shall not commit adultery* (27), *Whoever divorces his wife, let him give her a certificate of divorce* (31). Not until we come to the sixth and last antithesis do we see clearly that something is amiss. For this reads: *You shall love your neighbour and hate your enemy* (43). Now the first half of this sentence is a clear command of the law (Lv. 19:18), although even this is a truncated commandment, omitting the vital words which set the standard of our neighbour-love, namely 'as yourself'. The second half of the sentence, however, is not in the law at all. It comes neither in Leviticus 19:18, nor anywhere else. So here was a contemporary addition to the law, which was intended to interpret it, but in fact distorted it. When we look more closely at the other five antitheses (as we shall in the following chapters), it becomes plain that a similar distortion is implied. It is these distortions of the law which Jesus rejected, not the law itself. After all, the first two antitheses do not read 'It was said "you shall not commit murder and adultery", but I say you may'. Rather, 'but I say you shall not even have angry or lustful thoughts'.

Secondly, there is the introductory formula, beginning *you have heard that it was said to the men of old* (21, 33), or *you have heard that it was said* (27, 38, 43), or more briefly still, *it was also said* (31). The words common to these formulae are *it was said*, which represent the single Greek verb *errethē*. Now this was not the word which Jesus used when quoting Scripture. When he introduced a biblical quotation, both verb and tense were different, namely *gegraptai* (perfect, 'it stands written'), not *errethē* (aorist, 'it was said'). So in the six antitheses what Jesus was contradicting was not Scripture but tradition, not God's word which they had 'read'[1] but the oral instruction which was given 'to the men of old' and which they too had 'heard' since the scribes continued to give it in the synagogues.

Professor David Daube confirms this from his comprehensive knowledge of rabbinics. The verb 'hear' is associated, he says, with 'the superficial, literal meaning of Scripture'. So in the two parts of the introductory formula, 'the first gives a scriptural rule narrowly interpreted, the second a wider demand made by Jesus'. Again, 'These declarations "Ye have heard—But I say unto you" are intended to prove Jesus the Law's upholder, not destroyer . . . it is the revelation of a fuller meaning for a new age. The second member unfolds rather than sweeps away the first.'[2] One might sum it up by saying that in relation to scribal distortions of the law, the term 'antithesis' rightly describes the teaching of Jesus, whereas in relation to the law itself 'exegesis' would be a more accurate word. His quarrel was not over the law, for both the Jewish leaders and he accepted its divine authority, but over its true interpretation.

Thirdly, there is the immediate context. We have already seen that in the verses preceding and introducing the antitheses (17–20) Jesus affirmed in a quite unequivocal way what his own attitude to the law was and what his disciples' ought to be. This was 'fulfilment' in his case and 'obedience' in theirs. Not a dot or iota

[1] *Cf.* 12:3, 5; 19:4; 21:16, 42; 22:31.
[2] P. 55–60.

would pass away; all must be fulfilled. Not one of the least commandments might be disregarded; all must be obeyed. Are we now seriously to suppose that Jesus contradicted himself, that he proceeded at once in his teaching to do what he had just categorically said he had not come to do and they must not do? For this is the dilemma: if in the antitheses Jesus was contradicting Moses, he was thereby contradicting himself. 'Commentators have exhausted their ingenuity', writes W. C. Allen, 'in attempts to explain away this passage.'[1] He goes on to exercise his own ingenuity by supposing that verses 18 and 19 'did not originally belong to the Sermon, but have been placed here by the editor'. His reason is that in his view 'the attitude to the law here described is inconsistent with the general tenor of the Sermon'. But this is an entirely subjective judgment, and moreover it does not solve the dilemma. All it succeeds in doing is to remove the supposed discrepancy from the teaching of Jesus and attribute it instead either to the first evangelist or through him to some early Christian community. The better way is to accept the statements of verses 17 to 20 as genuine and to demonstrate that they are consistent not only with the Sermon as a whole but with the rest of Jesus' recorded teaching. This brings us to the last argument.

Fourthly, there is Christ's known attitude to the Old Testament. In the previous chapter Matthew has given an account of his temptations during forty gruelling days in the Judean desert. Each subtle enticement of the devil was countered by an appropriate quotation from Old Testament Scripture. Jesus had no need to debate or argue with the devil. Each issue was settled from the start by a simple appeal to what stood written (*gegraptai*). And this reverent submission of the incarnate Word to the written word continued throughout his life, not only in his personal behaviour but also in his mission. He was resolved to fulfil what was written of him, and could not be deflected from the path which Scripture had laid down for him. So his declaration in Matthew 5:17 that he had come not to abolish but to fulfil the law and the prophets is wholly consistent with his attitude to Scripture elsewhere.

From these four factors it is evident that the antitheses do not set in opposition to each other Christ and Moses, the New Testament and the Old Testament, the gospel and the law, but rather Christ's true interpretation of the law and the scribal mis-

[1] P. 45.

interpretations, and therefore Christian righteousness and pharisaic righteousness, as verse 19 anticipates.

What, then, were the scribes and Pharisees doing? What were the 'tortuous methods', as Calvin called them,[1] by which they debased the law? In general, they were trying to reduce the challenge of the law, to 'relax' (19) the commandments of God, and so make his moral demands more manageable and less exacting. They found Torah both a yoke and a burden (indeed they called it such), and wanted to make the yoke easier and the burden lighter. How they did it varied according to the form each law took, and in particular whether it was a commandment (either precept or prohibition) or a permission. Four of the six antitheses fall into the category of 'commandment', the first three of which are negative (forbidding murder, adultery and false swearing) and the last of which is positive (enjoining love for neighbour). These four are clear commands of God either to do or not to do something. The remaining two (the fourth and fifth antitheses) are best described as 'permissions'. They do not belong to the same category of moral command as the other four. Both lack the prescriptive words 'You shall' or 'You shall not'. The fourth antithesis concerns divorce, which was never commanded but was permitted in certain circumstances and on certain conditions. The fifth concerns retribution ('an eye for an eye . . .') which was permitted in the law courts and which restricted to an exact equivalent the penalties which Israelite judges might impose. Thus both these permissions were circumscribed by definite limits.

What the scribes and Pharisees were doing, in order to make obedience more readily attainable, was to restrict the commandments and extend the permissions of the law. They made the law's demands less demanding and the law's permissions more permissive. What Jesus did was to reverse both tendencies. He insisted instead that the full implications of God's commandments must be accepted without imposing any artificial limits, whereas the limits which God had set to his permissions must also be accepted and not arbitrarily increased. It may be helpful to see the application of these principles to the antitheses in summary before considering them in detail.

The scribes and Pharisees were evidently restricting the biblical prohibitions of murder and adultery to the act alone; Jesus

[1] P. 282.

extended them to include angry thoughts, insulting words and lustful looks. They restricted the command about swearing to certain oaths only (those involving the divine name) and the command about neighbour-love to certain people only (those of the same race and religion); Jesus said all promises must be kept and all people must be loved, without limitations.

But the scribes and Pharisees were not content merely to restrict the commands of the law to suit their convenience; they sought to serve their convenience still further by extending its permissions. Thus, they attempted to widen the permission of divorce beyond the single ground of 'some indecency' to include a husband's every whim, and to widen the permission of retribution beyond the law courts to include personal revenge. Jesus, however, reaffirmed the original restrictions. He called divorce on other grounds 'adultery' and insisted in personal relationships on the renunciation of all revenge.

This preliminary look at the antitheses has shown us that Jesus did not contradict the law of Moses. On the contrary, this is in effect what the Pharisees were doing. What Jesus did was rather to explain the true meaning of the moral law with all its uncomfortable implications. He extended the commands which they were restricting and restricted the permissions which they were extending. To him Moses' law was God's law, whose validity was permanent and whose authority must be accepted. In the Sermon on the Mount, as Calvin correctly expressed it, we see Jesus not 'as a new legislator, but as the faithful expounder of a law which had been already given'.[1] The Pharisees had 'obscured' the law; Jesus 'restored it to its integrity'.[2]

And in this matter Christian disciples must follow Christ, not the Pharisees. We have no liberty to try to lower the law's standards and make it easier to obey. That is the casuistry of Pharisees, not Christians. Christian righteousness must exceed pharisaic righteousness.

Yet the advocates of the 'new morality' or 'situational ethic' are in principle trying to do exactly what the Pharisees were doing. True, they claim to take Christ's part against the Pharisees, but they resemble the Pharisees in their dislike of the law. They regard the law as rigid and authoritarian, and (just like the Pharisees) they attempt to 'relax' its authority, to loosen its hold.

[1] P. 290.
[2] *Institutes*, I. viii. 7.

So they declare the category of law abolished (which Jesus said he had not come to abolish) and they set law and love at variance with each other (in a way in which Jesus never did). No. Jesus disagreed with the Pharisees' *interpretation* of the law; he never disagreed with their acceptance of its *authority*. Rather the reverse. In the strongest possible terms he asserted its authority as God's Word written, and called his disciples to accept its true and deeply exacting interpretation.

# Matthew 5:21-30
## A Christian's righteousness: avoiding anger and lust

The first two illustrations which Jesus gave of his theme (namely that he was deepening, not destroying the demands of the law) relate to the sixth and seventh of the ten commandments, the prohibitions against murder and adultery.

### 1. Avoiding anger (21-26)

*You have heard that it was said to the men of old, 'You shall not kill; and whoever kills shall be liable to judgment.' 22 But I say to you that every one who is angry with his brother shall be liable to judgment; whoever insults his brother shall be liable to the council, and whoever says, 'You fool!' shall be liable to the hell of fire. 23 So if you are offering your gift at the altar, and there remember that your brother has something against you, 24 leave your gift there before the altar and go; first be reconciled to your brother, and then come and offer your gift. 25 Make friends quickly with your accuser, while you are going with him to court, lest your accuser hand you over to the judge, and the judge to the guard, and you be put in prison; 26 truly, I say to you, you will never get out till you have paid the last penny.*

The commandment *You shall not kill* would be better expressed 'Do not commit murder' (NEB), for it is not a prohibition against taking all human life in any and every circumstance, but in particular against homicide or murder. This is clear from the fact that the same Mosaic law, which forbids killing in the decalogue, elsewhere enjoins it both in the form of capital punishment and in the wars designed to exterminate the corrupt pagan tribes which inhabited the promised land. Both war and the death penalty are vexed questions which have always perplexed sensitive Christian consciences. And there have always been Christians on both sides of both fences. What needs always to be asserted by Christians in these debates is that, if the concept of the 'just war' is tenable and if the retention of the death penalty is justifiable, the reason is not because human life is ever cheap and readily disposable but the very opposite, namely that it is precious as the life of creatures made in God's image. Those who campaign for the abolition of the death penalty on the ground that human life (the murderer's) should not be taken tend to forget the value of the life of the murderer's victim: 'Whoever sheds the blood of man, by man shall his blood be shed; *for God made man in his own image.*'[1] And those who campaign for unconditional pacifism tend to forget that, though the indiscriminate maiming and killing of civilians is utterly indefensible, God has given to society (whether the state or—by extension—some international body) the right and the responsibility to punish evildoers.[2] I mention these things now, not because the complex issues involved in war and the death penalty can be treated here, but to argue that they cannot be solved by a simplistic appeal to the commandment *You shall not kill.*

The scribes and Pharisees were evidently seeking to restrict the application of the sixth commandment to the deed of murder alone, to the act of spilling human blood in homicide. If they refrained from this, they considered that they had kept the commandment. And this apparently is what the rabbis taught the people. But Jesus disagreed with them. The true application of the prohibition was much wider, he maintained. It included thoughts and words as well as deeds, anger and insult as well as murder.

Anger is mentioned at the beginning of verse 22: *every one who is angry with his brother.* The additional words *without a cause* (AV) occur in most Greek MSS but not in the best. They are probably a later gloss and are therefore omitted in modern revisions and translations. Nevertheless, there is every reason to believe that the gloss correctly interprets what Jesus must have meant. Not all anger is evil, as is evident from the wrath of God, which is always holy and pure. And even fallen human beings may sometimes feel righteous anger, although, being fallen, we should

[1] Gn. 9:6.
[2] Rom. 13:1 ff.

ensure that even this is slow to rise and quick to die down.[1] Luther certainly knew in his own experience the meaning of righteous anger. He called it 'an anger of love, one that wishes no one any evil, one that is friendly to the person but hostile to the sin'.[2] The reference of Jesus, then, is to unrighteous anger, the anger of pride, vanity, hatred, malice and revenge.

Insults are mentioned at the end of verse 22. Jesus warns us against calling our brother either *Raca* (probably equivalent to an Aramaic word meaning 'empty') or *mōre* (the Greek word for a 'fool'). It appears that 'Raca' is an insult to a person's intelligence, calling him 'empty-headed', and commentators vie with one another in proposing English parallels like 'nitwit',[3] 'blockhead',[4] 'numskull' or 'bonehead'![5] A *moron* also is a fool, but it can hardly be used here in its ordinary sense, for Jesus himself called the Pharisees and his disciples 'fools'[6] and the apostles on occasions blamed their readers for their folly.[7] So we need to remember that the word had acquired both religious and moral overtones, being applied in the Old Testament to those who denied God's existence and as a result plunged into reckless evil doing.[8] Alternatively, as some scholars suggest, *mōre* may transliterate a Hebrew word which means a 'rebel', an 'apostate' or an 'outcast'.[9] In this case, Tasker proposes the sentiment: 'The man who tells his brother that he is doomed to hell is in danger of hell himself'.[10]

Some uncertainty remains about the precise meaning of these two terms of abuse. They were clearly derisive, insulting epithets, and NEB is content to replace them with a more general 'If he abuses his brother . . . if he sneers at him.' At the same time, A. B. Bruce probably preserves the major difference between the words when he writes: '*Raca* expresses contempt for a man's head = you stupid!; *mōre* expresses contempt for his heart and character = you scoundrel!'[11]

[1] *Cf.* Jas. 1:19 and Eph. 4:26, 27.
[2] P. 76.
[3] Tasker, p. 68.
[4] Hunter, p. 50.
[5] Lenski, pp. 217, 219.
[6] Mt. 23:17; Lk. 24:25.
[7] *E.g.* 1 Cor. 15:36; Gal. 3:1; Jas. 2:20.
[8] Ps. 14:1–4; Ps. 53:1–4.
[9] *E.g.* Ps. 78:8; Je. 5:23.
[10] P. 69.
[11] P. 107.

Now these things—angry thoughts and insulting words—may never lead to the ultimate act of murder. Yet they are tantamount to murder in God's sight. As John was later to write: 'Any one who hates his brother is a murderer.'[1] Anger and insult are ugly symptoms of a desire to get rid of somebody who stands in our way. Our thoughts, looks and words all indicate that, as we sometimes dare to say, we 'wish he were dead'. Such an evil wish is a breach of the sixth commandment. And it renders the guilty person liable to the very penalties to which the murderer exposes himself, not in each case literally in a human law court (for no court can charge a man with anger) but before the bar of God.

The exact meaning of the different judgments has been much discussed, but at least it is clear that Jesus was issuing a solemn warning of divine judgment. The rabbis may have been teaching not just that the only breach of the sixth commandment was murder, but also that the only penalty for murder was a human sentence: *Whoever kills shall be liable to judgment* (21). So Jesus added that *any one who is angry* without cause will equally *be liable to judgment*. Although the same Greek words are used for 'the judgment' in verse 22 as in verse 21, now the reference must be to the judgment of God, since no human court is competent to try a case of inward anger. Similarly, Jesus continued, insult will expose us not only to *the council* but even to *the hell of fire* (23). In both cases Jesus was extending the nature of the penalty as well as of the crime. Not only are anger and insult equivalent to murder, he said, but the punishment to which they render us liable is nothing less than the divine judgment of hell.

'So if . . .', Jesus continued (23), and proceeded to give a practical application of the principles he had just enunciated. His theme was that if anger and insult are so serious and so dangerous, then we must avoid them like the plague and take action as speedily as possible. He offered two illustrations, the first taken from going to the temple to offer sacrifice to God (23, 24), and the second from going to court to answer the charges of an accuser (25, 26). Jesus expressed them in the cultural terms of his own day, in which the temple still stood and its sacrifices were still being offered. Perhaps it would be legitimate to translate his illustrations into slightly more modern dress.

'If you are in church, in the middle of a service of worship, and you suddenly remember that your brother has a grievance against

[1] 1 Jn. 3:15.

85

you, leave church at once and put it right. Do not wait till the service has ended. Seek out your brother and ask his forgiveness. First go, then come. First go and be reconciled to your brother, then come and offer your worship to God.'

Again, 'If you have an unpaid debt, and your creditor takes you to court to get his money back, come to terms with him quickly. Make a settlement out of court. Even while you are on your way to court, pay your debt. Otherwise, once you reach the court, it will be too late. Your accuser will sue you before the judge and the judge will hand you over to the police, and you will find yourself in gaol. You will never get out till you've paid the last penny. So payment *before* prison would be much more sensible.'

The pictures are different: one is taken from church, the other from the law court. One concerns a 'brother' (23) and the other an enemy (25). But in both cases the basic situation is the same (somebody has a grievance against us) and the basic lesson is the same (the necessity of immediate, urgent action). In the very act of worship, if we remember the grievance, we are to break off our worship and go and put it right. In the very act of going to court, on our way there, we are to settle our debt.

Yet how seldom do we heed Christ's call for immediacy of action! If murder is a horrible crime, malicious anger and insult are horrible too. And so is every deed, word, look or thought by which we hurt or offend a fellow human being. We need to be more sensitive about these evils. We must never allow an estrangement to remain, still less to grow. We must not delay to put it right. We must not even allow the sun to set on our anger. But *immediately*, as soon as we are conscious of a broken relationship, we must take the initiative to mend it, to apologize for the grievance we have caused, to pay the debt we have left unpaid, to make amends. And these extremely practical instructions Jesus drew out from the sixth commandment as its logical implications! If we want to avoid committing murder in God's sight, we must take every possible positive step to live in peace and love with all men.

## 2. Avoiding lust (27–30)

Jesus now turns from the sixth commandment to the seventh, from the prohibition against murder to the prohibition against adultery.

*You have heard that it was said, 'You shall not commit adultery.' *[28]*But I say to you that every one who looks at a woman lustfully has already committed adultery with her in his heart. *[29]*If your right eye causes you to sin, pluck it out and throw it away; it is better that you lose one of your members than that your whole body be thrown into hell. *[30]*And if your right hand causes you to sin, cut it off and throw it away; it is better that you lose one of your members than that your whole body go into hell.*

Once again the rabbis were attempting to limit the scope of the commandment *you shall not commit adultery*. Although the sin of desiring another man's wife is included in the tenth commandment against covetousness, they evidently found it more comfortable to ignore this. In their view they and their pupils kept the seventh commandment, provided that they avoided the act of adultery itself. They thus gave a conveniently narrow definition of sexual sin and a conveniently broad definition of sexual purity.

But Jesus taught differently. He extended the implications of the divine prohibition. Rather, he affirmed that the true meaning of God's command was much wider than a mere prohibition of acts of sexual immorality. As the prohibition of murder included the angry thought and the insulting word, so the prohibition of adultery included the lustful look and imagination. We can commit murder with our *words*; we can commit adultery in our *hearts* or minds. Indeed (28), *every one who looks at a woman lustfully has already committed adultery with her in his heart.*

Perhaps two points should be made before we go any further. There is not the slightest suggestion here that natural sexual relations within the commitment of marriage are anything but God-given and beautiful. We may thank God that the Song of Solomon is contained in the canon of Scripture, for there is no Victorian prudery there but rather the uninhibited delight of lovers, of bride and bridegroom in each other. No. The teaching of Jesus here refers to unlawful sex outside marriage, whether practised by married or unmarried people. He is not even forbidding us to look at a woman, but to look lustfully. We all know the difference between looking and lusting.

This leads to the second point, that Jesus' allusion is to all forms of immorality. To argue that the reference is only to a man lusting after a woman and not vice versa, or only to a married man and not an unmarried, since the offender is said to commit 'adultery' not 'fornication', is to be guilty of the very casuistry

87

which Jesus was condemning in the Pharisees. His emphasis is that any and every sexual practice which is immoral in deed is immoral also in look and in thought.

What is particularly important to grasp is his equation of looking lustfully at a woman and committing adultery with her in the heart. It is the relation between the eyes and the heart which leads Jesus in the next two verses to give some very practical instruction about how to maintain sexual purity. The argument is this: If to look lustfully is to commit adultery in the heart, in other words, if heart-adultery is the result of eye-adultery (the eyes of the heart being stimulated by the eyes of the flesh), then the only way to deal with the problem is at its beginning, which is our eyes. Righteous Job claimed that he had learned this. 'I have made a covenant with my eyes,' he said; 'how then could I look upon a virgin?' Then he went on to speak of his heart: 'If . . . my heart has gone after my eyes, . . . if my heart has been enticed to a woman . . .,' he would acknowledge that he had sinned and that he deserved the judgment of God.[1] But Job had not done these things. The control of his heart was due to the control of his eyes.

This teaching of Jesus, confirmed in the experience of Job, is still true today. Deeds of shame are preceded by fantasies of shame, and the inflaming of the imagination by the indiscipline of the eyes. Our vivid imagination (one of many faculties which distinguish humans from animals) is a precious gift of God. None of the world's art and little of man's noblest achievement would have been possible without it. Imagination enriches the quality of life. But all God's gifts need to be used responsibly; they can readily be degraded and abused. This is certainly true of our imagination. I doubt if ever human beings have fallen victim to immorality, who have not first opened the sluicegates of passion through their eyes. Similarly, whenever men and women have learned sexual self-control in deed, it is because they have first learned it in the eyes of both flesh and fantasy. This may be an appropriate moment to refer in passing to the way girls dress. It would be silly to legislate about fashions, but wise (I think) to ask them to make this distinction: it is one thing to make yourself attractive; it is another to make yourself deliberately seductive. You girls know the difference; so do we men.

This brings us to verses 29 and 30: *If your right eye causes you to*

[1] Jb. 31:1, 7, 9. Contrast 2 Pet. 2:14 where the false teachers are described as having 'eyes full of adultery, insatiable for sin'.

*sin, pluck it out and throw it away . . . And if your right hand causes you
to sin, cut it off and throw it away . . .* This was evidently a favourite
saying of Jesus, for he quoted it more than once. It recurs later in
this same Gospel,[1] where the foot is added to the eye and the
hand, and the reference is a general one to 'temptations to sin',
not explicitly to sexual temptation. So the principle has a wider
application. Nevertheless, it is to this particular realm that Jesus
applied it in the Sermon on the Mount. What did he mean by
it?

On the surface it is a startling command to pluck out an offending eye, to cut off an offending hand or foot. A few Christians,
whose zeal greatly exceeded their wisdom, have taken Jesus *au
pied de la lettre* and mutilated themselves. Perhaps the best-known
example is the third-century scholar, Origen of Alexandria. He
went to extremes of asceticism, renouncing possessions, food and
even sleep, and in an over-literal interpretation of this passage and
of Matthew 19:12 actually made himself a eunuch. Not long after,
in AD 325, the Council of Nicea was right to forbid this barbarous
practice.

The command to get rid of troublesome eyes, hands and feet
is an example of our Lord's use of dramatic figures of speech.
What he was advocating was not a literal physical self-maiming,
but a ruthless moral self-denial. Not mutilation but mortification
is the path of holiness he taught, and 'mortification' or 'taking up
the cross' to follow Christ means to reject sinful practices so
resolutely that we die to them or put them to death.[2]

What does this involve in practice? Let me elaborate and so
interpret Jesus' teaching: 'If your eye causes you to sin because
temptation comes to you through your eyes (objects you see),
then pluck out your eyes. That is, don't look! Behave as if you
had actually plucked out your eyes and flung them away, and
were now blind and so *could* not see the objects which previously
caused you to sin. Again, if your hand or foot causes you to sin,
because temptation comes to you through your hands (things you
do) or your feet (places you visit), then cut them off. That is:
don't do it! Don't go! Behave as if you had actually cut off your
hands and feet, and had flung them away, and were now crippled
and so *could* not do the things or visit the places which previously
caused you to sin.' That is the meaning of 'mortification'.

[1] Mt. 18:8, 9.
[2] *Cf.* Mk. 8:34; Rom. 8:13; Gal. 5:24; Col. 3:5.

One wonders if there has ever been a generation in which this teaching of Jesus were more needed or more obviously applicable than our own, in which the river of filth (of pornographic literature and sex films) is in spate. Pornography is offensive to Christians (and indeed to all healthy-minded people) first and foremost because it degrades women from human beings into sex objects, but also because it presents the eye of the beholder with unnatural sexual stimulation. If we have a problem of sexual self-mastery, and if nonetheless our feet take us to these films, our hands handle this literature, and our eyes feast on the pictures they offer to us, we are not only sinning but actually inviting disaster.

In saying this I am very far from wishing to lay down any law or make any man-made rules about which books and magazines a Christian may read, which plays and films he may see (live or on television), and which art exhibitions he may visit. For we have to recognize that all men and women are made differently. Sexual desire is more easily aroused in some than in others, and different things arouse it. Sexual self-discipline and self-control come more naturally to some than to others. Some can see explicitly sexual pictures (on paper or film) and remain entirely unscathed, while others would find them terribly corrupting. Our temperaments and therefore our temptations vary. So we have no right to stand in judgment on others regarding what they feel able to permit themselves.

What we do have liberty to say is only this (for this is what Jesus said): *if* your eye causes you to sin, don't look; *if* your foot causes you to sin, don't go; and *if* your hand causes you to sin, don't do it. The rule Jesus laid down was hypothetical, not universal. He did not require all his disciples (metaphorically speaking) to blind or maim themselves, but only those whose eyes, hands and feet were a cause of sinning. It is they who have to take action; others may be able to retain both eyes, both hands and both feet with impunity. Of course even they may need to refrain from certain liberties out of loving concern for those with weaker consciences or weaker wills, but that is another principle which is not enunciated here.

What is necessary for all those with strong sexual temptations, and indeed for all of us in principle, is discipline in guarding the approaches of sin. The posting of sentries is a commonplace of *military* tactics; *moral* sentry-duty is equally indispensable. Are we so foolish as to allow the enemy to overwhelm us, simply because we have posted no sentries to warn us of his approach?

To obey this command of Jesus will involve for many of us a certain 'maiming'. We shall have to eliminate from our lives certain things which (though some may be innocent in themselves) either are, or could easily become, sources of temptation. In his own metaphorical language we may find ourselves without eyes, hands or feet. That is, we shall deliberately decline to read certain literature, see certain films, visit certain exhibitions. If we do this, we shall be regarded by some of our contemporaries as narrow-minded, untaught Philistines. 'What?' they will say to us incredulously, 'you've not read such and such a book? You've not seen such and such a film? Why, you're not educated, man!' They may be right. We may have had to become culturally 'maimed' in order to preserve our purity of mind. The only question is whether, for the sake of this gain, we are willing to bear that loss and endure that ridicule.

Jesus was quite clear about it. It is better to lose one member and enter life maimed, he said, than to retain our whole body and go to hell. That is to say, it is better to forgo some experiences this life offers in order to enter the life which is life indeed; it is better to accept some cultural amputation in this world than risk final destruction in the next. Of course this teaching runs clean counter to modern standards of permissiveness. It is based on the principle that eternity is more important than time and purity than culture, and that any sacrifice is worth while in this life if it is necessary to ensure our entry into the next. We have to decide, quite simply, whether to live for this world or the next, whether to follow the crowd or Jesus Christ.

# Matthew 5:31–37
# A Christian's righteousness: fidelity in marriage and honesty in speech

The third antithesis (about divorce) follows the second (about adultery) as a natural sequence. For in certain circumstances, Jesus now says, remarriage by or to a divorced person is tantamount to adultery. This third antithesis is essentially a call to fidelity in marriage.

I confess to a basic reluctance to attempt an exposition of these verses. This is partly because divorce is a controversial and complex subject, but even more because it is a subject which touches people's emotions at a deep level. There is almost no unhappiness so poignant as the unhappiness of an unhappy marriage, and almost no tragedy so great as the degeneration of what God meant for love and fulfilment into a non-relationship of bitterness, discord and despair. Although I believe that God's way in most cases is not divorce, I hope I shall write with sensitivity, for I know the pain which many suffer, and I have no wish to add to their distress. Yet it is because I am convinced that the teaching of Jesus on this and every subject is good—intrinsically good, good for individuals, good for society—that I take my courage in both hands and write on.

## 1. Fidelity in marriage (31, 32)

*It was also said, 'Whoever divorces his wife, let him give her a certificate of divorce.' [32] But I say to you that every one who divorces his wife, except on the ground of unchastity, makes her an adulteress; and whoever marries a divorced woman commits adultery.*

These two verses can hardly be thought to represent the sum total of our Lord's instruction on the mountain about divorce. They seem to give an abbreviated summary of his teaching, of which indeed Matthew records a fuller version in chapter 19. We shall be wise to take the two passages together and to interpret the shorter in the light of the longer. This is how his later debate with the Pharisees went:

19:3 *And Pharisees came up to him and tested him by asking, 'Is it lawful to divorce one's wife for any cause?'* 4 *He answered, 'Have you not read that he who made them from the beginning made them male and female,* 5 *and said, "For this reason a man shall leave his father and mother and be joined to his wife, and the two shall become one flesh"?* 6 *So they are no longer two but one flesh. What therefore God has joined together, let not man put asunder.'* 7 *They said to him, 'Why then did Moses command one to give a certificate of divorce, and to put her away?'* 8 *He said to them, 'For your hardness of heart Moses allowed you to divorce your wives, but from the beginning it was not so.* 9 *And I say to you: whoever divorces his wife, except for unchastity, and marries another, commits adultery.'*

We know that a current controversy about divorce was being conducted between the rival rabbinic schools of Hillel and Shammai. Rabbi Shammai took a rigorist line, and taught from Deuteronomy 24:1 that the sole ground for divorce was some grave matrimonial offence, something evidently 'unseemly' or 'indecent'. Rabbi Hillel, on the other hand, held a very lax view. If we can trust the Jewish historian Josephus, this was the common attitude, for he applied the Mosaic provision to a man who 'desires to be divorced from his wife for any cause whatsoever'.[1] Similarly Hillel, arguing that the ground for divorce was something 'unseemly', interpreted this term in the widest possible way to include a wife's most trivial offences. If she proved to be an incompetent cook and burnt her husband's food, or if he lost interest in her because of her plain looks and because he became enamoured of some other more beautiful woman, these things were 'unseemly' and justified him in divorcing her. The Pharisees seem to have been attracted by Rabbi Hillel's laxity, which will explain the form their question took: 'Is it lawful to divorce one's wife *for any cause*?'[2] In other words, they wanted to know whose side Jesus was on in the contemporary debate, and whether he belonged to the school of rigorism or of laxity.

[1] *Antiquities*, IV. viii. 23.
[2] 19:3.

Our Lord's reply to their question was in three parts. It is revealing to consider these separately and in the order in which he spoke them. In each he dissented from the Pharisees.

*a. The Pharisees were preoccupied with the grounds for divorce; Jesus with the institution of marriage.*

Their question was so framed as to draw Jesus on what he considered to be legitimate grounds for divorce. For what cause might a man divorce his wife? For one cause or several causes or any cause?

Jesus' reply was not a reply. He declined to answer their question. Instead, he asked a counter-question about their reading of Scripture. He referred them back to Genesis, both to the creation of mankind as male and female (chapter 1) and to the institution of marriage (chapter 2) by which a man leaves his parents and cleaves to his wife and the two become one. This biblical definition implies that marriage is both exclusive ('a man . . . his wife') and permanent ('cleave' or 'be joined' to his wife). It is these two aspects of marriage which Jesus selects for emphasis in his comments which follow (6). First, 'So they are no longer two but one flesh,' and secondly, 'What therefore God has joined together, let not man put asunder.' Thus marriage, according to our Lord's exposition of its origins, is a divine institution by which God makes permanently one two people who decisively and publicly leave their parents in order to form a new unit of society and then 'become one flesh'.

*b. The Pharisees called Moses' provision for divorce a command; Jesus called it a concession to the hardness of human hearts.*

The Pharisees responded to Jesus' exposition of the institution of marriage and its permanence by asking: 'Why then did Moses command one to give a certificate of divorce, and to put her away?'[1] Jesus' quotation of scribal teaching in the Sermon on the Mount was similar: 'It was also said, "Whoever divorces his wife, let him give her a certificate of divorce".'[2]

Both these were garbled versions of the Mosaic provision, typical of the Pharisees' disregard for what Scripture really said and implied. They laid their emphasis on the giving of a divorce certificate, as if this were the most important part of the Mosaic

[1] 19:7.
[2] 5:31.

94

provision, and then referred to both the certificate and the divorce as 'commands' of Moses.

A careful reading of Deuteronomy 24:1-4 reveals something quite different. To begin with, the whole paragraph hinges on a long series of conditional clauses. This may be brought out in the following paraphrase: 'After a man has married a wife, *if* he finds some indecency in her, and *if* he gives her a divorce-certificate and divorces her and she leaves, and *if* she marries again, and *if* her second husband gives her a divorce-certificate and divorces her, or *if* her second husband dies, *then* her first husband who divorced her is forbidden to remarry her . . .' The thrust of the passage is to prohibit the remarriage of one's own divorced partner. The reason for this regulation is obscure. It appears to be that if her 'indecency' had so 'defiled' her as to be a sufficient ground for divorce, it was also a sufficient reason for not taking her back. It may also have been intended to warn a husband against a hasty decision, because once made it could not be rescinded, and/or to protect the wife against exploitation. For our purposes here it is enough to observe that this prohibition is the only command in the whole passage; there is certainly no command to a husband to divorce his wife, nor even any encouragement to do so. All there is, instead, is a reference to certain necessary procedures *if* a divorce takes place; and therefore at the very most a reluctant permission is implied and a current practice is tolerated.

How, then, did Jesus respond to the Pharisees' question about the regulation of Moses? He attributed it to the hardness of people's hearts. In so doing he did not deny that the regulation was from God. He implied, however, that it was not a divine instruction, but only a divine concession to human weakness. It was for this reason that 'Moses allowed you to divorce . . . ', he said (8). But then he immediately referred again to the original purpose of God, saying: 'But from the beginning it was not so.' Thus even the divine concession was in principle inconsistent with the divine institution.

*c. The Pharisees regarded divorce lightly; Jesus took it so seriously that, with only one exception, he called all remarriage after divorce adultery.* This was the conclusion of his debate with the Pharisees, and this is what is recorded in the Sermon on the Mount. It may be helpful to see his two statements side by side.

*5:32: But I say to you that every one who divorces his wife, except on the ground of unchastity, makes her an adulteress; and whoever marries a divorced woman commits adultery.*

19:9: *And I say to you: whoever divorces his wife, except for unchastity, and marries another, commits adultery.*

It seems to be assumed that a divorce would lead to the remarriage of the divorced parties. Only this assumption can explain the statement that a man divorcing his wife without cause 'makes her an adulteress'. His action could have that result only if she married again. Besides, a separation without a divorce—in legal terms *a mensa et toro* (from table and bed) but not *a vinculo* (from the marriage bond)—is a modern arrangement unknown in the ancient world.

Since God instituted marriage as an exclusive and permanent union, a union which he makes and man must not break, Jesus draws the inevitable deduction that to divorce one's partner and marry another, or to marry a divorced person, is to enter a forbidden, adulterous relationship. For the person who may have secured a divorce in the eyes of human law is still in the eyes of God married to his or her first partner.

Only one exception is made to this principle: *except on the ground of unchastity* (5:32) or *except for unchastity* (19:9). The so-called 'exceptive clause' is a well-known crux. Commentators are not agreed about either its authenticity or its meaning.

First, its authenticity. I would wish to argue, as do virtually all conservative commentators, that we must accept this clause not only as a genuine part of Matthew's Gospel (for no MSS omit it) but also as an authentic word of Jesus. The reason why many have rejected it, regarding it as an interpolation by Matthew, is that it is absent from the parallel passages in the Gospels of Mark and Luke. Yet Plummer was right to dub 'a violent hypothesis'[1] this easy dismissal of the exceptive clause as an editorial gloss. It seems far more likely that its absence from Mark and Luke is due not to their ignorance of it but to their acceptance of it as something taken for granted. After all, under the Mosaic law adultery was punishable by death (although the death penalty for this offence seems to have fallen into disuse by the time of Jesus);[2] so

[1] P. 82.

[2] Dt. 22:22; Jn. 8:1-11. G. E. Ladd writes: 'The Old Testament condemned adultery with the death penalty. The New Testament says that an adulterer is to be considered as one dead, and the innocent party is freed from his marriage vows as though his mate had died' (*The Gospel of the kingdom*, Eerdmans, 1959, p. 85).

nobody would have questioned that marital unfaithfulness was a just ground for divorce. Even the rival Rabbis Shammai and Hillel were agreed about this. Their dispute was how much more widely than this the expression 'some indecency' in Deuteronomy 24:1 could be interpreted.

The second question about the exceptive clause concerns what is meant by *unchastity*. The Greek word is *porneia*. It is normally translated 'fornication', denoting the immorality of the unmarried, and is often distinguished from *moicheia* ('adultery'), the immorality of the married. For this reason some have argued that the exceptive clause permits divorce if some pre-marital sexual sin is later discovered. Some think that the 'indecency' of Deuteronomy 24:1 had the same meaning. But the Greek word is not precise enough to be limited in this way. *Porneia* is derived from *porne*, a prostitute, without specifying whether she (or her client) is married or unmarried. Further, it is used in the Septuagint for the unfaithfulness of Israel, Yahweh's bride, as exemplified in Hosea's wife Gomer.[1] It seems, therefore, that we must agree with R. V. G. Tasker's conclusion that *porneia* is 'a comprehensive word, including adultery, fornication and unnatural vice'.[2] At the same time we have no liberty to go to the opposite extreme and argue that *porneia* covers any and every offence which may be said in some vague sense to have a sexual basis. This would be virtually to equate *porneia* with 'incompatibility', and there is no etymological warrant for this. No, *porneia* means 'unchastity', some act of physical sexual immorality.

What, then, did Jesus teach? N. B. Stonehouse offers a good paraphrase of the first part of the antithesis in the Sermon on the Mount: 'Ye have heard of the appeal of Jewish teachers to Deuteronomy 24:1 in the interest of substantiating a policy which permits husbands freely at their own pleasure to divorce their wives—simply by providing them with a duly attested document of the transaction.'[3] 'But I say to you,' Jesus continued, that such irresponsible behaviour on the part of a husband will lead him and his wife and their second partners into unions which are not marriage but adultery. To this general principle there is one exception. The only situation in which divorce and remarriage are possible without breaking the seventh commandment is when

[1] Ho. 1:2, 3; 2:2, 4.
[2] P. 184.
[3] P. 203.

it has already been broken by some serious sexual sin. In this case, and in this case only, Jesus seems to have taught that divorce was permissible, or at least that it could be obtained without the innocent party contracting the further stigma of adultery. The modern tendency of Western countries to frame legislation for divorce on the basis rather of the 'irretrievable breakdown' or 'death' of a marriage than of a 'matrimonial offence' may make for better and juster law; it cannot be said to be compatible with the teaching of Jesus.

Nevertheless, the matter cannot be left there. For this reluctant permission of Jesus must still be seen for what it is, namely a continued accommodation to the hardness of human hearts. In addition, it must always be read both in its immediate context (Christ's emphatic endorsement of the permanence of marriage in God's purpose) and also in the wider context of the Sermon on the Mount and of the whole Bible which proclaim a gospel of reconciliation. Is it not of great significance that the Divine Lover was willing to woo back even his adulterous wife, Israel?[1] So one must never begin a discussion on this subject by enquiring about the legitimacy of divorce. To be preoccupied with the grounds for divorce is to be guilty of the very pharisaism which Jesus condemned. His whole emphasis in debating with the rabbis was positive, namely on God's original institution of marriage as an exclusive and permanent relationship, on God's 'yoking' of two people into a union which man must not break, and (one might add) on his call to his followers to love and forgive one another, and to be peacemakers in every situation of strife and discord. Chrysostom justly linked this passage with the beatitudes and commented in his homily on it: 'For he that is meek, and a peacemaker, and poor in spirit, and merciful, how shall he cast out his wife? He that is used to reconcile others, how shall he be at variance with her that is his own?'[2] From this divine ideal, purpose and call, divorce can be seen only as a tragic declension.

So, speaking personally as a Christian pastor, whenever somebody asks to speak with me about divorce, I have now for some years steadfastly refused to do so. I have made the rule never to speak with anybody about divorce, until I have first spoken with him (or her) about two other subjects, namely marriage and re-

[1] *Cf.* Je. 2:1; 3:1; 4:1; Ho. 2:1–23.
[2] P. 260.

conciliation. Sometimes a discussion on these topics makes a discussion of the other unnecessary. At the very least, it is only when a person has understood and accepted God's view of marriage and God's call to reconciliation that a possible context has been created within which one may regretfully go on to talk about divorce. This principle of pastoral priorities is, I believe, consistent with the teaching of Jesus.[1]

## 2. Honesty in speech (33)

If the rabbis tended to be permissive in their attitude to divorce, they were permissive also in their teaching about oaths. It is another example of their devious treatment of Old Testament Scripture, in order to make it more amenable to obedience. We must look first at the Mosaic law, then at the pharisaic distortion and finally at the true implication of the law on which Jesus insisted.

*Again you have heard that it was said to the men of old, 'You shall not swear falsely, but shall perform to the Lord what you have sworn.'*

This is not an accurate quotation of any one law of Moses. At the same time, it is a not inaccurate summary of several Old Testament precepts which require people who make vows to keep them. And the vows in question are, strictly speaking, 'oaths' in which the speaker calls upon God to witness his vow and to punish him if he breaks it. Moses often seems to have emphasized the evil of false swearing and the duty of performing to the Lord one's oaths. Here are a few examples:

'You shall not take the name of the Lord your God in vain' (Ex. 20:7, the third commandment).

'You shall not swear by my name falsely, and so profane the name of your God' (Lv. 19:12).

'When a man vows a vow to the Lord, . . . he shall not break his word' (Nu. 30:2).

'When you make a vow to the Lord your God, you shall not be slack to pay it' (Dt. 23:21).

Even a superficial reading of these commandments indicates

[1] For a fuller treatment of the scriptural material see the author's *Divorce: the biblical teaching* (Falcon, 1972).

plainly their intention. They prohibit false swearing or perjury, that is, making a vow and then breaking it.

But the casuistical Pharisees got to work on these awkward prohibitions and tried to restrict them. They shifted people's attention away from the vow itself and the need to keep it to the formula used in making it. They argued that what the law was really prohibiting was not taking the name of the Lord *in vain*, but taking *the name of the Lord* in vain. 'False swearing', they concluded, meant profanity (a profane use of the divine name), not perjury (a dishonest pledging of one's word). So they developed elaborate rules for the taking of vows. They listed which formulae were permissible, and they added that only those formulae which included the divine name made the vow binding. One need not be so particular, they said, about keeping vows in which the divine name had not been used.

Jesus expressed his contempt for this kind of sophistry in one of the 'woes' against the Pharisees ('blind guides' he called them) which Matthew records later (23:16–22):

*Woe to you, blind guides, who say, 'If any one swears by the temple, it is nothing; but if any one swears by the gold of the temple, he is bound by his oath.'* [17] *You blind fools! For which is greater, the gold or the temple that has made the gold sacred?* [18] *And you say, 'If any one swears by the altar, it is nothing; but if any one swears by the gift that is on the altar, he is bound by his oath.'* [19] *You blind men! For which is greater, the gift or the altar that makes the gift sacred?* [20] *So he who swears by the altar, swears by it and by everything on it;* [21] *and he who swears by the temple, swears by it and by him who dwells in it;* [22] *and he who swears by heaven, swears by the throne of God and by him who sits upon it.*

Our Lord's teaching in the Sermon on the Mount is similar. The second part of his antithesis, in which he set his teaching over against that of the rabbis, reads as follows:

5:34 *But I say to you, Do not swear at all, either by heaven, for it is the throne of God,* [35] *or by the earth, for it is his footstool, or by Jerusalem, for it is the city of the great King.* [36] *And do not swear by your head, for you cannot make one hair white or black.* [37] *Let what you say be simply 'Yes' or 'No'; anything more than this comes from evil.*

He begins by arguing that the question of the formula used in making vows is a total irrelevance, and in particular that the Pharisees' distinction between formulae which mention God and those which do not is entirely artificial. However hard you try, Jesus said, you cannot avoid some reference to God, for the whole world is God's world and you cannot eliminate him from any of it. If you vow by 'heaven', it is God's throne; if by 'earth' it is his footstool; if by 'Jerusalem' it is his city, *the city of the great King*. If you swear by your head, it is indeed yours in the sense that it is nobody else's, and yet it is God's creation and under God's control. You cannot even change the natural colour of a single hair, black in youth and white in old age.

So if the precise wording of a vow-formula is irrelevant, then a preoccupation with formulae was not the point of the law at all. Indeed, since anybody who makes a vow must keep it (whatever formula of attestation he uses), strictly speaking all formulae are superfluous. For the formula does not add to the solemnity of the vow. A vow is binding irrespective of its accompanying formula. That being so, the real implication of the law is that we must keep our promises and be people of our word. Then vows become unnecessary. *Do not swear at all* (34), but rather *let what you say be simply 'Yes' or 'No'* (37). As the apostle James was to put it later: 'Let your yes be yes and your no be no.'[1] And *anything more than this*, Jesus added, *comes from evil*, either from the evil of our hearts and its fundamental deceit, or from the evil one whom Jesus described as 'a liar and the father of lies'.[2] If divorce is due to human hard-heartedness, swearing is due to human untruthfulness. Both were permitted by the law; neither was commanded;[3] neither should be necessary.

Two questions may arise in our minds at this point. First, if swearing is forbidden, why has God himself used oaths in Scripture? Why, for example, did he say to Abraham: 'By myself I have sworn . . . I will indeed bless you . . .'?[4] To this I think we must answer that the purpose of the divine oaths was not to increase his credibility (since 'God is not man that he should lie'[5]), but to elicit and confirm our faith. The fault which made God condescend to this human level lay not in any untrustworthiness of his but in our unbelief.

Secondly, if swearing is forbidden, is the prohibition absolute? For example, should Christians, in order to be consistent in their

---

[1] Jas. 5:12.　　　[2] Jn. 8:44.　　　[3] *Cf.* Dt. 23:22.
[4] Gn. 22:16, 17. *Cf.* Heb. 6:13-18.　　　[5] Nu. 23:19.

obedience, decline to swear an affidavit for any purpose before a Commissioner of Oaths and to give evidence on oath in a court of law? The Anabaptists took this line in the sixteenth century and most Quakers still do today. While admiring their desire not to compromise, one can still perhaps question whether their interpretation is not excessively literalistic. After all, Jesus himself, Matthew later records, did not refuse to reply when the high priest put him on oath, saying: 'I adjure you by the living God, tell us if you are the Christ, the Son of God.' He confessed that he was and that later they would see him enthroned at God's right hand.[1] What Jesus emphasized in his teaching was that honest men do not need to resort to oaths; it was not that they should refuse to take an oath if required by some external authority to do so.

The modern application is not far to seek, for the teaching of Jesus is timeless. Swearing (*i.e.* oath-taking) is really a pathetic confession of our own dishonesty. Why do we find it necessary to introduce our promises by some tremendous formula, 'I swear by the archangel Gabriel and all the host of heaven' or 'I swear by the Holy Bible'? The only reason is that we know our simple word is not likely to be trusted. So we try to induce people to believe us by adding a solemn oath. Interestingly, the Essenes (a Jewish sect contemporary with Jesus) had high standards in this matter. Josephus wrote of them: 'They are eminent for fidelity and are the ministers of peace. Whatsoever they say also is firmer than an oath. But swearing is avoided by them, and they esteem it worse than perjury, for they say that he who cannot be believed without (swearing by) God, is already condemned.'[2] As A. M. Hunter puts it, 'Oaths arise because men are so often liars.'[3] The same is true of all forms of exaggeration, hyperbole and the use of superlatives. We are not content to say we had an enjoyable time; we have to describe it as 'fantastic' or 'fabulous' or even 'fantabulous' or some other invention. But the more we resort to such expressions, the more we devalue human language and human promises. Christians should say what they mean and mean what they say. Our unadorned word should be enough, 'yes' or 'no'. And when a monosyllable will do, why waste our breath by adding to it?

[1] Mt. 26:63, 64.
[2] *War*, II. viii. 6.
[3] P. 55.

# Matthew 5:38–48

## A Christian's righteousness: non-retaliation and active love

The two final antitheses bring us to the highest point of the Sermon on the Mount, for which it is both most admired and most resented, namely the attitude of total love which Christ calls us to show towards *one who is evil* (39) and our *enemies* (44). Nowhere is the challenge of the Sermon greater. Nowhere is the distinctness of the Christian counter-culture more obvious. Nowhere is our need of the power of the Holy Spirit (whose first fruit is love) more compelling.

### 1. Passive non-retaliation (38–42)

*You have heard that it was said, 'An eye for an eye and a tooth for a tooth.'* [39] *But I say to you, Do not resist one who is evil. But if any one strikes you on the right cheek, turn to him the other also;* [40] *and if any one would sue you and take your coat, let him have your cloak as well;* [41] *and if any one forces you to go one mile, go with him two miles.* [42] *Give to him who begs from you, and do not refuse him who would borrow from you.*

The excerpt from the oral teaching of the rabbis which Jesus quoted comes straight out of the Mosaic law. As we consider it, we need to remember that the law of Moses was a civil as well as a moral code. For example, Exodus 20 contains the ten commandments (the distillation of the moral law). Exodus 21 to 23, on the other hand, contain a series of 'ordinances' in which the standards of the ten commandments are applied to the young nation's life. A wide variety of 'case-laws' is given, with a particular emphasis on damage to person and property. It is in the course of this legislation that these words occur: 'When men strive together

... if any harm follows, then you shall give life for life, eye for eye, tooth for tooth, hand for hand, foot for foot, burn for burn, wound for wound, stripe for stripe.'[1]

The context makes it clear beyond question that this was an instruction to the judges of Israel. Indeed, they are mentioned in Deuteronomy 19:17, 18. It expressed the *lex talionis*, the principle of an exact retribution, whose purpose was both to lay the foundation of justice, specifying the punishment which a wrong-doer deserved, and to limit the compensation of his victim to an exact equivalent and no more. It thus had the double effect of defining justice and restraining revenge. It also prohibited the taking of the law into one's own hands by the ghastly vengeance of the family feud.

Similarly, in Islamic law the *lex talionis* specified the maximum punishment allowable. It was administered literally (and still is in *e.g.* Saudi Arabia) unless the wounded person waived the penalty or his heirs (in a case of murder) demanded blood-money instead.[2]

It is almost certain that by the time of Jesus literal retaliation for damage had been replaced in Jewish legal practice by money penalties or 'damages'. Indeed there is evidence of this much earlier. The verses immediately following the *lex talionis* in Exodus enact that if a man strikes his slave so as to destroy his eye or knock out his tooth, instead of losing his own eye or tooth (which he would deserve but which would be no compensation to the disabled slave), he must lose his slave: 'He shall let the slave go free for the eye's (or tooth's) sake.'[3] We may be quite sure that in other cases too this penalty was not physically exacted, except in the case of murder ('life for life'); it was commuted to a payment of damages.

But the scribes and Pharisees evidently extended this principle of just retribution from the law courts (where it belongs) to the realm of personal relationships (where it does not belong). They tried to use it to justify personal revenge, although the law explicitly forbade this: 'You shall not take vengeance or bear any grudge against the sons of your own people.'[4] Thus, 'This excellent, if stern, principle of judicial retribution was being

---

[1] Ex. 21:22–25. *Cf.* Lv. 24:19, 20; Dt. 19:21.
[2] I owe these facts to Sir Norman Anderson, an expert in Islamic law.
[3] Ex. 21:26, 27.
[4] Lv. 19:18.

utilized as an excuse for the very thing it was instituted to abolish, namely personal revenge.'[1]

In his reply Jesus did not contradict the principle of retribution, for it is a true and just principle. Later in the Sermon he himself stated it in the form: 'Judge not, that you be not judged' (7:1), and all his teaching about the terrible reality of divine judgment on the last day rests upon the same foundation principle. What Jesus affirmed in the antithesis was rather that this principle, though it pertains to the law courts and to the judgment of God, is not applicable to our personal relationships. These are to be based on love, not justice. Our duty to individuals who wrong us is not retaliation, but the acceptance of injustice without revenge or redress: *Do not resist one who is evil* (39).

But what exactly is the meaning of this call to non-resistance? The Greek verb (*anthistēmi*) is plain: it is to resist, oppose, withstand or set oneself against someone or something. So whom or what are we forbidden to resist?

Perhaps the other uses of the verb in the New Testament will help to set the context for our thinking. According to its major negative use, we are above all not to resist God, his will, his truth or his authority.[2] We are constantly urged, however, to resist the devil. The apostles Paul, Peter and James all tell us to oppose him who is 'the evil one' *par excellence*, and all the powers of evil at his disposal.[3] So how is it possible that Jesus told us *not* to resist evil? We cannot possibly interpret his command as an invitation to compromise with sin or Satan. No, the first clue to a correct understanding of his teaching is to recognize that the words *tō ponērō* ('the evil') are here masculine not neuter. What we are forbidden to resist is not evil as such, evil in the abstract, nor 'the evil one' meaning the devil, but an evil person, *one who is evil* (as RSV rightly translates) or 'the man who wrongs you' (NEB). Jesus does not deny that he is evil. He asks us neither to pretend that he is other than he is, nor to condone his evil behaviour. What he does not allow is that we retaliate. 'Do not take revenge on someone who wrongs you' (GNB).

The four mini-illustrations which follow all apply the prin-

---

[1] John W. Wenham, *Christ and the Bible* (Tyndale Press, 1972), p. 35.
[2] For resisting his will *cf.* Rom. 9:19; his truth, 2 Tim. 3:8; 4:15; Lk. 21:15; Acts 6:10; 13:8; and his authority delegated to the state, Rom. 13:2.
[3] *Cf.* Eph. 6:13; 1 Pet. 5:9; Jas. 4:7.

ciple of Christian non-retaliation, and indicate the lengths to
which it must go. They are vivid little cameos drawn from
different life-situations. Each introduces a person (in the context a
person who in some sense is 'evil') who seeks to do us an injury,
one by hitting us in the face, another by prosecuting us at law, a
third by commandeering our service and a fourth by begging
money from us. All have a very modern ring except the third,
which sounds a bit archaic. The verb translated *forces* (*angareusei*),
Persian in origin, was used by Josephus with reference to 'the
compulsory transportation of military baggage'.[1] It could be
applied today to any form of service in which we find ourselves
conscripts rather than volunteers. In each of the four situations,
Jesus said, our Christian duty is so completely to forbear revenge
that we even allow the 'evil' person to double the injury.

Let it be said at once, albeit to our great discomfort, that there
will be occasions when we cannot dodge this demand but must
obey it literally. It may seem fantastic that we should be expected
to offer our left cheek to someone who has already struck our
right, especially when we recall that 'the striking on the right
cheek, the blow with the back of the hand, is still today in the
East the insulting blow' and that Jesus probably had in mind not
an ordinary insult but 'a quite specific insulting blow: the blow
given to the disciples of Jesus as heretics'.[2] Yet this is the standard
which Jesus asks, and it is the standard which he himself fulfilled.
It had been written of him in Old Testament Scripture: 'I gave
my back to the smiters, and my cheeks to those who pulled out
the beard; I hid not my face from shame and spitting.' And in the
event first the Jewish police spat on him, blindfolded him and
struck him in the face, and then the Roman soldiers followed suit.
They crowned him with thorns, clothed him in the imperial
purple, invested him with a sceptre of reed, jeered at him, 'Hail,
King of the Jews,' knelt before him in mock homage, spat in
his face and struck him with their hands.[3] And Jesus, with the
infinite dignity of self-control and love, held his peace. He
demonstrated his total refusal to retaliate by allowing them to
continue their cruel mockery until they had finished. Further,
before we become too eager to evade the challenge of his teaching and behaviour as mere unpractical idealism, we need to

[1] Allen, p. 54.
[2] Jeremias, pp. 27, 28.
[3] Is. 50:6; Mk. 14:65; 15:16-20.

remember that Jesus called his disciples to what Bonhoeffer termed a 'visible participation in his cross'.[1] This is how Peter put it: 'Christ . . . suffered for you, leaving you an example, that you should follow in his steps . . . When he was reviled, he did not revile in return; when he suffered, he did not threaten; but he trusted to him who judges justly.'[2] In Spurgeon's arresting phrase, we 'are to be as the anvil when bad men are the hammers'.[3]

Yes, but an anvil is one thing, a doormat is another. Jesus' illustrations and personal example depict not the weakling who offers no resistance. He himself challenged the high priest when questioned by him in court.[4] They depict rather the strong man whose control of himself and love for others are so powerful that he rejects absolutely every conceivable form of retaliation. Further, however conscientious we may be in our determination not to sidestep the implications of Jesus' teaching, we still cannot take the four little cameos with wooden, unimaginative literalism. This is partly because they are given not as detailed regulations but as illustrations of a principle, and partly because they must be seen to uphold the principle they are intended to illustrate. That principle is love, the selfless love of a person who, when injured, refuses to satisfy himself by taking revenge, but studies instead the highest welfare of the other person and of society, and determines his reactions accordingly. He will certainly never hit back, returning evil for evil, for he has been entirely freed from personal animosity. Instead, he seeks to return good for evil. So he is willing to give to the uttermost—his body, his clothing, his service, his money in so far as these gifts are required by love.

Thus the only limit to the Christian's generosity will be a limit which love itself may impose. For example the apostle Paul once 'resisted' (same Greek word) the apostle Peter to his face. Peter's behaviour had been wrong, evil. He had withdrawn from fellowship with Gentile brothers and so contradicted the gospel. Did Paul give in to him and let him get away with it? No. He opposed him, publicly rebuking him and denouncing his action. And I think we must defend Paul's conduct as a true expression of love. For on the one hand there was no personal animosity towards Peter (he did not punch him or insult him or injure him), while on the other there was a strong love for the Gentile Christians Peter had affronted and for the gospel he had denied.[5]

[1] P. 130.　　[2] I Pet. 2:21–23.
[3] P. 30.　　[4] Jn. 18:19–23.　　[5] Gal. 2:11–14.

Similarly, Christ's illustrations are not to be taken as the charter for any unscrupulous tyrant, ruffian, beggar or thug. His purpose was to forbid revenge, not to encourage injustice, dishonesty or vice. How can those who seek as their first priority the extension of God's righteous rule at the same time contribute to the spread of unrighteousness? True love, caring for both the individual and society, takes action to deter evil and to promote good. And Christ's command was 'a precept of love, not folly'.[1] He teaches not the irresponsibility which encourages evil but the forbearance which renounces revenge. Authentic Christian non-resistance is non-retaliation.

The familiar words of the Authorized Version, 'Resist not evil,' have been taken by some as the basis for an uncompromising pacifism, as the prohibition of the use of force in any and every situation.

One of the most absurd instances of this is 'the crazy saint' whom Luther describes, 'who let the lice nibble at him and refused to kill any of them on account of this text, maintaining that he had to suffer and could not resist evil'![2]

A more reputable example, though also an extreme one, was Leo Tolstoy, the distinguished nineteenth-century Russian novelist and social reformer. In *What I Believe* (1884) he describes how in a time of deep personal perplexity about life's meaning he was 'left alone with my heart and the mysterious book'. As he read and re-read the Sermon on the Mount, 'I suddenly understood what I had not formerly understood' and what, in his view, the whole church for 1800 years had misunderstood. 'I understood that Christ says just what he says,' in particular in his command 'Resist not evil.' 'These words . . . , understood in their direct meaning, were for me truly a key opening everything else.'[3] In the second chapter ('The Command of Non-Resistance') he interprets Jesus' words as a prohibition of all physical violence to both persons and institutions. 'It is impossible at one and the same time to confess Christ as God, the basis of whose teaching is non-resistance to him that is evil, and consciously and calmly to work for the establishment of property, law courts, government and military forces . . .'[4] Again, 'Christ totally forbids the human institution of any law court' because they resist evil and even return evil for evil.[5] The same principle applies, he says, to the

[1] Glover, p. 55.  [2] P. 110.
[3] Tolstoy, pp. 315-319.  [4] P. 323.  [5] P. 331.

police and the army. When Christ's commands are at last obeyed 'all men will be brothers, and everyone will be at peace with others . . . Then the Kingdom of God will have come.'[1] When in the last chapter he tries to defend himself against the charge of naivety because 'enemies will come . . . , and if you do not fight, they will slaughter you', he betrays his ingenuous (indeed mistaken) doctrine of human beings as basically rational and amiable. Even 'the so-called criminals and robbers . . . love good and hate evil as I do'. And when they come to see, through the truth Christians teach and exhibit, that the non-violent devote their lives to serving others, 'no man will be found so senseless as to deprive of food or to kill those who serve him'.[2]

One man whom Tolstoy's writings profoundly influenced was Gandhi. Already as a child he had learnt the doctrine of *ahimsa*, 'refraining from harming others'. But then as a young man he read first in London the *Baghavad Gita* and the Sermon on the Mount ('It is that Sermon which has endeared Jesus to me'), and then in South Africa Tolstoy's *The kingdom of God is within you*. When he returned to India about ten years later, he was determined to put Tolstoy's ideals into action. Strictly speaking, his policy was neither 'passive resistance' (which he regarded as too negative), nor 'civil disobedience' (which was too defiant) but *satyagraha* or 'truth-force', the attempt to win his opponents by the power of truth and 'by the example of suffering willingly endured'. His theory approached very close to anarchy. 'The State represents violence in a concentrated and organized form.' In the perfect state which he envisaged, although the police would exist, they would seldom use force; punishment would end; prisons would be turned into schools; and litigation be replaced by arbitration.[3]

It is impossible not to admire Gandhi's humility and sincerity of purpose. Yet his policy must be judged unrealistic. He said he would resist the Japanese invaders (if they came) by a peace brigade, but his claim never had to be put to the test. He urged the Jews to offer a non-violent resistance to Hitler, but they did not heed him. In July 1940 he issued an appeal to every Briton for the cessation of hostilities, in which he claimed: 'I have been

[1] P. 406.
[2] Pp. 535, 536.
[3] Most of the quotations are taken from George Woodstock, *Gandhi* (Fontana 'Modern Masters' series, 1972).

practising, with scientific precision, non-violence and its possibilities for an unbroken period of over fifty years. I have applied it in every walk of life—domestic, institutional, economic and political. I know no single case in which it has failed.'[1] But his appeal fell on deaf ears. Jacques Ellul makes the perceptive comment that 'an essential factor in Gandhi's success' was the people involved. These were on the one hand India, 'a people shaped by centuries of concern for holiness and the spiritual, . . . a people . . . uniquely capable of understanding and accepting his message' and on the other Britain which 'officially declared itself a Christian nation' and 'could not remain insensible to Gandhi's preachment of non-violence'. 'But put Gandhi into the Russia of 1925 or the Germany of 1933. The solution would be simple: after a few days he would be arrested and nothing more would be heard of him.'[2]

Our main disagreement with Tolstoy and Gandhi, however, must not be that their views were unrealistic, but that they were unbiblical. For we cannot take Jesus' command, 'Resist not evil,' as an absolute prohibition of the use of all force (including the police) unless we are prepared to say that the Bible contradicts itself and the apostles misunderstood Jesus. For the New Testament teaches that the state is a divine institution, commissioned (through its executive office-bearers) both to punish the wrongdoer (i.e., to 'resist one who is evil' to the point of making him bear the penalty of his evil) and to reward those who do good.[3] This revealed truth may not be twisted, however, to justify the institutionalized violence of an oppressive regime. Far from it. Indeed, the same state—the Roman Empire—which in Romans 13 is termed 'the servant of God', wielding his authority, is pictured in Revelation 13 as an ally of the devil wielding his authority. But these two aspects of the state complement one another; they are not contradictory. The fact that the state has been instituted by God does not preserve it from abusing its power and becoming a tool of Satan. Nor does the historical truth that the state has sometimes persecuted good men alter the biblical truth that its real function is to punish bad men. And

[1] Reuters' text of Gandhi's appeal is quoted in F. W. Dillistone, *Charles Raven* (Hodder, 1975), pp. 230 ff.
[2] Jacques Ellul, *Violence* (SCM, 1970), p. 15.
[3] Rom. 13:1 ff.

when the state exercises its God-given authority to punish, it is 'the servant of God to execute his wrath on the wrongdoer'.[1]

How does this principle apply to war? No slick or easy answer either for or against war seems possible, although all Christians will surely agree that in its very nature war is brutalizing and horrible. Certainly too the concept of the 'just war' developed by Thomas Aquinas, a war whose cause, methods and results must be 'just', is difficult to relate to the modern world. Nevertheless, I would want to argue on the one hand that war cannot be absolutely repudiated on the basis of 'Resist not evil' any more than police and prisons can, and on the other that its only possible justification (from a biblical viewpoint) would be as a kind of glorified police action. Further, it is of the essence of police action to be discriminate; to arrest specific evildoers in order to bring them to justice. It is because so much modern warfare lacks anything approaching this precision either in defining the evildoers or in punishing the evil that Christian consciences revolt against it. Certainly the indiscriminate horrors of atomic war, engulfing the innocent with the guilty, are enough to condemn it altogether.

The point I have been labouring is that the duties and functions of the state are quite different from those of the individual. The individual's responsibility towards a wrongdoer was laid down by the apostle Paul at the end of Romans 12: 'Repay no one evil for evil (surely an echo of "Do not resist one who is evil"), but take thought for what is noble in the sight of all . . . Beloved, never avenge yourselves, but leave it to the wrath of God; for it is written, "Vengeance is mine, I will repay, says the Lord." No, "if your enemy is hungry, feed him; if he is thirsty, give him drink; for by so doing you will heap burning coals upon his head" (*i.e.* shame him into repentance). Do not be overcome by evil, but overcome evil with good.'[2] It will be seen that Paul's prohibition of vengeance is not because retribution is in itself wrong, but because it is the prerogative of God, not man. 'Vengeance is mine,' says the Lord. His purpose is to express his wrath or vengeance now through the law courts (as Paul goes on to write in Romans 13), and finally on the day of judgment.

This difference of God-given function between two 'servants of God'—the state to punish the evildoer, the individual Christian

[1] Rom. 13:4.
[2] Rom. 12:17–21.

not to repay evil for evil, but to overcome evil with good—is bound to create a painful tension in all of us, specially because all of us in different degrees are both individuals and citizens of the state, and therefore share in both functions. For example, if my house is burgled one night and I catch the thief, it may well be my duty to sit him down and give him something to eat and drink, while at the same time telephoning the police.

Luther explained this tension by making a helpful distinction between our 'person' and our 'office'. It was part of his teaching about the 'two kingdoms' which has, however, been justly criticized. He derived it from the text 'Render to Caesar the things that are Caesar's, and to God the things that are God's'. He saw in these words the existence of both a divine or spiritual realm, 'the kingdom of Christ', and a secular or temporal realm, 'the kingdom of the world' (or 'of the emperor'). In the first, which he also called 'the kingdom of God's right hand', the Christian lives as a 'person'; in the second 'the kingdom of God's left hand', he occupies an 'office' of some kind, whether as 'father', 'master', 'prince' or 'judge'. 'You must not confuse the two,' Luther wrote, 'your person or your office.'[1]

Here is part of his application of this distinction to the command not to resist evil: a Christian 'lives simultaneously as a Christian toward everyone, personally suffering all sorts of things in the world, and as a secular person, maintaining, using and performing all the functions required by the law of his territory or city . . .' 'A Christian should not resist any evil; but within the limits of his office a secular person should oppose every evil.' 'In short, the rule in the kingdom of Christ is the toleration of everything, forgiveness, and the recompense of evil with good. On the other hand, in the realm of the emperor, there should be no tolerance shown towards any injustice, but rather a defence against wrong and a punishment of it, . . . according to what each one's office or station may require.' 'Christ . . . is not saying "No one should ever resist evil" for that would completely undermine all rule and authority. But this is what he is saying: "You, you shall not do it".'[2]

Luther's clear-cut distinction between the two 'realms' was certainly overdrawn. 'It is difficult to escape the feeling,' writes Harvey McArthur, 'that his teaching gave to the secular sphere

[1] P. 83.
[2] Pp. 113–114.

an autonomy to which it has no rightful claim.'[1] He went as far as to tell the Christian that in the secular kingdom 'you do not have to ask Christ about your duty', for it can be learnt from the emperor. But Scripture does not allow us to set the two kingdoms over against each other in such total contrast, as if the church were Christ's sphere ruled by love and the state the emperor's ruled by justice. For Jesus Christ has universal authority, and no sphere may be excluded from his rule. Further, the state's administration of justice needs to be tempered with love, while in the church love has sometimes to be expressed in terms of discipline. Jesus himself spoke of the painful necessity of excommunicating an obstinate and unrepentant offender.'

Nevertheless, I think Luther's distinction between 'person' and 'office', or, as we might say, between individual and institution, holds. The Christian is to be wholly free from revenge, not only in action, but in his heart as well; as an office-bearer in either state or church, however, he may find himself entrusted with authority from God to resist evil and to punish it.

To sum up the teaching of this antithesis, Jesus was not prohibiting the administration of justice, but rather forbidding us to take the law into our own hands. 'An eye for an eye' is a principle of justice belonging to courts of law. In personal life we must be rid not only of all retaliation in word and deed, but of all animosity of spirit. We can and must commit our cause to the good and righteous Judge, as Jesus himself did,[2] but it is not for us to seek or to desire any personal revenge. We must not repay injury but suffer it, and so overcome evil with good.

So the command of Jesus not to resist evil should not properly be used to justify either temperamental weakness or moral compromise or political anarchy or even total pacifism. Instead, what Jesus here demands of all his followers is a personal attitude to evildoers which is prompted by mercy not justice, which renounces retaliation so completely as to risk further costly suffering, which is governed never by the desire to cause them harm but always by the determination to serve their highest good.

I do not know anybody who has expressed this in more relevant modern terms than Martin Luther King, who had learnt as much from Gandhi as Gandhi had learnt from Tolstoy, although I think he understood Jesus' teaching better than either. There

[1] P. 135.
[2] 1 Pet. 2:23.

can be no doubt of the unjust sufferings which Luther King had to endure. Dr Benjamin Mays listed them at his funeral: 'If any man knew the meaning of suffering, King knew. House bombed; living day by day for thirteen years under constant threats of death; maliciously accused of being a Communist; falsely accused of being insincere . . . ; stabbed by a member of his own race; slugged in a hotel lobby; jailed over twenty times; occasionally deeply hurt because friends betrayed him—and yet this man had no bitterness in his heart, no rancour in his soul, no revenge in his mind; and he went up and down the length and breadth of this world preaching non-violence and the redemptive power of love.'[1]

One of his most moving sermons, based on Matthew 5:43-45, was entitled 'Loving your enemies' and was written in a Georgia gaol. Wrestling with the questions why and how Christians are to love, he described how 'hate multiplies hate . . . in a descending spiral of violence' and is 'just as injurious to the person who hates' as to his victim. But above all 'love is the only force capable of transforming an enemy into a friend' for it has 'creative' and 'redemptive' power. He went on to apply his theme to the racial crisis in the United States. For over three centuries American Negroes had suffered oppression, frustration and discrimination. But Luther King and his friends were determined to 'meet hate with love'. Then they would win both freedom and their oppressors, 'and our victory will be a double victory'.[2]

## 2. Active love (43–48)

*You have heard that it was said, 'You shall love your neighbour and hate your enemy.'* [44] *But I say to you, love your enemies and pray for those who persecute you,* [45] *so that you may be sons of your Father who is in heaven; for he makes his sun rise on the evil and on the good, and sends rain on the just and on the unjust.* [46] *For if you love those who love you, what reward have you? Do not even the tax collectors do the same?* [47] *And if you salute only your brethren, what more are you doing than others? Do not even the Gentiles do the same?* [48] *You, therefore, must be perfect, as your heavenly Father is perfect.*

[1] Coretta Scott King, *My life with Martin Luther King Jr* (Hodder & Stoughton, 1970), pp. 365-369.
[2] *Strength to love* (1963; Fontana, 1969), pp. 47-55.

We have already seen how blatant a perversion of the law is the instruction, 'Love your neighbour and hate your enemy,' because of what it omits from the commandment and adds to it. It deliberately narrows both the standard of love (leaving out the crucial words 'as yourself', which pitch the standard very high) and its objects (qualifying the category of 'neighbour' by specifically excluding enemies from it and adding the command to hate them instead). I call the perversion 'blatant' because it is totally lacking in justification, and yet the rabbis would have defended it as a legitimate interpretation. They seized on the immediate context of the inconvenient command to love the neighbour, pointing out that Leviticus 19 is addressed 'to all the congregation of the people of Israel'. It gives instructions to Israelites on their duties to their own parents, and more widely to their 'neighbour' and their 'brother'. They were not to oppress or rob him, whatever his social status might be. 'You shall not hate your brother in your heart . . . You shall not take vengeance or bear any grudge against the sons of your own people, but you shall love your neighbour as yourself' (vv. 17, 18).

It was easy enough for ethical casuists (consciously or unconsciously anxious to ease the burden of this command) to twist it to their own convenience. 'My neighbour', they argued, 'is one of my own people, a fellow Jew, my own kith and kin, who belongs to my race and my religion. The law says nothing about strangers or enemies. So, since the command is to love only my neighbour, it must be taken as a permission, even an injunction, to hate my enemy. For he is not my neighbour that I should love him.' The reasoning is rational enough to convince those who wanted to be convinced, and to confirm them in their own racial prejudice. But it is a rationalization, and a specious one at that. They evidently ignored the instruction earlier in the same chapter to leave the gleanings of field and vineyard 'for the poor *and the sojourner*', who was not a Jew but a resident alien, and the unequivocal statement against racial discrimination at the end of the chapter: 'the stranger who sojourns with you shall be to you as the native among you, and you shall love him as yourself' (34). Similarly, 'There shall be one law for the native and for the stranger who sojourns among you.'[1]

They also turned a blind eye to other commandments which regulated their conduct towards their enemies. For example, 'If

[1] Ex. 12:49.

you meet your enemy's ox or his ass going astray, you shall bring it back to him. If you see the ass of one who hates you lying under its burden, you shall refrain from leaving him with it, you shall help him to lift it up.'[1] Almost identical instruction was given regarding a brother's ox or ass,[2] indicating that love's requirement was the same whether the beasts belonged to a 'brother' or to an 'enemy'. The rabbis must also have known very well the teaching of the book of Proverbs, which the apostle Paul was later to quote as an illustration of overcoming rather than avenging evil: 'If your enemy is hungry, give him bread to eat; and if he is thirsty, give him water to drink.'[3]

It is quite true that the scribes and Pharisees may have adduced as biblical warrant to hate their enemies either the Israelite wars against the Canaanites or the imprecatory psalms. But if so they misunderstood both these wars and these psalms. The Canaanites are known from modern near eastern studies to have been utterly corrupt in religion and culture. So nauseating were their abominable practices that the land itself is described as having 'vomited them out'. Indeed if Israel were to follow their customs, she would share their fate.[4] 'The wars of Israel', wrote Bonhoeffer, 'were the only "holy wars" in history, for they were the wars of God against the world of idols. It is not this enmity which Jesus condemns, for then he would have condemned the whole history of God's dealings with his people. On the contrary, he affirms the old covenant. But from now on there will be no more wars of faith.'[5]

As for the imprecatory psalms, in them the psalmist speaks not with any personal animosity but as a representative of God's chosen people Israel, regards the wicked as the enemies of God, counts them his own enemies only because he has completely identified himself with the cause of God, hates them because he loves God, and is so confident that this 'hatred' is 'perfect hatred' that he calls upon God in the next breath to search him and know his heart, to try him and know his thoughts, in order to see if there is any wickedness in him.[6] That we cannot easily aspire to

[1] Ex. 23:4, 5.
[2] Dt. 22:1–4.
[3] Pr. 25:21; cf. Rom. 12:20.
[4] Cf. Lv. 18:25, 28; 20:22.
[5] P. 132.
[6] Ps. 139:19–24. Cf. Homilies, p. 404.

this is an indication not of our spirituality but of our lack of it, not of our superior love for men but of our inferior love for God, indeed of our inability to hate the wicked with a hatred that is 'perfect' and not 'personal'.

The truth is that evil men should be the object simultaneously of our 'love' and of our 'hatred', as they are simultaneously the objects of God's (although his 'hatred' is expressed as his 'wrath'). To 'love' them is ardently to desire that they will repent and believe, and so be saved. To 'hate' them is to desire with equal ardour that, if they stubbornly refuse to repent and believe, they will incur God's judgment. Have you never prayed for the salvation of wicked men (*e.g.*, who blaspheme God or exploit their fellow humans for profit as if they were animals), and gone on to pray that if they refuse God's salvation, then God's judgment will fall upon them? I have. It is a natural expression of our belief in God, that he is the God both of salvation and of judgment, and that we desire his perfect will to be done.

So there is such a thing as perfect hatred, just as there is such a thing as righteous anger. But it is a hatred for *God's* enemies, not our own enemies. It is entirely free of all spite, rancour and vindictiveness, and is fired only by love for God's honour and glory. It finds expression now in the prayer of the martyrs who have been killed for the word of God and for their witness.[1] And it will be expressed on the last day by the whole company of God's redeemed people who, seeing God's judgment come upon the wicked, will concur in its perfect justice and will say in unison, 'Hallelujah! Salvation and glory and power belong to our God, for his judgments are true and just . . . Amen. Hallelujah!'[2]

It will surely now be conceded that such pure 'hatred' of evil and of evil men, unmixed with any taint of personal malice, gave the rabbis no possible justification for changing God's command to love our neighbour into a permission also to hate those who hate us, our personal enemies. The words 'and hate your enemy' were a 'parasitical growth'[3] upon God's law; they had no business there. God did not teach his people a double standard of morality, one for a neighbour and another for an enemy.

So Jesus contradicted their addition as a gross distortion of the law: *But I say to you, Love your enemies* (44). For our neighbour, as

[1] Rev. 6:10.
[2] Rev. 19:1, 3, 4.
[3] Spurgeon, p. 31.

he later illustrated so plainly in the parable of the good Samaritan,[1] is not necessarily a member of our own race, rank or religion. He may not even have any connection with us. He may be our enemy, who is after us with a knife or a gun. Our 'neighbour' in the vocabulary of God includes our enemy. What constitutes him our neighbour is simply that he is a fellow human being in need, whose need we know and are in a position in some measure to relieve.

What, then, is our duty to our neighbour, whether he be friend or foe? We are to love him. Moreover, if we add the clauses in Luke's account of the Sermon, our love for him will be expressed in our deeds, our words and our prayers. First, our deeds. 'Love your enemies, do good to those who hate you ... Love your enemies, and do good ...'[2] 'Do-gooders' are despised in today's world, and, to be sure, if philanthropy is self-conscious and patronizing, it is not what Jesus meant by 'doing good'. The point he is making is that true love is not sentiment so much as service —practical, humble, sacrificial service. As Dostoyevsky put it somewhere, 'Love in action is much more terrible than love in dreams.' Our enemy is seeking our harm; we must seek his good. For this is how God has treated us. It is 'while we were enemies' that Christ died for us to reconcile us to God.[3] If he gave himself for his enemies, we must give ourselves for ours.

Words can also express our love, however, both words addressed to our enemies themselves and words addressed to God on their behalf. 'Bless those who curse you.' If they call down disaster and catastrophe upon our heads, expressing in words their wish for our downfall, we must retaliate by calling down heaven's blessing upon them, declaring in words that we wish them nothing but good. Finally, we direct our words to God. Both evangelists record this command of Jesus: 'Pray for those who persecute (or abuse) you.'[4] Chrysostom saw this responsibility to pray for our enemies as 'the very highest summit of self-control'.[5] Indeed, looking back over the requirements of these last two antitheses, he traces nine ascending steps, with intercession as the topmost one. First, we are not to take any evil initiative ourselves. Secondly, we are not to avenge another's evil. Thirdly, we are to be quiet, and fourthly, to suffer wrongfully. Fifthly, we are to surrender to the evildoer even more than he demands. Sixthly, we are

[1] Lk. 10:29-37.    [2] Lk. 6:27, 35.
[3] Rom. 5:10.    [4] Mt. 5:44; Lk. 6:28.    [5] P. 281.

not to hate him, but (steps 7 and 8) to love him and do him good. As our ninth duty, we are 'to entreat God Himself on his behalf'.[1]

Modern commentators also have seen such intercession as the summit of Christian love. 'This is the supreme command,' wrote Bonhoeffer. 'Through the medium of prayer we go to our enemy, stand by his side, and plead for him to God.'[2] Moreover, if intercessory prayer is an expression of what love we have, it is a means to increase our love as well. It is impossible to pray for someone without loving him, and impossible to go on praying for him without discovering that our love for him grows and matures. We must not, therefore, wait before praying for an enemy until we feel some love for him in our heart. We must begin to pray for him before we are conscious of loving him, and we shall find our love break first into bud, then into blossom. Jesus seems to have prayed for his tormentors actually while the iron spikes were being driven through his hands and feet; indeed the imperfect tense suggests that he kept praying, kept repeating his entreaty 'Father, forgive them; for they know not what they do'.[3] If the cruel torture of crucifixion could not silence our Lord's prayer for his enemies, what pain, pride, prejudice or sloth could justify the silencing of ours?

I find I am quoting Bonhoeffer in this chapter more than any other commentator. I suppose the reason is that although he wrote his exposition before the outbreak of war, he could see where Nazism was leading, and we know to what fate his Christian testimony against it brought him in the end. He quoted a certain A. F. C. Villmar of 1880, but his words sound almost prophetic of Bonhoeffer's own day: 'This commandment, that we should love our enemies and forgo revenge, will grow even more urgent in the holy struggle which lies before us ... The Christians will be hounded from place to place, subjected to physical assault, maltreatment and death of every kind. We are approaching an age of wide-spread persecution ... Soon the time will come when we shall pray ... It will be a prayer of earnest love for these very sons of perdition who stand around and gaze at us with eyes aflame with hatred, and who have perhaps already raised their hands to kill us ... Yes, the Church which is really waiting for its Lord, and which discerns the signs

[1] Pp. 276 f.
[2] P. 134.
[3] Lk. 23:34.

of the times of decision, must fling itself with its utmost power and with the panoply of its holy life, into this prayer of love.'[1]

Having indicated that our love for our enemies will express itself in deeds, words and prayers, Jesus goes on to declare that only then shall we prove conclusively whose sons we are, for only then shall we be exhibiting a love like the love of our heavenly Father's. *For he makes his sun rise* (notice, in passing, to whom the sun belongs!) *on the evil and on the good, and sends rain on the just and on the unjust* (45). Divine love is indiscriminate love, shown equally to good men and bad. The theologians (following Calvin) call this God's 'common grace'. It is not 'saving grace', enabling sinners to repent, believe and be saved; but grace shown to all mankind, the penitent and the impenitent, believers and unbelievers alike. This common grace of God is expressed, then, not in the gift of salvation but in the gifts of creation, and not least in the blessings of rain and sunshine, without which we could not eat and life on the planet could not continue. This, then, is to be the standard of Christian love. We are to love like God, not men.

*For if you love those who love you, what reward have you?* Or what credit is that to you? 'Even sinners love those who love them.'[2] Fallen man is not incapable of loving. The doctrine of total depravity does not mean (and has never meant) that original sin has rendered men incapable of doing anything good at all, but rather that every good they do is tainted to some degree by evil. Unredeemed sinners can love. Parental love, filial love, conjugal love, the love of friends—all these, as we know very well, are the regular experience of men and women outside Christ. *Even the tax collectors* (the petty customs officials who because of their extortion had a reputation for greed) love those who love them. *Even the Gentiles* (those 'dogs', as the Jews called them, those outsiders who loathed the Jews and would look the other way when they passed one in the street), even they salute each other. None of this is in dispute.

But all human love, even the highest, the noblest and the best, is contaminated to some degree by the impurities of self-interest. We Christians are specifically called to love our enemies (in which love there is no self-interest), and this is impossible without the supernatural grace of God. If we love only those who love us, we

[1] Pp. 135 f.
[2] Lk. 6:32.

are no better than swindlers. If we greet only our brothers and sisters, our fellow Christians, we are no better than pagans; they too greet one another. The question Jesus asked is: *What more are you doing than others?* (47). This simple word *more* is the quintessence of what he is saying. It is not enough for Christians to *resemble* non-Christians; our calling is to outstrip them in virtue. Our righteousness is to exceed (*perisseusē . . . pleion*) that of the Pharisees (20) and our love is to surpass, to be more than (*perisson*) that of the Gentiles (47). Bonhoeffer puts it well: 'What makes the Christian different from other men is the "peculiar", the *perisson*, the "extraordinary", the "unusual", that which is not "a matter of course" . . . It is "the more", the "beyond-all-that". The natural is *to auto* (one and the same) for heathen and Christian, the distinctive quality of the Christian life begins with the *perisson* . . . For him (*sc.* Jesus) the hallmark of the Christian is the "extraordinary".'[1]

And what is this *perisson*, this 'plus' or 'extra' which Christians must display? Bonhoeffer's reply was: 'It is the love of Jesus Christ himself, who went patiently and obediently to the cross . . . The cross is the differential of the Christian religion.'[2] What he writes is true. Yet, to be more precise, the way Jesus put it was to say that this 'super-love' is not the love of men, but the love of God, which in common grace gives sun and rain to the wicked. So *you, therefore* (the 'you' is emphatic, distinguishing Christians from non-Christians), *must be perfect, as your heavenly Father is perfect* (48). The concept that God's people must imitate God rather than men is not new. The book of Leviticus repeated some five times as a refrain the command, 'I am the Lord your God; . . . you shall therefore be holy, for I am holy.'[3] Yet here Christ's call to us is not to be 'holy' but to be 'perfect'.

Some holiness teachers have built upon this verse great dreams of the possibility of reaching in this life a state of sinless perfection. But the words of Jesus cannot be pressed into meaning this without causing discord in the Sermon. For he has already indicated in the beatitudes that a hunger and thirst after righteousness is a perpetual characteristic of his disciples,[4] and in the next chapter he will teach us to pray constantly, 'Forgive us our

[1] Pp. 136 f.
[2] P. 137.
[3] Lv. 11:44, 45; 19:2; 20:7, 26. *Cf.* 1 Pet. 1:16.
[4] 5:6.

debts.'[1] Both the hunger for righteousness and the prayer for forgiveness, being continuous, are clear indications that Jesus did not expect his followers to become morally perfect in this life. The context shows that the 'perfection' he means relates to love, that perfect love of God which is shown even to those who do not return it. Indeed, scholars tell us that the Aramaic word which Jesus may well have used meant 'all-embracing'. The parallel verse in Luke's account of the Sermon confirms this: 'Be merciful, even as your Father is merciful.'[2] We are called to be perfect in love, that is, to love even our enemies with the merciful, the inclusive love of God.

Christ's call to us is new not only because it is a command to be 'perfect' rather than 'holy', but also because of his description of the God we are to imitate. In the Old Testament it was always 'I am the Lord who brought you up out of the land of Egypt, to be your God; you shall therefore be holy, for I am holy.' But now in New Testament days it is not the unique Redeemer of Israel whom we are to follow and obey; it is our *Father who is in heaven* (45), our *heavenly Father* (48). And our obedience will come from our hearts as the manifestation of our new nature. For we are the sons of God, through faith in Jesus Christ, and we can demonstrate whose sons we are only when we exhibit the family likeness, only when we become peacemakers as he is (9), only when we love with an all-embracing love like his (45, 48).

The last two antitheses of the series reveal a progression. The first is a negative command: *Do not resist one who is evil*; the second is positive: *Love your enemies* and seek their good. The first is a call to passive non-retaliation, the second to active love. As Augustine put it, 'Many have learned how to offer the other cheek, but do not know how to love him by whom they were struck.'[3] For we are to go beyond forbearance to service, beyond the refusal to repay evil to the resolve to overcome evil with good. Alfred Plummer summed up the alternatives with admirable simplicity: 'To return evil for good is devilish; to return good for good is human; to return good for evil is divine.'[4]

Throughout his exposition Jesus sets before us alternative models by which he contrasts secular culture and Christian counter-culture. Ingrained in non-Christian culture is the notion of retaliation, both the retaliation of evil and the retaliation of

[1] 6:12.  [2] 6:63.
[3] I. 58.  [4] P. 89.

good. The first is obvious, for it means revenge. But the second is sometimes overlooked. Jesus expressed it as 'doing good to those who do good to you'.[1] So the first says, 'You do me a bad turn, and I'll do you a bad turn,' and the second, 'You do me a good turn and I'll do you a good turn,' or (more colloquially) 'You scratch my back and I'll scratch yours.' So retaliation is the way of the world; revenge on the one hand and recompense on the other, paying back injuries and paying back favours. Then we are quits, we are no man's debtors, we keep even with everybody. It is the device of the proud who cannot bear to be indebted to anybody. It is an attempt to order society by a rough and ready justice which we administer ourselves, so that nobody gets the better of us in any way.

But it will not do in the kingdom of God! Sinners, Gentiles and tax collectors behave that way. It is the highest to which they can rise. But it is not high enough for the citizens of God's kingdom: *What more are you doing than others?* Jesus asks (47). So the model he sets before us as an alternative to the world around us is our Father above us. Since he is kind to the evil as well as the good, his children must be too. The life of the old (fallen) humanity is based on rough justice, avenging injuries and returning favours. The life of the new (redeemed) humanity is based on divine love, refusing to take revenge but overcoming evil with good.

Jesus accused the Pharisees of placing two serious restrictions on their love. Of course they believed in love. Everybody believes in love. Yes, but not love for those who had injured them, and not love for those Gentile outsiders either. The spirit of pharisaism is still abroad. It is the spirit of revenge and of racialism. The first says, 'I'll love nice harmless people, but I'll get even with those who wrong me.' The second says, 'I'll love my own kith and kin, but you can't expect me to love people who have no claim on me.' In fact Jesus *does* expect of his followers the very things which others think cannot reasonably be expected of anybody. He calls us to renounce all those convenient restrictions we like to put on love (especially revenge and racialism) and instead to be all-embracing and constructive in our love, like God.

Looking back over all six antitheses, it has become clear what the 'greater' righteousness is to which Christians are summoned. It is a deep inward righteousness of the heart where the Holy Spirit has written God's law. It is new fruit exhibiting the new-

[1] Lk. 6:33.

ness of the tree, new life burgeoning from a new nature. So we have no liberty to try to dodge or duck the lofty demands of the law. Law-dodging is a pharisaic hobby; what is characteristic of Christians is a keen appetite for righteousness, hungering and thirsting after it continuously. And this righteousness, whether expressed in purity, honesty or charity, will show to whom we belong. Our Christian calling is to imitate not the world, but the Father. And it is by this imitation of him that the Christian counter-culture becomes visible.

# Matthew 6: 1–6, 16–18
# A Christian's religion: not hypocritical but real

Jesus began his instruction on the hill by portraying in the beatitudes the essential elements of Christian *character*, and went on to indicate by his metaphors of salt and light the *influence* for good which Christians will exert in the community if they exhibit this character. He then described Christian *righteousness* which must exceed the righteousness of scribes and Pharisees by accepting the full implications of God's law without dodging anything or setting artificial limits. Christian righteousness is righteousness unlimited. It must be allowed to penetrate beyond our actions and words to our heart, mind and motives, and to master us even in those hidden, secret places.

Jesus now continues his teaching on 'righteousness'. Chapter 6 begins (literally), 'Beware of doing your righteousness before men.' The word used (according to the correct reading) is *dikaiosune*, the same as in 5:6, 20. Yet, although the word is the same, the emphasis has shifted. Previously 'righteousness' related to kindness, purity, honesty and love; now it concerns such practices as almsgiving, praying and fasting. Thus Jesus moves from a Christian's moral righteousness to his 'religious' righteousness. Most versions recognize this change of subject in their translation. RSV renders the sentence, 'Beware of practising your piety before men,' and NEB, 'Be careful not to make a show of your religion before men.'

It is important to acknowledge that according to Jesus Christian 'righteousness' has these two dimensions, moral and religious. Some speak and behave as if they imagine their major duty as Christians lies in the sphere of religious activity, whether in public (church-going) or in private (devotional exercises). Others have reacted so sharply against such an overemphasis on piety that they talk of a 'religionless' Christianity. For them the church has become the secular city, and prayer a loving encounter with their neighbour. But there is no need to choose between piety and morality, religious devotion in church and active service in the world, loving God and loving our neighbour, since Jesus taught that authentic Christian 'righteousness' includes both.

Moreover, in both spheres of righteousness Jesus issues his insistent call to his followers to be different. In Matthew 5 he teaches that our righteousness must be greater than that of the Pharisees (because they obeyed the letter of the law, while our obedience must include our heart) and greater also (in the form of love) than that of the pagans (because they love each other, while our love must include our enemies as well). Now in Matthew 6, with regard to 'religious' righteousness, he draws the same two contrasts. He takes the ostentatious religion of the Pharisees first and says: *You must not be like the hypocrites* (5). He then moves on to the mechanical formalism of the heathen and says: *Do not be like them* (8). Thus again Christians are to be different from both Pharisees and pagans, the religious and irreligious, the church and the world. That Christians are not to conform to the world is a familiar concept of the New Testament. It is not so well known that Jesus also saw (and foresaw) the worldliness of the church itself and called his followers not to conform to the nominal church either, but rather to be a truly Christian community distinct in its life and practice from the religious establishment, an *ecclesiola* (little church) *in ecclesia*. The essential difference in religion as in morality is that authentic Christian righteousness is not an external manifestation only, but one of the secret things of the heart.

**6:1** *Beware of practising your piety before men in order to be seen by them; for then you will have no reward from your Father who is in heaven.*

The fundamental warning Jesus issues is against *practising your piety before men in order to be seen by them*. At first sight these words appear to contradict his earlier command to 'let your light shine before men, that they may see . . .'.[1] In both verses he speaks of doing good works 'before men' and in both the objective is stated, namely in order to be 'seen' by them. But in the earlier

[1] 5:16.

case he commands it, while in the later one he prohibits it. How can this discrepancy be resolved? The contradiction is only verbal, not substantial. The clue lies in the fact that Jesus is speaking against different sins. It is our human cowardice which made him say 'Let your light shine before men', and our human vanity which made him tell us to beware of practising our piety before men. A. B. Bruce sums it up well when he writes that we are to 'show when tempted to *hide*' and 'hide when tempted to *show*'.[1] Our good works must be public so that our light shines; our religious devotions must be secret lest we boast about them. Besides, the end of both instructions of Jesus is the same, namely the glory of God. Why are we to keep our piety secret? It is in order that glory may be given to God, rather than men. Why are we to let our light shine and do good works in the open? It is that men may glorify our heavenly Father.

The three examples of 'religious' righteousness which Jesus gives—almsgiving, praying and fasting—occur in some form in every religion. They are prominent, for example, in the Koran. Certainly all Jews were expected to give to the poor, to pray and to fast, and all devout Jews did so. Evidently Jesus expected his disciples to do the same. For he did not begin each paragraph, '*If* you give, pray, fast, then this is how you should do it' but '*When*' you do so (2, 5, 16). He took it for granted that they would.

Further, this trio of religious obligations expresses in some degree our duty to God, to others and to ourselves. For to give alms is to seek to serve our neighbour, especially the needy. To pray is to seek God's face and to acknowledge our dependence on him. To fast (that is, to abstain from food for spiritual reasons) is intended at least partly as a way to deny and so to discipline oneself. Jesus does not raise the question whether his followers will engage in these things but, assuming that they will, teaches them why and how to do so.

The three paragraphs follow an identical pattern. In vivid and deliberately humorous imagery Jesus paints a picture of the hypocrite's way of being religious. It is the way of ostentation. Such receive the reward they want, the applause of men. With this he contrasts the Christian way, which is secret, and the only reward which Christians want, the blessing of God who is their heavenly Father and who sees in secret.

[1] P. 116.

## 1. Christian giving (2–4)

*Thus, when you give alms, sound no trumpet before you, as the hypocrites*
*do in the synagogues and in the streets, that they may be praised by men.*
*Truly, I say to you, they have their reward.* [3] *But when you give alms, do*
*not let your left hand know what your right hand is doing,* [4] *so that your*
*alms may be in secret; and your Father who sees in secret will reward you.*

There is much teaching in the Old Testament on compassion
for the poor. The Greek word for almsgiving in verse 2 (*eleēmo-*
*sunē*) means a deed of mercy or pity. Since our God is a merciful
God, as Jesus has just emphasized, 'kind to the ungrateful and the
selfish',[1] his people must be kind and merciful too. Jesus obviously expected his disciples to be generous givers. His words
condemn 'the selfish stinginess of many', as Ryle put it.[2]

Generosity is not enough, however. Our Lord is concerned
throughout this Sermon with motivation, with the hidden
thoughts of the heart. In his exposition of the sixth and seventh
commandments he indicated that both murder and adultery can
be committed in our heart, unwarranted anger being a kind of
heart-murder and lustful looks a kind of heart-adultery. In the
matter of giving he has the same concern about secret thoughts.
The question is not so much what the hand is doing (passing over
some cash or a cheque) but what the heart is thinking while the
hand is doing it. There are three possibilities. Either we are
seeking the praise of men, or we preserve our anonymity but are
quietly congratulating ourselves, or we are desirous of the approval of our divine Father alone.

A ravenous hunger for the praise of men was the besetting sin
of the Pharisees. 'You . . . receive glory from one another,' Jesus
said to them, 'and do not seek the glory that comes from the only
God.'[3] Similarly John the evangelist commented: 'They loved
the praise of men more than the praise of God.'[4] So insatiable was
their appetite for human commendation that it quite spoiled their
giving. Jesus ridicules the way they turned it into a public performance. He pictures a pompous Pharisee on his way to put money
into the special box at the temple or synagogue, or to take a gift

---

[1] Lk. 6:35, 36. *Cf.* Mt. 5:45, 48.
[2] P. 47.
[3] Jn. 5:44.
[4] Jn. 12:43.

to the poor. In front of him march the trumpeters, blowing a fanfare as they walk, and quickly attracting a crowd. 'They pretended, no doubt,' comments Calvin, 'that it was to call the poor, as apologies (*sc.* excuses) are never wanting: but it was perfectly obvious that they were hunting for applause and commendation.'[1] Whether Pharisees sometimes did this literally or whether Jesus was painting an amusing caricature does not really matter. In either case he was rebuking our childish anxiety to be highly esteemed by men. As Spurgeon put it, 'To stand with a penny in one hand and a trumpet in the other is the posture of hypocrisy.'[2]

And 'hypocrisy' is the word which Jesus used to characterize this display. In classical Greek the *hupokritēs* was first an orator and then an actor. So figuratively the word came to be applied to anybody who treats the world as a stage on which he plays a part. He lays aside his true identity and assumes a false one. He is no longer himself but in disguise, impersonating somebody else. He wears a mask. Now in a theatre there is no harm or deceit in the actors playing their parts. It is an accepted convention. The audience know they have come to a drama; they are not taken in by it. The trouble with the religious hypocrite, on the other hand, is that he deliberately sets out to deceive people. He is like an actor in that he is pretending (so that what we are seeing is not the real person but a part, a mask, a disguise), yet he is quite unlike the actor in this respect: he takes some religious practice which is a real activity and he turns it into what it was never meant to be, namely a piece of make-believe, a theatrical display before an audience. And it is all done for applause.

It is easy to poke fun at those Jewish Pharisees of the first century. Our Christian pharisaism is not so amusing. We may not employ a troop of trumpeters to blow a fanfare each time we give to a church or a charity. Yet, to use the familiar metaphor, we like to 'blow our own trumpet'. It boosts our ego to see our name as subscribers to charities and supporters of good causes. We fall to the very same temptation: we draw attention to our giving in order to 'be praised by men'.

Of such people, who seek the praise of men, Jesus says with emphasis: *they have their reward.* The verb translated 'have' (*apechō*) was at that time a technical term in commercial transactions; it meant to 'receive a sum in full and give a receipt for

[1] P. 309.
[2] P. 32.

it'.[1] It was often so used in the papyri. So the hypocrites who seek applause will get it, but then 'they have had all the reward they are going to get'.[2] Nothing further is due to them, nothing but judgment on the last day.

Having forbidden his followers to give to the needy in the ostentatious manner of the Pharisees, Jesus now tells us the Christian way, which is the way of secrecy. He expresses it by another negative: *But when you give alms, do not let your left hand know what your right hand is doing, so that your alms may be in secret.* The right hand is normally the active hand. So Jesus assumes we shall use it when handing over our gift. Then he adds that our left hand must not be watching. There is no difficulty in grasping his meaning. Not only are we not to tell other people about our Christian giving; there is a sense in which we are not even to tell ourselves. We are not to be self-conscious in our giving, for our self-consciousness will readily deteriorate into self-righteousness. So subtle is the sinfulness of the heart that it is possible to take deliberate steps to keep our giving secret from men while simultaneously dwelling on it in our own minds in a spirit of self-congratulation.

It would be hard to exaggerate the perversity of this. For giving is a real activity involving real people in real need. Its purpose is to alleviate the distress of the needy. The Greek word for almsgiving, as we have seen, indicates that it is a work of mercy. Yet it is possible to turn an act of mercy into an act of vanity, so that our principal motive in giving is not the benefit of the person receiving the gift but our own benefit who give it. Altruism has been displaced by a distorted egotism.

So then, in order to 'mortify' or put to death our sinful vanity, Jesus urges us to keep our giving secret from ourselves as well as from others. By his words 'Do not let your left hand know what your right hand is doing,' writes Bonhoeffer, Jesus 'was sounding the death-knell of the old man,'[3] For self-centredness belongs to the old life; the new life in Christ is one of uncalculating generosity. Of course it is not possible to obey this command of Jesus in precise literalness. If we keep accounts and plan our giving, as conscientious Christians should, we are bound to know how much we give away. We cannot very well close our eyes while writing

[1] AG.
[2] JBP.
[3] P. 144.

out our cheques! Nevertheless, as soon as the giving of a gift is decided and done, it will be in keeping with this teaching of Jesus that we forget it. We are not to keep recalling it in order to gloat over it, or to preen ourselves on how generous, disciplined or conscientious our giving may have been. Christian giving is to be marked by self-sacrifice and self-forgetfulness, not by self-congratulation.

What we should seek when giving to the needy is neither the praise of men, nor a ground for self-commendation, but rather the approval of God. This is implied in our Lord's reference to our right and left hands. 'By this expression', Calvin writes, 'he means that we ought to be satisfied with having God for our only witness.'[1] Although we can keep our giving secret from others, and to some extent secret even from ourselves, we cannot keep it secret from God. No secrets are hidden from him. So *your Father who sees in secret will reward you.*

Some people rebel against this teaching of Jesus. They neither want nor expect a reward of any kind from anybody, they say. More than that, they find in our Lord's promise of a reward an inherent inconsistency. How can he forbid the desire for praise from others or from ourselves and then command us to seek it from God? Surely, they say, this merely exchanges one form of vanity for another? Should we not rather give purely for the sake of giving? To seek praise from any quarter—from man, self or God—seems to them to vitiate the act of giving.

The first reason why such arguments are mistaken has to do with the nature of rewards. When people say that the idea of rewards is distasteful to them, I always suspect that the picture in their mind is prize-giving at school, with silver trophies gleaming on the platform table and everybody clapping! The conjuring up of this kind of scene may be due to the AV words 'shall reward thee *openly*'. This adverb should be omitted, however. The contrast is not between a secret gift and a public reward, but between the men who neither see nor reward the gift and the God who does both.

C. S. Lewis wisely wrote in an essay entitled 'The weight of glory': 'We must not be troubled by unbelievers when they say that this promise of reward makes the Christian life a mercenary affair. There are different kinds of reward. There is the reward

[1] P. 310.

which has no natural connection with the things you do to earn it, and is quite foreign to the desires that ought to accompany those things. Money is not the natural reward of love; that is why we call a man mercenary if he marries a woman for the sake of her money. But marriage is the proper reward for a real lover, and he is not mercenary for desiring it.' Similarly we might say that a silver cup is not a very suitable reward for a schoolboy who works hard, whereas a scholarship at the university would be. C. S. Lewis concludes his argument: 'The proper rewards are not simply tacked on to the activity for which they are given, but are the activity itself in consummation.'[1]

What, then, is the 'reward' which the heavenly Father gives the secret giver? It is neither public nor necessarily future. It is probably the only reward which genuine love wants when making a gift to the needy, namely to see the need relieved. When through his gifts the hungry are fed, the naked clothed, the sick healed, the oppressed freed and the lost saved, the love which prompted the gift is satisfied. Such love (which is God's own love expressed through man) brings with it its own secret joys, and desires no other reward.

To sum up, our Christian giving is to be neither before men (waiting for the clapping to begin), nor even before ourselves (our left hand applauding our right hand's generosity) but 'before God', who sees our secret heart and rewards us with the discovery that, as Jesus said, 'It is more blessed to give than to receive.'[2]

## 2. Christian praying (5, 6)

*And when you pray, you must not be like the hypocrites; for they love to stand and pray in the synagogues and at the street corners, that they may be seen by men. Truly, I say to you, they have their reward.* [6]*But when you pray, go into your room and shut the door and pray to your Father who is in secret; and your Father who sees in secret will reward you.*

In his second example of the 'religious' kind of righteousness Jesus depicts two men at prayer. Again the basic difference is between hypocrisy and reality. He contrasts the reason for their praying, and its reward.

[1] *They asked for a paper* (Bles, 1962), p. 198.
[2] Acts 20:35.

What he says of the hypocrites sounds fine at first: 'They love . . . to pray.' But unfortunately it is not prayer which they love, nor the God they are supposed to be praying to. No, they love themselves and the opportunity which public praying gives them to parade themselves.

Of course the discipline of regular prayer is good; all devout Jews prayed three times a day like Daniel.[1] And there was nothing wrong in standing to pray, for this was the usual posture for prayer among Jews. Nor were they necessarily mistaken to pray *at the street corners* as well as *in the synagogues* if their motive was to break down segregated religion and bring their recognition of God out of the holy places into the secular life of every day. But Jesus uncovered their true motive as they stood in synagogue or street with hands uplifted to heaven in order that they might *be seen by men*. Behind their piety lurked their pride. What they really wanted was applause. They got it. 'They have received their reward in full' (NIV).

Religious pharisaism is far from dead. The accusation of hypocrisy has often been levelled at us church-goers. It is possible to go to church for the same wrongheaded reason which took the Pharisee to the synagogue: not to worship God, but to gain for ourselves a reputation for piety. It is possible to boast of our private devotions in the same way. What stands out is the perversity of all hypocritical practice. The giving of praise to God, like the giving of alms to men, is an authentic act in its own right. An ulterior motive destroys both. It degrades the service of God and men into a mean kind of self-service. Religion and charity become an exhibitionist display. How can we pretend to be praising God, when in reality we are concerned that men will praise us?

How, then, should Christians pray? *Go into your room and shut the door*, Jesus said. We are to close the door against disturbance and distraction but also to shut out the prying eyes of men and to shut ourselves in with God. Only then can we obey the Lord's next command: *Pray to your Father who is in secret*, or, as the Jerusalem Bible clarifies it, 'who is in that secret place'. Our Father is there, waiting to welcome us. Just as nothing destroys prayer like side-glances at human spectators, so nothing enriches it like a sense of the presence of God. For he sees not the outward appearance only but the heart, not the one who is praying only but the motive for which he prays. The essence of Christian prayer is to

[1] Dn. 6:10.

MATTHEW 6: 1-6, 16-18

seek God. Behind all true prayer lies the conversation which God
initiates:

> Thou hast said, 'Seek ye my face.'
> My heart says to thee,
> 'Thy face, Lord, do I seek.'[1]

We seek him in order to acknowledge him as the person he is,
God the Creator, God the Lord, God the Judge, God our
heavenly Father through Jesus Christ our Saviour. We desire to
meet him in the secret place in order to bow down before him in
humble worship, love and trust. Then, Jesus went on, *your Father
who sees in secret will reward you.* R. V. G. Tasker points out that the
Greek word for the 'room' into which we are to withdraw to pray
(*tameion*) 'was used for the store-room where treasures might be
kept'. The implication may be, then, that 'there are treasures
already awaiting' us when we pray.[2] Certainly the hidden rewards
of prayer are too many to enumerate. In words of the apostle
Paul, when we cry, 'Abba, Father,' the Holy Spirit witnesses with
our spirit that we are indeed God's children, and we are granted a
strong assurance of his fatherhood and love.[3] He lifts the light of
his face upon us and gives us his peace.[4] He refreshes our soul,
satisfies our hunger, quenches our thirst. We know we are no
longer orphans for the Father has adopted us; no longer prodigals
for we have been forgiven; no longer alienated, for we have come
home.

Our Lord's emphasis on the need for secrecy should not be
driven to extremes. To interpret it with rigid literalism would be
guilty of the very pharisaism against which he is warning us. If all
our praying were to be kept secret, we would have to give up
church-going, family prayers and prayer meetings. His reference
here is to private prayer. The Greek words are in the singular, as
the AV indicates: 'But thou, when thou prayest, enter thy closet,
. . . shut thy door, pray to thy Father.' Jesus has not yet come to
public prayer. When he does, he tells us to pray in the plural 'Our
Father', and one can scarcely pray that prayer in secret alone.

Rather than becoming absorbed in the mechanics of secrecy, we
need to remember that the purpose of Jesus' emphasis on 'secret'
prayer is to purify our motives in praying. As we are to give out
of a genuine love for people, so we are to pray out of a genuine

---

[1] Ps. 27:8.    [2] P. 73.
[3] Rom. 5:5; 8:16.    [4] Nu. 6:26.

love for God. We must never use either of these exercises as a pious cloak for self-love.

## 3. Christian fasting (16–18)

*And when you fast, do not look dismal, like the hypocrites, for they disfigure their faces that their fasting may be seen by men. Truly, I say to you, they have received their reward.* [17] *But when you fast, anoint your head and wash your face,* [18] *that your fasting may not be seen by men but by your Father who is in secret; and your Father who sees in secret will reward you.*

The Pharisees fasted 'twice a week',[1] on Mondays and Thursdays. John the Baptist and his disciples also fasted regularly, even 'often', but the disciples of Jesus did not.[2] So how is it that in these verses of the Sermon on the Mount Jesus not only expected his followers to fast, but gave them instructions how to do so? Here is a passage of Scripture which is commonly ignored. I suspect that some of us live our Christian lives as if these verses had been torn out of our Bibles. Most Christians lay stress on daily prayer and sacrificial giving, but few lay any stress on fasting. Evangelical Christianity in particular, whose characteristic emphasis is on an inward religion of heart and spirit, does not readily come to terms with an outward bodily practice like fasting. Is it not an Old Testament exercise, we ask, enjoined by Moses for the Day of Atonement, and after the return from Babylonian exile required on some other annual days, but now abrogated by Christ? Did not people come to Jesus and ask: 'Why do John's disciples and the disciples of the Pharisees fast, but your disciples do *not* fast'? And is fasting not a Roman Catholic practice, so that the medieval church developed an elaborate calendar of 'feast days' and 'fast days'? Did it not also become associated with a superstitious view of the mass and of 'fasting communion'?

We can answer 'yes' to all these questions. But it is easy to be selective in our knowledge and use of both Scripture and church history. Here are some other and balancing facts: Jesus himself, our Lord and Master, fasted for forty days and nights in the wilderness; in reply to the question people asked him, he said,

[1] Lk. 18:12.
[2] Mt. 9:14; Lk. 5:33.

'When the bridegroom is taken away, ... *then* they (*sc.* my disciples) will fast.'[1] In the Sermon on the Mount he told us how to fast, on the assumption that we would. And in the Acts and the New Testament letters there are several references to the apostles fasting. So we cannot dismiss fasting as either an Old Testament practice abrogated in the New or a Catholic practice rejected by Protestants.

First, then, what is fasting? Strictly speaking, it is a total abstention from food. It can be legitimately extended, however, to mean going without food partially or totally, for shorter or longer periods. Hence of course the naming of each day's first meal as 'breakfast', since at it we 'break our fast', the night period during which we ate nothing.

There can be no doubt that in Scripture fasting has to do in various ways with self-denial and self-discipline. First and foremost, to 'fast' and to 'humble ourselves before God' are virtually equivalent terms (*e.g.* Ps. 35:13; Is. 58:3, 5). Sometimes this was an expression of penitence for past sin. When people were deeply distressed over their sin and guilt, they would both weep and fast. For example, Nehemiah assembled the people 'with fasting and in sackcloth', and they 'stood and confessed their sins'; the people of Nineveh repented at Jonah's preaching, proclaimed a fast and put on sackcloth; Daniel sought God 'by prayer and supplications with fasting, sackcloth and ashes', prayed to the Lord his God and made confession of the sins of his people; and Saul of Tarsus after his conversion, moved to penitence for his persecution of Christ, for three days neither ate nor drank.[2]

Sometimes still today, when the people of God are convicted of sin and moved to repentance, it is not inappropriate as a token of penitence to mourn, to weep and to fast. The Anglican Homily entitled 'Of good works, and first of fasting' suggests this as the way to apply to ourselves the word of Jesus that 'when the bridegroom is taken away, *then* my disciples will fast'. It argues that Christ the bridegroom may be said to be 'with us' and we may be said to be enjoying the marriage feast, when we are rejoicing in him and his salvation. But the bridegroom may be said to be 'taken away from us' and the feast to be suspended when we are oppressed by defeat, affliction and adversity. 'Then is it a fit time', says the Homily, 'for that man to humble himself

[1] Mt. 9:15.
[2] Ne. 9:1, 2; Jon. 3:5; Dn. 9:2 ff.; 10:2 ff.; Acts 9:9.

to Almighty God by fasting, and to mourn and bewail his sins with a sorrowful heart.'[1]

We are not to humble ourselves before God only in penitence for past sin, however, but also in dependence on him for future mercy. And here again fasting may express our self-humbling before God. For if 'penitence and fasting' go together in Scripture, 'prayer and fasting' are even more often coupled. This is not so much a regular practice, so that whenever we pray we fast, as an occasional and special arrangement, so that when we need to seek God for some particular direction or blessing we turn aside from food and other distractions in order to do so. Thus Moses fasted on mount Sinai immediately after the covenant was renewed by which God had taken Israel to be his people; Jehoshaphat, seeing the armies of Moab and Ammon advancing towards him, 'set himself to seek the Lord and proclaimed a fast throughout all Judah'; Queen Esther, before she took her life in her hands by approaching the king, urged Mordecai to gather the Jews and 'hold a fast' on her behalf, while she and her maids did the same; Ezra 'proclaimed a fast' before leading the exiles back to Jerusalem, 'that we might humble ourselves before our God to seek from him a straight way'; not least, as already mentioned, our Lord Jesus himself fasted immediately before his public ministry began; and the early church followed his example, the church of Antioch before Paul and Barnabas were sent out on the first missionary journey, and Paul and Barnabas themselves before appointing elders in every new church which they had planted.[2] The evidence is plain that special enterprises need special prayer, and that special prayer may well involve fasting.

There is another biblical reason for fasting. Hunger is one of our basic human appetites, and greed one of our basic human sins. So 'self-control' is meaningless unless it includes the control of our bodies, and is impossible without self-discipline. Paul uses the athlete as his example. To compete in the games he must be physically fit, and therefore he goes into training. His training will include a disciplined regime of food, sleep and exercise: 'every athlete exercises self-control in all things'. And Christians engaged in the Christian race should do the same. Paul writes of 'pommeling' his body (beating it black and blue) and 'subduing'

[1] P. 307.
[2] Ex. 24:18; 2 Ch. 20:1 ff.; Est. 4:16; Ezr. 8:21 ff.; Mt. 4:1, 2; Acts 13:1-3; 14:23.

it (leading it about as a slave).[1] This is neither masochism (finding pleasure in self-inflicted pain), nor false asceticism (like wearing a hair shirt or sleeping on a bed of spikes), nor an attempt to win merit like the Pharisee in the temple.[2] Paul would reject all such ideas, and so must we. We have no cause to 'punish' our bodies (for they are God's creation), but must discipline them to make them obey us. And fasting (a voluntary abstinence from food) is one way of increasing our self-control.

One further reason for fasting should be mentioned, namely a deliberate doing without in order to share what we might have eaten (or its cost) with the undernourished. There is biblical warrant for this practice. Job could say that he had not 'eaten his morsel alone' but shared it with orphans and widows.'[3] By contrast, when through Isaiah God condemned the hypocritical fasting of the inhabitants of Jerusalem, his complaint was that they were seeking their own pleasure and oppressing their workers *on the very day of their fast*. This meant partly that there was no correlation in their mind or actions between the food they did without and the material need of their employees. Theirs was a religion without justice or charity. So God said: 'Is not this the fast that I choose: to loose the bonds of wickedness, . . . to let the oppressed go free? Is it not to share your bread with the hungry, and bring the homeless poor into your house . . . ?'[4] Jesus implied something similar when he told of the rich man feasting sumptuously every day while the beggar lay at his gate, desiring to be fed with the crumbs which fell from his table.[5]

It is not difficult to find more modern applications. In sixteenth-century England abstinence from meat was enjoined on certain days, and the eating of fish instead, not by the church but by the state, in order to help maintain 'fishertowns bordering upon the seas' and thereby to reduce 'victuals to a more moderate price, to the better sustenance of the poor'.[6] In our own day, the plight of the hungry millions in some developing countries is brought before us daily on our television screens. To have an occasional (or, better, regular) 'hunger-lunch', or miss a meal once or twice a week, and at all times to avoid being overweight by overeating—these are forms of fasting which please God because they express a sense of solidarity with the poor.

So whether for penitence or for prayer, for self-discipline or for

[1] I Cor. 9:24–27.   [2] Lk. 18:12.   [3] 31:16 ff.
[4] 58:1 ff.   [5] Lk. 16:19–31.   [6] *Homilies*, pp. 301–303.

solidary love, there are good biblical reasons for fasting. Whatever our reasons, Jesus took it for granted that fasting would have a place in our Christian life. His concern was that, as with our giving and praying so with our fasting, we should not, like the hypocrites, draw attention to ourselves. Their practice was to *look dismal* and *disfigure their faces*. The word translated 'disfigure' (*aphanizo*) means literally to 'make to disappear' and so to 'render invisible or unrecognizable'.[1] They may have neglected personal hygiene, or covered their heads with sackcloth, or perhaps smeared their faces with ashes in order to look pale, wan, melancholy and so outstandingly holy. All so that their fasting might be seen and known by everybody. The admiration of the onlookers would be all the reward they got. 'But as for you, my disciples,' Jesus went on, *when you fast, anoint your head and wash your face*, that is, 'brush your hair and wash your face'.[2] Jesus was not recommending anything unusual, as if they were now to affect a particular kind of gaiety. For, as Calvin justly comments, 'Christ does not withdraw us from one kind of hypocrisy, to lead us into another.'[3] He assumed that they would have a 'wash and brush up' every day, and on fast days they were to do it as usual, so that nobody would suspect that they were fasting. Then once again *your Father who sees in secret will reward you*. For the purpose of fasting is not to advertise ourselves but to discipline ourselves, not to gain a reputation for ourselves but to express our humility before God and our concern for others in need. If these purposes are fulfilled, it will be reward enough.

Looking back over these verses, it is evident that throughout Jesus has been contrasting two alternative kinds of piety, pharisaic and Christian. Pharisaic piety is ostentatious, motivated by vanity and rewarded by men. Christian piety is secret, motivated by humility and rewarded by God.

In order to grasp the alternative even more clearly, it may be helpful to look at the cause and effect of both forms. First the effect. Hypocritical religion is perverse because it is destructive. We have seen that praying, giving and fasting are all authentic activities in their own right. To pray is to seek God, to give is to serve others, to fast is to discipline oneself. But the effect of

[1] AG.
[2] JBP.
[3] P. 331.

hypocrisy is to destroy the integrity of these practices by turning each of them into an occasion for self-display.

What, then, is the cause? If we can isolate this, we can also find the remedy. Although one of the refrains of this passage is 'before men in order to be seen and praised by men', it is not men with whom the hypocrite is obsessed, but himself. 'Ultimately', writes Dr Lloyd-Jones, 'our only reason for pleasing men around us is that we may please ourselves.'[1] The remedy then is obvious. We have to become so conscious of God that we cease to be self-conscious. And it is on this that Jesus concentrates.

Perhaps I can put it in this way: absolute secrecy is impossible for any of us. It is not possible to do, say or think anything in the absence of spectators. For even if no human being is there, God is watching us. Not as a species of celestial policeman 'snooping' in order to catch us out, but as our loving heavenly Father, who is ever looking for opportunities to bless us. So the question is: which spectator matters to us the more, earthly or heavenly, men or God? The hypocrite performs his rituals 'in order to be seen by men'. The Greek verb is *theathēnai*. That is, they are in a theatre giving a performance. Their religion is a public spectacle. The true Christian is also aware that he is being watched, but for him the audience is God.

But why is it, someone may ask, that a different audience causes a different performance? Surely the answer is this. We can bluff a human audience; they can be taken in by our performance. We can fool them into supposing that we are genuine in our giving, praying, fasting, when we are only acting. But God is not mocked; we cannot deceive him. For God looks on the heart. That is why to do anything in order to be seen by men is bound to degrade it, while to do it to be seen by God is equally bound to ennoble it.

So we must choose our audience carefully. If we prefer human spectators, we shall lose our Christian integrity. The same will happen if we become our own audience. As Bonhoeffer put it: 'It is even more pernicious if I turn myself into a spectator of my own prayer performance . . . I can lay on a very nice show for myself even in the privacy of my own room.'[2] So we must choose God for our audience. As Jesus watched the people putting their

[1] P. 330.
[2] P. 146.

gifts into the temple treasury,[1] so God watches us as we give. As we pray and fast secretly, he is there in the secret place. God hates hypocrisy but loves reality. That is why it is only when we are aware of his presence that our giving, praying and fasting will be real.

[1] Mk. 12:41 ff.

## Matthew 6:7-15

## A Christian's prayer:
## not mechanical but thoughtful

*And in praying do not heap up empty phrases as the Gentiles do; for they think that they will be heard for their many words. [8] Do not be like them, for your Father knows what you need before you ask him. [9] Pray then like this:*

> *Our Father who art in heaven,*
> *Hallowed be thy name.*
> *[10] Thy kingdom come,*
> *Thy will be done,*
> *   On earth as it is in heaven.*
> *[11] Give us this day our daily bread;*
> *[12] And forgive us our debts,*
> *   As we also have forgiven our debtors;*
> *[13] And lead us not into temptation,*
> *   But deliver us from evil.*

*[14] For if you forgive men their trespasses, your heavenly Father also will forgive you; [15] but if you do not forgive men their trespasses, neither will your Father forgive your trespasses.*

Hypocrisy is not the only sin to avoid in prayer; 'vain repetition' or meaningless, mechanical utterance is another. The former is the folly of the Pharisee, the latter of the Gentile or pagan (7). Hypocrisy is a misuse of the *purpose* of prayer (diverting it from the glory of God to the glory of self); verbosity is a misuse of the very *nature* of prayer (degrading it from a real and personal approach to God into a mere recitation of words).

We see again that the method of Jesus is to paint a vivid contrast between two alternatives, in order to indicate his way the more plainly. Regarding the practice of piety in general, he has contrasted the pharisaic way (ostentatious and selfish) with the Christian way (secret and godly). Now regarding the practice of prayer in particular, he contrasts the pagan way of meaningless loquacity with the Christian way of meaningful communion with God. Thus Jesus is always calling his followers to something higher than the attainments of those around them, whether religious people or secular people. He emphasizes that Christian righteousness is greater (because inward), Christian love broader (because inclusive of enemies) and Christian prayer deeper (because sincere and thoughtful) than anything to be found in the non-Christian community.

## 1. The pagan way of prayer

*Do not heap up empty phrases as the Gentiles do,* he says (7). The Greek verb *battalogeō* is unique not only in biblical literature but elsewhere as well; no other use of the word is known beyond quotations of this verse. So nobody knows for certain either its derivation or its meaning. Some (like Erasmus) 'suppose the word to be derived from Battus, a king of Cyrene, who is said to have stuttered (so Herodotus); others from Battus, an author of tedious and wordy poems'.[1] But this is a bit far-fetched. Most regard it as an onomatopoeic expression, the sound of the word indicating its meaning. Thus *battarizō* meant to stammer; and any foreigner whose speech sounded to Greek ears like the interminable repetition of the syllable 'bar' was called *barbaros*, a barbarian. *Battalogeō* is perhaps similar. William Tyndale was the first translator to choose 'babble' as an equivalent English onomatopoeia, and NEB has taken it up: 'Do not go babbling on like the heathen.'

The familiar AV rendering, 'Use not vain repetitions,' is therefore misleading, unless it is clear that the emphasis is on 'vain' rather than on 'repetitions'. Jesus cannot be prohibiting all repetition, for he repeated himself in prayer, notably in Gethsemane when 'he went away and prayed for the third time, saying the same words'.[2] Perseverance and even importunity in prayer are commended by him also; rather is he condemning verbosity, especially in those who 'speak without thinking'.[3] So RSV's 'heap

[1] C. L. W. Grimm and J. H. Thayer, *A Greek–English lexicon of the New Testament* (T. and T. Clark, 1901).

[2] Mt. 26:44.

[3] AG.

up empty phrases' is helpful. The word describes any and every prayer which is all words and no meaning, all lips and no mind or heart. *Battalogia* is explained in the same verse (7) as *polulogia*, 'much speaking', that is, a torrent of mechanical and mindless words.

How are we to apply our Lord's prohibition today? It is certainly applicable to the prayer wheel, and even more to prayer flags by which the wind conveniently does the 'praying'. I think we must apply it also to Transcendental Meditation, for Maharishi Mahesh Yogi has himself expressed regret at his misleading choice of the word 'meditation'. True meditation involves the conscious use of the mind, but Transcendental Meditation is a simple and essentially mechanical technique for the relaxing of both body and mind. Instead of stimulating thought, it is designed to bring a person to a state of complete stillness and inactivity.

Turning from non-Christian to Christian practices of prayer, it seems that our Lord's condemnation would certainly include a mindless use of the rosary in which nothing happens but the fingering of beads and reciting of words, in which (that is) the rosary distracts instead of concentrating the mind. Does it also apply to liturgical forms of worship? Are Anglicans guilty of *battalogia*? Yes, no doubt some are, for the use of set forms does permit an approach to God with the lips while the heart is far from him. But then it is equally possible to use 'empty phrases' in extempore prayer and to lapse into religious jargon while the mind wanders. To sum up, what Jesus forbids his people is any kind of prayer with the mouth when the mind is not engaged.

The next words expose the folly of such a pretence at praying: *for they think that they will be heard for their many words*. NEB: 'They imagine that the more they say, the more likely they are to be heard.' What an incredible notion! What sort of a God is this who is chiefly impressed by the mechanics and the statistics of prayer, and whose response is determined by the volume of words we use and the number of hours we spend in praying?

*Do not be like them*, Jesus says (8). Why not? Because Christians do not believe in that kind of God. That is, we are not to do as they do because we are not to think as they think. On the contrary, *your Father knows what you need before you ask him*. He is neither ignorant, so that we need to instruct him, nor hesitant, so that we need to persuade him. He is our Father—a Father who loves his children and knows all about their needs. If that be so, somebody asks, then what is the point of praying? Let Calvin answer your question: 'Believers do not pray with the view of informing God about things unknown to him, or of exciting him to do his duty, or of urging him as though he were reluctant. On the contrary, they pray in order that they may arouse themselves to seek him, that they may exercise their faith in meditating on his promises, that they may relieve themselves from their anxieties by pouring them into his bosom; in a word, that they may declare that from him alone they hope and expect, both for themselves and for others, all good things.'[1] Luther put it more succinctly still: 'By our praying . . . we are instructing ourselves more than we are him.'[2]

## 2. The Christian way of prayer

If the praying of Pharisees was hypocritical and that of pagans mechanical, then the praying of Christians must be real—sincere as opposed to hypocritical, thoughtful as opposed to mechanical. Jesus intends our minds and hearts to be involved in what we are saying. Then prayer is seen in its true light—not as a meaningless repetition of words, nor as a means to our own glorification, but as a true communion with our heavenly Father.

The so-called 'Lord's Prayer' was given by Jesus as a model of what genuine Christian prayer is like. According to Matthew he gave it as a pattern to copy (*Pray then like this*), according to Luke as a form to use (11:2, 'When you pray, say . . .'). We are not obliged to choose, however, for we can both use the prayer as it stands and also model our own praying upon it.

The essential difference between pharisaic, pagan and Christian praying lies in the kind of God we pray to. Other gods may like mechanical incantations; but not the living and true God revealed by Jesus Christ. Jesus told us to address him as (literally) 'our Father in the heavens'. This implies first that he is personal, as much 'he' as I am 'I'. He may indeed be, in C. S. Lewis's well-known phrase, 'beyond personality'; he is certainly not less. One of the reasons for rejecting the attempts of modern radical theologians to reconstruct the doctrine of God is that they depersonalize him. The concept of God as 'the ground of our

[1] P. 314.
[2] P. 144.

(human) being' is simply not compatible with the notion of his divine fatherhood. God is just as personal as we are, in fact more so. Secondly, he is loving. He is not an ogre who terrifies us with hideous cruelty, nor the kind of father we sometimes read or hear about—autocrat, playboy, drunkard—but he himself fulfils the ideal of fatherhood in his loving care for his children. Thirdly, he is powerful. He is not only good but great. The words 'in the heavens' denote not the place of his abode so much as the authority and power at his command as the creator and ruler of all things. Thus he combines fatherly love with heavenly power, and what his love directs his power is able to perform.

In telling us to address God as 'our Father in heaven', the concern of Jesus is not with protocol (teaching us the correct etiquette in approaching the Deity) but with truth (that we may come to him in the right frame of mind). It is always wise, before we pray, to spend time deliberately recalling who he is. Only then shall we come to our loving Father in heaven with appropriate humility, devotion and confidence.

Further, when we have taken time and trouble to orientate ourselves towards God and recollect what manner of God he is, our personal, loving, powerful Father, then the content of our prayers will be radically affected in two ways. First, God's concerns will be given priority . . . ('your name, your kingdom . . . , your will . . . '). Secondly, our own needs, though demoted to second place, will yet be comprehensively committed to him ('Give us . . . , forgive us . . . , deliver us . . .'). Everybody knows that the Lord's prayer is in these two parts, concerned first with the glory of God and then with the needs of man, but I think Calvin[1] was the first commentator to suggest a parallel with the ten commandments. For they also are divided in two and express the same priority: the first table outlines our duty to God and the second our duty to our neighbour.

The first three petitions in the Lord's Prayer express our concern for God's glory in relation to his name, rule and will. If our concept of God were of some impersonal force, then of course he would have no personal name, rule or will to be concerned about. Again, if we were to think of him as 'the Ultimate within ourselves' or 'the ground of our being', it would be impossible to distinguish between his concerns and ours. But if he is in reality

[1] Pp. 316, 321.

'our Father in heaven', the personal God of love and power fully revealed by Jesus Christ, Creator of all, who cares about the creatures he has made and the children he has redeemed, then and then only does it become possible (indeed, essential) to give his concerns priority and to become preoccupied with his name, his kingdom and his will.

The name of God is not a combination of the letters G, O and D. The name stands for the person who bears it, for his character and activity. So God's 'name' is God himself as he is in himself and has revealed himself. His name is already 'holy' in that it is separate from and exalted over every other name. But we pray that it may be *hallowed*, 'treated as holy', because we ardently desire that due honour may be given to it, that is to him whose name it is, in our own lives, in the church and in the world.

The kingdom of God is his royal rule. Again, as he is already holy so he is already King, reigning in absolute sovereignty over both nature and history. Yet when Jesus came he announced a new and special break-in of the kingly rule of God, with all the blessings of salvation and the demands of submission which the divine rule implies. To pray that his kingdom may 'come' is to pray both that it may grow, as through the church's witness people submit to Jesus, and that soon it will be consummated when Jesus returns in glory to take his power and reign.

The will of God is 'good, acceptable and perfect',[1] for it is the will of 'our Father in heaven' who is infinite in knowledge, love and power. It is, therefore, folly to resist it, and wisdom to discern, desire and do it. As his name is already holy and he is already King, so already his will is being done 'in heaven'. What Jesus bids us pray is that life on earth may come to approximate more nearly to life in heaven. For the expression *on earth as it is in heaven* seems to apply equally to the hallowing of God's name, the spreading of his kingdom and the doing of his will.

It is comparatively easy to repeat the words of the Lord's Prayer like a parrot (or indeed a heathen 'babbler'). To pray them with sincerity, however, has revolutionary implications, for it expresses the priorities of a Christian. We are constantly under pressure to conform to the self-centredness of secular culture. When that happens we become concerned about our own little name (liking to see it embossed on our notepaper or hitting the headlines in the press, and defending it when it is attacked), about

[1] Rom. 12:2.

our own little empire (bossing, 'influencing' and manipulating people to boost our ego), and about our own silly little will (always wanting our own way and getting upset when it is frustrated). But in the Christian counter-culture our top priority concern is not our name, kingdom and will, but God's. Whether we can pray these petitions with integrity is a searching test of the reality and depth of our Christian profession.

In the second half of the Lord's Prayer the possessive adjective changes from 'your' to 'our', as we turn from God's affairs to our own. Having expressed our burning concern for his glory, we now express our humble dependence on his grace. A true understanding of the God we pray to, as heavenly Father and great King, although putting our personal needs into a second and subsidiary place, will not eliminate them. To decline to mention them at all in prayer (on the ground that we do not want to bother God with such trivialities) is as great an error as to allow them to dominate our prayers. For since God is 'our Father in heaven' and loves us with a father's love, he is concerned for the total welfare of his children and wants us to bring our needs trustingly to him, our need of food and of forgiveness and of deliverance from evil.

*Give us this day our daily bread.* Some early commentators could not believe that Jesus intended our first request to be for literal bread, bread for the body. It seemed to them improper, especially after the noble three opening petitions relating to God's glory, that we should abruptly descend to so mundane and material a concern. So they allegorized the petition. The bread he meant must be spiritual, they said. Early church fathers like Tertullian, Cyprian and Augustine thought the reference was either to 'the invisible bread of the Word of God'[1] or to the Lord's Supper. Jerome in the Vulgate translated the Greek word for 'daily' by the monstrous adjective 'supersubstantial'; he also meant the

---

[1] This is Augustine's expression. He begins by listing three alternative interpretations, *viz*. 'all those things which meet the wants of this life', 'the sacrament of the body of Christ' and 'the spiritual food', namely 'divine precepts which we ought daily to meditate and to labour after'. He himself prefers the latter explanation. But he concludes that if anyone wishes to understand 'daily bread' as referring also to 'food necessary for the body' or to 'the sacrament of the Lord's body', then 'we must take all three meanings conjointly'. That is, 'We are to ask for all at once as daily bread, both the bread necessary for the body, and the visible hallowed bread (*sc.* Holy Communion) and the invisible bread of the word of God' (VI. 25, 27).

Holy Communion. We should be thankful for the greater, down-to-earth, biblical understanding of the Reformers. Calvin's comment on the spiritualizing of the fathers was: 'This is exceedingly absurd.'[1] Luther had the wisdom to see that 'bread' was a symbol for 'everything necessary for the preservation of this life, like food, a healthy body, good weather, house, home, wife, children, good government and peace',[2] and probably we should add that by 'bread' Jesus meant the necessities rather than the luxuries of life.

The petition that God will 'give' us our food does not, of course, deny that most people have to earn their own living, that farmers have to plough, sow and reap to provide basic cereals or that we are commanded to feed the hungry ourselves.[3] Instead, it is an expression of ultimate dependence on God who normally uses human means of production and distribution through which to fulfil his purposes. Moreover, it seems that Jesus wanted his followers to be conscious of a day-to-day dependence. The adjective *epiousios* in 'our daily bread' was so completely unknown to the ancients that Origen thought the evangelists had coined it. Moulton and Milligan are of the same opinion in our generation.[4] It is probably to be translated either 'for the current day' or 'for the following day'.[5] Whichever is correct, it is a prayer for the immediate and not the distant future. As A. M. Hunter comments: 'Used in the morning, this petition would ask bread for the day just beginning. Used in the evening, it would pray for tomorrow's bread.'[6] Thus we are to live a day at a time.

Forgiveness is as indispensable to the life and health of the soul as food is for the body. So the next prayer is, *Forgive us our debts.* Sin is likened to a 'debt' because it deserves to be punished. But when God forgives sin, he remits the penalty and drops the charge against us. The addition of the words *as we also have forgiven our debtors* is further emphasized in verses 14 and 15 which follow the prayer and state that our Father will forgive us if we forgive others but will not forgive us if we refuse to forgive others. This certainly does not mean that our forgiveness of others earns us the right to be forgiven. It is rather that God forgives only the penitent and that one of the chief evidences of true penitence is a forgiving spirit. Once our eyes have been opened to see the enormity of our offence against God, the injuries which others

[1] P. 322.          [2] P. 147.          [3] Mt. 25:35.
[4] J. H. Moulton and G. Milligan, *The Vocabulary of the Greek Testament* (Hodder, 1949).          [5] AG.          [6] P. 75.

have done to us appear by comparison extremely trifling. If, on the other hand, we have an exaggerated view of the offences of others, it proves that we have minimized our own. It is the disparity between the size of debts which is the main point of the parable of the unmerciful servant.[1] Its conclusion is: 'I forgave you *all that debt* (which was huge) . . . ; should not you have had mercy on your fellow servant, as I had mercy on you?' (33).

The last two petitions should probably be understood as the negative and positive aspects of one: *Lead us not into temptation, but deliver us from evil.* The sinner whose evil in the past has been forgiven longs to be delivered from its tyranny in the future. The general sense of the prayer is plain. But two problems confront us. First, the Bible says that God does not (indeed cannot) tempt us with evil.[2] So what is the sense of praying that he will not do what he has promised never to do? Some answer this question by interpreting 'tempting' as 'testing',[3] explaining that though God never entices us to sin he does test our faith and character. This is possible. A better explanation seems to me to be that 'lead us not' must be understood in the light of its counterpart 'but deliver us', and that 'evil' should be rendered 'evil one' (as in 13:19). In other words, it is the devil who is in view, who tempts God's people to sin, and from whom we need to be 'rescued' (*rusai*).

The second problem concerns the fact that the Bible says temptation and trial are good for us: 'Count it all joy, my brethren, when you meet various trials' or 'various temptations'.[4] If then they are beneficial, why should we pray not to be led into them? The probable answer is that the prayer is more that we may overcome temptation, than that we may avoid it. Perhaps we could paraphrase the whole request as 'Do not allow us so to be led into temptation that it overwhelms us, but rescue us from the evil one'. So behind these words that Jesus gave us to pray are the implications that the devil is too strong for us, that we are too weak to stand up to him, but that our heavenly Father will deliver us if we call upon him.

Thus the three petitions which Jesus puts upon our lips are beautifully comprehensive. They cover, in principle, all our human need—material (daily bread), spiritual (forgiveness of

[1] Mt. 18:23-35.
[2] Jas. 1:13.
[3] *Cf.* NEB, 'Do not bring us to the test.'
[4] Jas. 1:2.

sins) and moral (deliverance from evil). What we are doing whenever we pray this prayer is to express our dependence upon God in every area of our human life. Moreover, a trinitarian Christian is bound to see in these three petitions a veiled allusion to the Trinity, since it is through the Father's creation and providence that we receive our daily bread, through the Son's atoning death that we may be forgiven and through the Spirit's indwelling power that we are rescued from the evil one. No wonder some ancient manuscripts (though not the best) end with the doxology, attributing 'the kingdom and the power and the glory' to this triune God to whom alone it belongs.

Jesus seems then to have given the Lord's Prayer as a model of *real* prayer, *Christian* prayer, in distinction to the prayers of Pharisees and heathen. To be sure, one could recite the Lord's Prayer either hypocritically or mechanically or both. But if we mean what we say, then the Lord's Prayer is the divine alternative to both forms of false prayer. I do not myself think it fanciful to see this in both halves of the prayer.

The error of the hypocrite is selfishness. Even in his prayers he is obsessed with his own self-image and how he looks in the eyes of the beholder. But in the Lord's Prayer Christians are obsessed with God—with his name, his kingdom and his will, not with theirs. True Christian prayer is always a preoccupation with God and his glory. It is therefore the exact opposite of the exhibitionism of hypocrites who use prayer as a vehicle for their own glory.

The error of the heathen is mindlessness. He just goes babbling on, giving voice to his meaningless liturgy. He does not think about what he is saying, for his concern is with volume, not content. But God is not impressed by verbiage. Over against this folly Jesus invites us to make all our needs known to our heavenly Father with humble thoughtfulness, and so express our daily dependence on him.

Thus Christian prayer is seen in contrast to its non-Christian alternatives. It is *God-centred* (concerned for God's glory) in contrast to the self-centredness of the Pharisees (preoccupied with their own glory). And it is *intelligent* (expressive of thoughtful dependence) in contrast to the mechanical incantations of the heathen. Therefore when we come to God in prayer, we do not come hypocritically like play actors seeking the applause of men, nor mechanically like pagan babblers, whose mind is not in their mutterings, but thoughtfully, humbly and trustfully like little children to their father.

It will be seen that the fundamental difference between various kinds of prayer is in the fundamentally different images of God which lie behind them. The tragic mistake of Pharisees and pagans, of hypocrites and heathen, is to be found in their false image of God. Indeed, neither is really thinking of God at all, for the hypocrite thinks only of himself while the heathen thinks of other things. What sort of God is it who might be interested in such selfish and mindless prayers? Is God a commodity that we can use him to boost our own status, or a computer that we can feed words into him mechanically?

From these unworthy notions we turn back with relief to the teaching of Jesus that God is our Father in the heavens. We need to remember that he loves his children with most tender affection, that he sees his children even in the secret place, that he knows his children and all their needs before they ask him, and that he acts on behalf of his children by his heavenly and kingly power. If we thus allow Scripture to fashion our image of God, if we recall his character and practise his presence, we shall never pray with hypocrisy but always with integrity, never mechanically but always thoughtfully, like the children of God that we are.

# Matthew 6:19-34
## A Christian's ambition: not material security but God's rule

In the first half of Matthew 6 (1–18) Jesus describes the Christian's *private* life 'in the secret place' (giving, praying, fasting); in the second half (19–34) he is concerned with our *public* business in the world (questions of money, possessions, food, drink, clothing and ambition). Or the same contrast could be expressed in terms of our 'religious' and our 'secular' responsibilities. This distinction is misleading, because we cannot separate these into watertight compartments. Indeed, the divorce of the sacred from the secular in church history has been disastrous. If we are Christians, everything we do, however 'secular' it may seem (like shopping, cooking, totting up figures in the office, *etc.*) is 'religious' in the sense that it is done in God's presence and according to God's will. One of the emphases Jesus makes in this chapter is precisely on this point, that God is equally concerned with both areas of our life—private and public, religious and secular. For on the one hand, 'Your heavenly Father sees in secret' (4, 6, 18), and on the other, 'Your heavenly Father knows that you need' food, drink and clothing (32).

In both spheres also the same insistent summons of Jesus is heard, the call to be different from the popular culture: different from the hypocrisy of the religious (1–18) and now different also from the materialism of the irreligious (19–34). For although the Pharisees were largely in his mind at the beginning of the chapter, it is 'the Gentiles' whose value-system he now bids us renounce (32). In fact Jesus places the alternatives before us at every stage. There are two treasures (on earth and in heaven, 19–21), two bodily conditions (light and darkness, 22, 23), two masters (God and mammon, 24) and two preoccupations (our bodies and God's kingdom, 25–34). We cannot sit on the fence.

But how shall we make our choice? Worldly ambition has a strong fascination for us. The spell of materialism is hard to break. So in this section Jesus helps us to choose well. He points out the folly of the wrong way and the wisdom of the right. As in the previous sections on piety and prayer, so here regarding ambition, he sets the false and the true over against each other in such a way as to invite us to compare them and see for ourselves.

This topic confronts us with fresh urgency in our generation. As the world's population continues to mushroom and the economic problems of the nations become more complex, the rich are still getting richer and the poor poorer. We can no longer turn a blind eye to the facts. The old complacency of bourgeois Christianity has been disturbed. The sleepy social conscience of many has been stabbed awake. There has been a fresh discovery that the God of the Bible is on the side of the poor and the deprived. Responsible Christians are uneasy about affluence and are seeking to develop a simple life-style which is appropriate both in face of world need and out of loyalty to their Master's teaching and example.

## 1. A question of treasure (19–21)

*Do not lay up for yourselves treasures on earth, where moth and rust consume and where thieves break in and steal, 20 but lay up for yourselves treasures in heaven, where neither moth nor rust consumes and where thieves do not break in and steal. 21 For where your treasure is, there will your heart be also.*

Here the point to which Jesus directs our attention is the comparative durability of the two treasures. It ought to be easy to decide which to collect, he implies, because *treasures on earth* are corruptible and therefore insecure, whereas *treasures in heaven* are incorruptible and therefore secure. After all, if our object is to lay up treasure, we shall presumably concentrate on the kind which will last and can be stored without either depreciation or deterioration.

It is important to face squarely and honestly the question: what was Jesus prohibiting when he told us not to lay up treasure for ourselves on earth? It may help if we begin by listing what he was (and is) not forbidding. First, there is no ban on possessions in themselves; Scripture nowhere forbids private property.

Secondly, 'saving for a rainy day' is not forbidden to Christians, or for that matter a life assurance policy which is only a kind of saving by self-imposed compulsion. On the contrary, Scripture praises the ant for storing in the summer the food it will need in the winter, and declares that the believer who makes no provision for his family is worse than an unbeliever.[1] Thirdly, we are not to despise, but rather to enjoy, the good things which our Creator has given us richly to enjoy.[2] So neither having possessions, nor making provision for the future, nor enjoying the gifts of a good Creator are included in the ban on earthly treasure-storage.

What then? What Jesus forbids his followers is the *selfish* accumulation of goods (NB 'Do not lay up *for yourselves* treasures on earth'); extravagant and luxurious living; the hardheartedness which does not feel the colossal need of the world's under-privileged people; the foolish fantasy that a person's life consists in the abundance of his possessions;[3] and the materialism which tethers our hearts to the earth. For the Sermon on the Mount repeatedly refers to 'the heart', and here Jesus declares that our heart always follows our treasure, whether down to earth or up to heaven (21). In a word to 'lay up treasure on earth' does not mean being provident (making sensible provision for the future) but being covetous (like misers who hoard and materialists who always want more). This is the real snare of which Jesus warns here. 'Whenever the Gospel is taught', wrote Luther, 'and people seek to live according to it, there are two terrible plagues that always arise: false preachers who corrupt the teaching, and then Sir Greed, who obstructs right living.'[4]

The earthly treasure we covet, Jesus reminds us, 'grows rusty and moth-eaten, and thieves break in to steal it' (NEB). The Greek word for 'rust' (*brōsis*) actually means 'eating'; it could refer to the corrosion caused by rust, but equally to any devouring pest or vermin. Thus in those days moths would get into people's clothes, rats and mice eat the stored grain, worms take whatever they put underground, and thieves break into their home and steal what they kept there. Nothing was safe in the ancient world. And for us moderns, who try to protect our treasure by insecticides, rat poison, mouse-traps, rustproof paints and burglar alarms, it disintegrates instead through inflation or devaluation or an economic slump. Even if some of it lasts through this life, we

[1] Pr. 6:6 ff.; 1 Tim. 5:8.  [2] 1 Tim. 4:3, 4; 6:17.
[3] Lk. 12:15.  [4] P. 166.

*Naked?
Funeral?*

can take none of it with us to the next. Job was right: 'Naked I came from my mother's womb, and naked I shall return.'[1]

But 'treasure in heaven' is incorruptible. What is this? Jesus does not explain. Yet surely we may say that to 'lay up treasure in heaven' is to do anything on earth whose effects last for eternity. Jesus was certainly not teaching a doctrine of merit or a 'treasury of merits' (as the medieval Roman Catholic Church called it), as if we could accumulate by good deeds done on earth a kind of credit account in heaven on which we and others might draw, for such a grotesque notion contradicts the gospel of grace which Jesus and his apostles consistently taught. And in any case Jesus is addressing disciples who have already received the salvation of God. It seems rather to refer to such things as these: the development of Christlike character (since all we can take with us to heaven is ourselves); the increase of faith, hope and charity, all of which (Paul said) 'abide';[2] growth in the knowledge of Christ whom one day we shall see face to face; the active endeavour (by prayer and witness) to introduce others to Christ, so that they too may inherit eternal life; and the use of our money for Christian causes, which is the only investment whose dividends are everlasting.

All these are temporal activities with eternal consequences. This then is 'treasure in heaven'. No burglar can steal this, and no vermin destroy it. For there are neither moths, nor mice, nor marauders in heaven. So treasure in heaven is secure. Precautionary measures to protect it are unnecessary. It needs no insurance cover. It is indestructible. Therefore, Jesus seems to be saying to us, 'If it's a safe investment you're after, nothing could be safer than this; it's the only gilt-edged security whose gilt will never tarnish.'

## 2. A question of vision (22, 23)

*The eye is the lamp of the body. So, if your eye is sound, your whole body will be full of light;* [23] *but if your eye is not sound, your whole body will be full of darkness. If then the light in you is darkness, how great is the darkness!*

Jesus turns from the comparative durability of the two treasures to the comparative benefit to be derived from two conditions. The contrast now is between a blind person and a sighted person,

[1] Jb. 1:21.      [2] 1 Cor. 13:13.

and so between the light and darkness in which they respectively live. *The eye is the lamp of the body.* This is not literal, of course, as if the eye were a kind of window letting light into the body, but it is a readily intelligible figure of speech. Almost everything the body does depends on our ability to see. We need to see in order to run, jump, drive a car, cross a road, cook, embroider, paint. The eye, as it were, 'illumines' what the body does through its hands and feet. True, blind people often cope wonderfully, learn to do many things without eyes, and develop their other faculties to compensate for their lack of sight. Yet the principle holds good: a sighted person walks in the light, while a blind person is in darkness. And the great difference between the light and the darkness of the body is due to this small but intricate organ, the eye. *If your eye is sound, your whole body will be full of light; but if your eye is not sound, your whole body will be full of darkness.* In total blindness the darkness is complete.

✳ All this is factual description. But it is also metaphorical. Not infrequently in Scripture the 'eye' is equivalent to the 'heart'. That is, to 'set the heart' and to 'fix the eye' on something are synonyms. One example may be enough, from Psalm 119. In verse 10 the psalmist writes: 'With my whole heart I seek thee; let me not wander from thy commandments,' and in verse 19, 'I have fixed my eyes on all thy commandments.' Similarly, here in the Sermon on the Mount, Jesus passes from the importance of having our *heart* in the right place (21) to the importance of having our *eye* sound and healthy.

✳ The argument seems to go like this: just as our eye affects our whole body, so our ambition (where we fix our eyes and heart) affects our whole life. Just as a seeing eye gives light to the body, so a noble and singleminded ambition to serve God and man adds meaning to life and throws light on everything we do. Again, just as blindness leads to darkness, so an ignoble and selfish ambition (*e.g.* to lay up treasure for ourselves on earth) plunges us into moral darkness. It makes us intolerant, inhuman, ruthless and deprives life of all ultimate significance.

It is all a question of vision. If we have physical vision, we can see what we are doing and where we are going. So too if we have spiritual vision, if our spiritual perspective is correctly adjusted, then our life is filled with purpose and drive. But if our vision becomes clouded by the false gods of materialism, and we lose our sense of values, then our whole life is in darkness and we cannot see where we are going. Perhaps the emphasis lies even more strongly than I have so far suggested on the loss of vision caused by covetousness, because according to biblical thought an 'evil eye' is a niggardly, miserly spirit, and a 'sound' one is generous. At all events Jesus adds this new reason for laying up treasure in heaven. The first was its greater durability; the second the resulting benefit now on earth of such a vision.

### 3. A question of worth (24)

*No one can serve two masters; for either he will hate the one and love the other, or he will be devoted to the one and despise the other. You cannot serve God and mammon.*

Jesus now explains that behind the choice between two treasures (where we lay them up) and two visions (where we fix our eyes) there lies the still more basic choice between two masters (whom we are going to serve). It is a choice between God and mammon, that is between the living Creator himself and any object of our own creation we term 'money' ('mammon' being the transliteration of an Aramaic word for wealth). For we cannot serve both.

Some people disagree with this saying of Jesus. They refuse to be confronted with such a stark and outright choice, and see no necessity for it. They blandly assure us that it is perfectly possible to serve two masters simultaneously, for they manage it very nicely themselves. Several possible arrangements and adjustments appeal to them. Either they serve God on Sundays and mammon on weekdays, or God with their lips and mammon with their hearts, or God in appearance and mammon in reality, or God with half their being and mammon with the other half.

It is this popular compromise solution which Jesus declares to be impossible: *No one can serve two masters . . . You cannot serve God and mammon* (notice the 'can' and the 'cannot'). Would-be compromisers misunderstand his teaching, for they miss the picture of slave and slave-owner which lies behind his words. As McNeile puts it, 'Men can work for two employers, but no slave can be the property of two owners,'[1] for 'single ownership and fulltime service are of the essence of slavery'.[2] So anybody who divides his allegiance between God and mammon has already given it to mammon, since God can be served only with an entire

[1] P. 85.     [2] Tasker, p. 76.

and exclusive devotion. This is simply because he is God: 'I am the Lord, that is my name; my glory I give to no other.'[1] To try to share him with other loyalties is to have opted for idolatry.

And when the choice is seen for what it is—a choice between Creator and creature, between the glorious personal God and a miserable thing called money, between worship and idolatry—it seems inconceivable that anybody could make the wrong choice. For now it is a question not just of comparative durability and comparative benefit, but of comparative worth: the intrinsic worth of the One and the intrinsic worthlessness of the other.

### 4. A question of ambition (25-34)

*Therefore I tell you, do not be anxious about your life, what you shall eat or what you shall drink, nor about your body, what you shall put on. Is not life more than food, and the body more than clothing?* [26]*Look at the birds of the air; they neither sow nor reap nor gather into barns, and yet your heavenly Father feeds them. Are you not of more value than they?* [27]*And which of you by being anxious can add one cubit to his span of life?* [28]*And why are you anxious about clothing? Consider the lilies of the field, how they grow; they neither toil nor spin;* [29]*yet I tell you, even Solomon in all his glory was not arrayed like one of these.* [30]*But if God so clothes the grass of the field, which today is alive and tomorrow is thrown into the oven, will he not much more clothe you, O men of little faith?* [31]*Therefore do not be anxious, saying 'What shall we eat?' or 'What shall we drink?' or 'What shall we wear?'* [32]*For the Gentiles seek all these things; and your heavenly Father knows that you need them all.* [33]*But seek first his kingdom and his righteousness, and all these things shall be yours as well.* [34]*Therefore do not be anxious about tomorrow, for tomorrow will be anxious for itself. Let the day's own trouble be sufficient for the day.*

It is a pity that this passage is often read on its own in church, isolated from what has gone before. Then the significance of the introductory *Therefore I tell you* is missed. So we must begin by relating this 'therefore', this conclusion of Jesus, to the teaching which has led up to it. He calls us to thought before he calls us to action. He invites us to look clearly and coolly at the alternatives before us and to weigh them up carefully. We want to accumulate treasure? Then which of the two possibilities is the more durable? We wish to be free and purposive in our movements? Then what must our eyes be like to facilitate this? We wish to serve the best

[1] Is. 42:8; 48:11.

master? Then we must consider which is the more worthy of our devotion. Only when we have grasped with our minds the comparative durability of the two treasures (corruptible and incorruptible), the comparative usefulness of the two eye conditions (light and darkness) and the comparative worth of the two masters (God and mammon), are we ready to make our choice. And only when we have made our choice—for heavenly treasure, for light, for God—*therefore I tell you* this is how you must go on to behave: *do not be anxious about your life . . . nor about your body . . . But seek first his kingdom and his righteousness* (25, 33). In other words, our basic choice of which of two masters we intend to serve will radically affect our attitude to both. We shall not be anxious about the one (for we have rejected it), but concentrate our mind and energy on the other (for we have chosen him); we shall refuse to become engrossed in our own concerns, but instead *seek first* the concerns of God.

Christ's language of search (contrasting what *the Gentiles seek* with what his followers are to *seek first*, 32, 33) introduces us to the subject of ambition. Jesus took it for granted that all human beings are 'seekers'. It is not natural for people to drift aimlessly through life like plankton. We need something to live for, something to give meaning to our existence, something to 'seek', something on which to set our 'hearts'[1] and our 'minds'.[2] Although few people today would use the language of ancient Greek philosophers, yet what we are seeking is, in fact, what they called 'the Supreme Good' to which to dedicate our lives. Probably 'ambition' is the best modern equivalent. True, in dictionary terms it means 'a strong desire to achieve success' and therefore often has a bad image, a selfish flavour. It is in this sense that Shakespeare in his *King Henry VIII* brings this appeal to Thomas Cromwell: 'Cromwell, I charge thee, fling away Ambition. By that sin fell the angels . . .' But 'ambition' can equally refer to other strong desires—unselfish rather than selfish, godly rather than worldly. In a word, it is possible to be 'ambitious for God'. Ambition concerns our goals in life and our incentives for pursuing them. A person's ambition is what makes him 'tick'; it uncovers the mainspring of his actions, his secret inner motivation. This, then, is what Jesus was talking about when he defined what in the Christian counter-culture we are to 'seek first'.

[1] JBP.
[2] JB.

Once again our Lord simplifies the issue for us by reducing the alternative possible life-goals to only two. He puts them over against each other in this section, urging his followers not to be preoccupied with their own security (food, drink and clothing), for that is the obsession of 'the Gentiles' who do not know him, but rather with God's rule and God's righteousness, and with their spread and triumph in the world.

### a. False or secular ambition: our own material security

Most of this paragraph is negative. Three times Jesus repeats his prohibition *Do not be anxious* (25, 31, 34) or 'Don't worry.'[1] And the preoccupation he forbids us is food, drink and clothing: *What shall we eat? What shall we drink? What shall we wear?* (31). Yet this is precisely 'the world's Trinity of cares':[2] *for the Gentiles seek all these things* (32). We have only to glance at the advertisements on television, in newspapers and in public transport to find a vivid modern illustration of what Jesus taught nearly two millennia ago.

A few years ago I was sent a complimentary copy of *Accent*, a new glossy magazine whose full title was *Accent on good living*. It included enticing advertisements for champagne, cigarettes, food, clothing, antiques and carpets, together with the description of an esoteric weekend's shopping in Rome. There were articles on how to have a computer in your kitchen; how to win a luxury cabin cruiser or 100 twelve-bottle cases of Scotch whisky instead; and how 15 million women cannot be wrong about their cosmetic choices. We were then promised in the following month's issue alluring articles on Caribbean holidays, staying in bed, high fashion warm underwear and the delights of reindeer meat and snowberries. From beginning to end it concerned the welfare of the body and how to feed it, clothe it, warm it, cool it, refresh it, relax it, entertain it, titivate and titillate it.

Now please do not misunderstand this. Jesus Christ neither denies nor despises the needs of the body. As a matter of fact, he made it himself. And he takes care of it. He has just taught us to pray, 'Give us this day our daily bread.' What is he saying then? He is emphasizing that to become engrossed in material comforts is a false preoccupation. For one thing, it is unproductive (except perhaps of ulcers and yet more worry); for another it is unneces-

[1] JBP.
[2] Spurgeon, p. 39.

sary (because 'your Father knows what you need', 8 and 32); but especially it is unworthy. It betrays a false view of human beings (as if they were only bodies needing to be fed, watered, clothed and housed) and of human life (as if it were merely a physiological mechanism needing to be protected, lubricated and fuelled). An exclusive preoccupation with food, drink and clothing could be justified only if physical survival were the be-all and end-all of existence. We just live to live. Then indeed how to sustain the body would be our proper first concern. So it is understandable that in emergency famine conditions the struggle to survive must take precedence over other things. But for this to be so in ordinary circumstances would express a reductionist concept of man which is totally unacceptable. It would downgrade him to the level of animals, indeed to that of birds and plants. Yet the great majority of today's advertisements are directed towards the body—underwear to display it at its shapeliest, deodorants to keep it smelling sweet, and alcoholic beverages to pep it up when it is languishing. This preoccupation prompts these questions: is physical well-being a worthy object to which to devote our lives? Has human life no more significance than this? *The Gentiles seek all these things.* Let them. But as for you, my disciples, Jesus implies, they are a hopelessly unworthy goal. For they are not the 'Supreme Good' in life.

We need now to clarify what Jesus is prohibiting, and what reasons he gives for his prohibition. First, he is not forbidding thought. On the contrary, he is encouraging it when he goes on to bid us look at the birds and the flowers and 'consider' how God looks after them. So the familiar AV 'Take no thought' is mistaken and misleading. Secondly, he is not forbidding forethought. I have already mentioned the Bible's approval of the ant. Birds too, which Jesus commends, make provision for the future by building their nests, laying and incubating their eggs, and feeding their young. Many migrate to warmer climes before the winter (which is an outstanding example of provident—though instinctive—forethought), and some even store food, like shrikes which stock their own larder by impaling insects on thorns. So there is nothing here to stop Christians making plans for the future or taking sensible steps for their own security. No, what Jesus forbids is neither thought nor forethought, but anxious thought. This is the meaning of the command *mē merimnate*. It is the word used of Martha who was 'distracted' with much serving, of the good seed sown among thorns which was choked by the 'cares' of life, and by Paul in his injunction, 'Have no anxiety about anything.'[1] As Bishop Ryle expressed it: 'Prudent provision for the future is right; wearing, corroding, self-tormenting anxiety is wrong.'[2]

Why is it wrong? Jesus replies by arguing that obsessional worry of this kind is incompatible both with Christian faith (25-30) and with common sense (34), but he spends more time on the first.

1. *Worry is incompatible with Christian faith* (25-30). In verse 30 Jesus dubs those who get het up over food and clothing 'men of little faith'. The reasons he gives why we should trust God instead of being anxious are both *a fortiori* ('how much more') arguments. One is taken from human experience and argues from the greater to the lesser; the other comes from sub-human experience (birds and flowers) and argues from the lesser to the greater.

Our human experience is this: God created and now sustains our life; he also created and continues to sustain our body. This is a fact of everyday experience. We neither made ourselves, nor keep ourselves alive. Now, our 'life' (for which God is responsible) is obviously more important than the food and drink which nourish it. Similarly our 'body' (for which God is also responsible) is more important than the clothing which covers and warms it. Well then, if God already takes care of the greater (our life and our body), can we not trust him to take care of the lesser (our food and our clothing)? The logic is inescapable, and Jesus enforces it in verse 27 with the question: *Which of you by being anxious can add one cubit to his span of life?* It is uncertain whether the last word of his question (*hēlikia*) should be translated 'span of life' (RSV) or 'stature' (AV). It can mean either. To add half a metre to our stature would be a remarkable feat indeed, although God does it to all of us between our childhood and adult life. To add a period of time to our lifespan is also outside our competence. A human being cannot achieve this by himself. Indeed, far from lengthening his life, worry 'may very well shorten it',[3] as we all know. So just as we leave these matters to God (for they are

[1] Lk. 10:40; 8:14; Phil. 4:6.
[2] P. 59.
[3] Tasker, p. 77.

certainly beyond us), would it not be sensible to trust him for lesser things like food and clothes?

Next, Jesus turns to the subhuman world and argues the other way round. He uses birds as an illustration of God's supply of food (26) and flowers to illustrate his supply of clothing (28–30). In both cases he tells us to 'look at' or 'consider' them, that is, to think about the facts of God's providential care in their case. Some readers may know that I happen myself to have been since boyhood an enthusiastic bird-watcher. I know, of course, that bird-watching is regarded by some as a rather eccentric pastime; they view the likes of me with quizzical and patronizing amusement. But I claim biblical—indeed dominical—warrant for this activity. 'Consider the fowls of the air,' said Jesus according to the AV, and this in basic English could be translated 'watch birds'! Indeed, I am quite serious, for the Greek verb in his command (*emblepsate eis*) means 'fix your eyes on, so as to take a good look at'.[1] If we do take an interest in birds and flowers (and we should surely, like our Master, be gratefully aware of the natural world around us), then we will know that although birds *neither sow nor reap nor gather into barns*, yet our *heavenly Father feeds them*, and that although *the lilies of the field* (anemones, poppies, irises and gladioli have all been suggested as alternatives to lilies, although the reference may be general to all the beautiful spring flowers of Galilee) . . . *neither toil nor spin*, yet our heavenly Father *clothes* them, indeed more gorgeously than *Solomon in all his glory*. This being so, can we not trust him to feed and clothe us who are of much more value than birds and flowers? Why, he even clothes the common grass *which today is alive and tomorrow is thrown into the oven*!

'You see,' writes Martin Luther with great charm, 'he is making the birds our schoolmasters and teachers. It is a great and abiding disgrace to us that in the Gospel a helpless sparrow should become a theologian and a preacher to the wisest of men . . . Whenever you listen to a nightingale, therefore, you are listening to an excellent preacher . . . It is as if he were saying "I prefer to be in the Lord's kitchen. He has made heaven and earth, and he himself is the cook and the host. Every day he feeds and nourishes innumerable little birds out of his hand." '[2] Similarly, this time

[1] Bruce, p. 125.
[2] Pp. 197 f.

quoting Spurgeon: 'Lovely lilies, how ye rebuke our foolish nervousness!'[1]

More familiar to most of us will be the doggerel:

> Said the robin to the sparrow:
> 'I should really like to know
> Why these anxious human beings
> Rush about and worry so.'
>
> Said the sparrow to the robin:
> 'Friend, I think that it must be
> That they have no heavenly Father,
> Such as cares for you and me.'

It is a delightful sentiment, yet not a strictly accurate reflection of the teaching of Jesus. For he did not say that birds have a heavenly Father, but rather that we have, and that if the Creator cares for his creatures, we may be even more sure that the Father will look after his children.

2. *Problems relating to Christian faith.* I need at this point to allow myself a digression in order to comment on three problems related to the child-like Christian faith which Jesus asks of us. All three are big problems and can only be touched on here, but because they arise in our minds from our Lord's basic promise that our heavenly Father can be trusted to feed and clothe us, it would be wrong to evade them. I will state them negatively in terms of the three liberties which faith does *not* take in the light of God's promise, or of the three immunities which his promise does *not* give us.

First, *believers are not exempt from earning their own living.* We cannot sit back in an armchair, twiddle our thumbs, mutter 'my heavenly Father will provide' and do nothing. We have to work. As Paul put it later: 'If anyone will not work, let him not eat.'[2] With characteristic earthiness Luther writes: 'God ... wants nothing to do with the lazy, gluttonous bellies who are neither concerned nor busy; they act as if they just had to sit and wait for him to drop a roasted goose into their mouth.'[3]

[1] P. 39.
[2] 2 Thes. 3:10.
[3] P. 209.

Jesus used birds and flowers as evidences of God's ability to feed and clothe us, as we have seen. But how does God feed the birds? One answer would be that he does not, for they feed themselves! Jesus was an acute observer. He knew perfectly well about birds' feeding habits, that some are seed-eaters, others carrion-eaters or fish-eaters, while yet others are insectivores, predators or scavengers. God feeds them all right. But the way in which he does so is not by stretching out to them a divine hand filled with food, but by providing in nature the wherewithal to feed themselves. One could say something similar about plants. 'The flowers perform neither men's work in the field ("toil"), nor women's work at home ("spin"),'[1] yet God clothes them. How? Not miraculously, but by a complex process he has arranged in which they draw their sustenance from the sun and the soil.

It is the same, then, with human beings. God provides, but we still have to co-operate. Hudson Taylor learnt this lesson on his first voyage to China in 1853. When a violent storm off the Welsh coast threatened disaster, he felt it would be dishonouring to God to wear a life-belt. So he gave his away. Later, however, he saw his mistake: 'The use of means ought not to lessen our faith in God, and our faith in God ought not to hinder our using whatever means he has given us for the accomplishment of his own purposes.'[2]

Similarly, God does not cast all his children in the role of the prophet Elijah and supply our food miraculously through angels or ravens, but rather through the more normal means of farmers, millers, market gardeners, fishermen, butchers, grocers and the rest. Jesus urges upon us the necessity of a simple trust in our heavenly Father, but his understanding of faith was neither naive (ignorant of second causes) nor archaic (incompatible with modern science).

Secondly, *believers are not exempt from responsibility for others.* I say this in relation to the second problem, which is one of providence, rather than of science. If God promises to feed and clothe his children, how is it that many are ill-clad and under-nourished? It will not do, I think, to say rather glibly that God does look after his own children, and that the poor who lack adequate food and clothing are all unbelievers outside his family circle, for there

[1] McNeile, p. 88.
[2] Marshall Broomhall, *The man who believed God* (China Inland Mission, 1929), p. 53.

are certainly Christian people in some drought- and famine-stricken areas of the world in very severe need. It does not seem to me that there is a simple solution to this problem. But one important point should be made, namely that the most basic cause of hunger is not an inadequate divine provision, but an inequitable human distribution. The truth is that God has provided ample resources in earth and sea. The earth brings forth plants yielding seed and trees bearing fruit. The animals, birds and fish he has made are fruitful and multiply. But men hoard or spoil or waste these resources, and do not share them out. It seems significant that in this same Gospel of Matthew the Jesus who here says that our heavenly Father feeds and clothes his children, later says that *we* must ourselves feed the hungry and clothe the naked, and will be judged accordingly. It is always important to allow Scripture to interpret Scripture. The fact that God feeds and clothes his children does not exempt us from the responsibility of being the agents through whom he does it.

Thirdly, *believers are not exempt from experiencing trouble.* It is true that Jesus forbids his people to worry. But to be free from *worry* and to be free from *trouble* are not the same thing. Christ commands us not to be anxious, but does not promise that we shall be immune to all misfortune. On the contrary, there are many indications in his teaching that he knew all about calamity. Thus, although God *clothes the grass of the field*, it is still cut down and burnt. God protects even sparrows, which are so common and of such minimal value that two are sold for a farthing and five for two farthings, one being thrown in for luck. 'Not one of them will fall to the ground without your Father's will,' Jesus said.[1] But sparrows do fall to the ground and get killed. His promise was not that they would not fall, but that this would not happen without God's knowledge and consent. People fall too, and aeroplanes. Christ's words cannot be taken as a promise that the law of gravity will be suspended on our behalf, but again that God knows about accidents and allows them. Further, it is significant that at the end of this paragraph the reason Jesus gives why we are not to be *anxious about tomorrow* is: *Let the day's own trouble be sufficient for the day* (34). So there will be 'trouble' (*kakia*, 'evil'). A Christian's freedom from anxiety is not due to some guaranteed freedom from trouble, but to the folly of worry (to which we shall come later) and especially to the confidence that God is our

[1] Mt. 10:29; *cf.* 12:6.

Father, that even permitted suffering is within the orbit of his care,[1] and that 'in everything God works for good with those who love him, who are called according to his purpose'.[2]

This was the assurance which fortified Dr Helmut Thielicke while he preached a course of sermons on the Sermon on the Mount in St Mark's Church, Stuttgart, during the terrible years (1946–1948) which immediately followed the second world war. He often alluded to the scream of the air-raid sirens, alerting people to yet more devastation and death from allied bombs. What could freedom from anxiety mean in such circumstances? 'We know the sight and the sound of homes collapsing in flames . . . Our own eyes have seen the red blaze and our own ears have heard the sound of crashing, falling and shrieking.' Against that background the command to look at the birds and the lilies might well have sounded hollow. 'Nevertheless,' Dr Thielicke went on, 'I think we must stop and listen when *this* man, whose life on earth was anything but birdlike and lilylike, points us to the carefreeness of the birds and lilies. Were not the sombre shadows of the Cross already looming over this hour of the Sermon on the Mount?'[3] In other words, it is reasonable to trust in our heavenly Father's love, even in times of grievous trouble, because we have been privileged to see it revealed in Christ and his cross.

So then God's children are promised freedom neither from work, nor from responsibility, nor from trouble, but only from worry. Worry is forbidden us: it is incompatible with Christian faith.

3. *Worry is incompatible with common sense* (34). Returning from our digression on the problems of faith, we have now to notice that worry is as inconsistent with common sense as it is with Christian faith. In verse 34 Jesus mentions both *today* and *tomorrow*. All worry is about *tomorrow*, whether about food or clothing or anything else; but all worry is experienced *today*. Whenever we are anxious, we are upset in the present about some event which may happen in the future. However, these fears of ours about *tomorrow*, which we feel so acutely *today*, may not be fulfilled. The popular advice 'Don't worry, it may never happen,' is doubtless

[1] *Cf.* Jb. 2:10.
[2] Rom. 8:28.
[3] Pp. 124, 134.

unsympathetic, but perfectly true. People worry that they may not pass an exam, or find a job, or get married, or retain their health, or succeed in some enterprise. But it is all fantasy. 'Fears may be liars;' they often are. Many worries, perhaps most, never materialize.

So then worry is a waste—a waste of time, thought and nervous energy. We need to learn to live a day at a time. We should plan for the future, of course, but not worry about the future. 'One day's trouble is enough for one day,'[1] or, 'Each day has troubles enough of its own.'[2] So why anticipate them? If we do, we double them. For if our fear does not materialize, we have worried once for nothing; if it does materialize, we have worried twice instead of once. In both cases it is foolish: worry doubles trouble.

It is time to sum up Jesus' exposition of the world's false ambition. To become preoccupied with material things in such a way that they engross our attention, absorb our energy and burden us with anxiety is incompatible with both Christian faith and common sense. It is distrustful of our heavenly Father, and it is frankly stupid. This is what pagans do; but it is an utterly unsuitable and unworthy ambition for Christians. So just as Jesus has already called us in the Sermon to a greater righteousness, a broader love and a deeper piety, he now calls us to a higher ambition.

### b. True or Christian ambition: God's rule and righteousness

It is important to see verses 31 to 33 together. Verse 31 repeats the prohibition against being anxious about food, drink and clothing. Verse 32 adds: *For the Gentiles seek all these things.* This shows that in the vocabulary of Jesus 'to seek' and 'to be anxious' are interchangeable. He is not talking so much about anxiety as about ambition. Now heathen ambition focuses on material necessities. But this cannot be right for Christians partly because *your heavenly Father knows that you need them all*, but mostly because these things are not an appropriate or worthy object for the Christian's quest. He must have something else, something higher, as the Supreme Good which he will energetically seek: not material things, but spiritual values; not his own good but God's; in fact not food and clothing, but the kingdom and the

[1] JBP.
[2] NEB.

righteousness of God. This is no more than an elaboration of teaching already implicit in the Lord's Prayer. According to this, Christians must and do recognize the needs of the body ('give us our daily bread'), although our priority concerns are with God's name, kingdom and will. We cannot pray the Lord's Prayer until our ambitions have been purified. Jesus tells us to 'seek first God's kingdom and righteousness'; in the Lord's Prayer we turn this supreme quest into petition.

1. *Seeking first God's kingdom.* When Jesus spoke of the kingdom of God he was not referring to the general sovereignty of God over nature and history, but to that specific rule over his own people which he himself had inaugurated, and which begins in anybody's life when he humbles himself, repents, believes, submits and is born again. God's kingdom is Jesus Christ ruling over his people in total blessing and total demand. To 'seek first' this kingdom is to desire as of first importance the spread of the reign of Jesus Christ. Such a desire will start with ourselves, until every single department of our life—home, marriage and family, personal morality, professional life and business ethics, bank balance, tax returns, life-style, citizenship—is joyfully and freely submissive to Christ. It will continue in our immediate environment, with the acceptance of evangelistic responsibility towards our relatives, colleagues, neighbours and friends. And it will also reach out in global concern for the missionary witness of the church.

We must be clear, then, about true missionary motivation. Why do we desire the spread of the gospel throughout the world? Not out of a sinful imperialism or triumphalism, whether for ourselves or the church or even 'Christianity'. Nor just because evangelism is part of our Christian obedience (though it is). Nor primarily to make other people happy (though it does). But especially because the glory of God and of his Christ is at stake. God is King, has inaugurated his saving reign through Christ, and has a right to rule in the lives of his creatures. Our ambition, then, is to seek first his kingdom, to cherish the passionate desire that his name should receive from men the honour which is due to it.

To accord priority to the interests of the kingdom of God here and now is not to lose sight of its goal beyond history. For the present manifestation of the kingdom is only partial. Jesus spoke also of a future kingdom of glory and told us to pray for its coming. So to 'seek first' the kingdom includes the desire and the prayer for the consummation at the end of time when all the King's enemies have become his footstool and his reign is undisputed.

2. *Seeking first God's righteousness.* It is not clear why Jesus distinguished between *his kingdom* and *his righteousness* as twin but separate objects of our priority Christian quest. For God's rule is a righteous rule, and already in the Sermon on the Mount Jesus has taught us to hunger and thirst for righteousness, to be willing to be persecuted for it and to exhibit a righteousness greater than that of the scribes and Pharisees. Now we are told to *seek first* the righteousness of God in addition to seeking first the kingdom of God.

Let me make a tentative suggestion about the difference between the two. God's kingdom exists only where Jesus Christ is consciously acknowledged. To be in his kingdom is synonymous with enjoying his salvation. Only the born again have seen and entered the kingdom. And to seek it first is to spread the good news of salvation in Christ.

But God's 'righteousness' is (arguably, at least) a wider concept than God's 'kingdom'. It includes that individual and social righteousness to which reference has been made earlier in the Sermon. And God, because he is himself a righteous God, desires righteousness in every human community, not just in every Christian community. The Hebrew prophets denounced injustice not only in Israel and Judah, but in the surrounding heathen nations as well. The prophet Amos, for example, warned that God's judgment would fall on Syria, Philistia, Tyre, Edom, Ammon and Moab because of their cruelty in warfare and other atrocities, as well as on God's people. God hates injustice and loves righteousness everywhere. The Lausanne Covenant, framed at the Congress on World Evangelization in July 1974, includes a paragraph on 'Christian social responsibility' which begins: 'We affirm that God is both the Creator and the Judge of all men. We therefore should share his concern for justice and reconciliation throughout human society.'

Now one of God's purposes for his new and redeemed community is through them to make his righteousness attractive (in personal, family, business, national and international life), and so commend it to all men. Then people outside God's kingdom will see it and desire it, and the righteousness of God's kingdom will, as it were, spill over into the non-Christian world. Of course the deep righteousness of the heart which Jesus emphasizes in the Sermon is impossible to any but the regenerate; but some degree of righteousness is possible in unregenerate society—in personal life, in family standards and in public decency. To be sure, Christians want to go much further than this and see people actually brought into God's kingdom through faith in Jesus Christ. At the same time, we should not be shy of maintaining that outside the circle of the kingdom righteousness is more pleasing to God than unrighteousness, justice than injustice, freedom than oppression, love than hate, peace than war.

If this is so (and I do not see how it can be gainsaid), then to *seek first his kingdom and his righteousness* may be said to embrace our Christian evangelistic and social responsibilities, much as do the 'salt' and 'light' metaphors of Matthew 5. In order to seek first God's kingdom we must evangelize, since the kingdom spreads only as the gospel of Christ is preached, heard, believed and obeyed. In order to seek first God's righteousness we shall still evangelize (for the inward righteousness of the heart is impossible otherwise), but we shall also engage in social action and endeavour to spread throughout the community those higher standards of righteousness which are pleasing to God.

What, then, is our Christian ambition? Everybody is ambitious to be or to do something, often from early years. Childhood ambitions tend to follow certain stereotypes—*e.g.* to be a cowboy, astronaut or ballerina. Adults have their own narrow stereotypes too—*e.g.* to be wealthy, famous or powerful. But ultimately there are only two possible ambitions for human beings. So far we have seen how Jesus contrasted a false with a true ambition, a secular ('Gentile') with a Christian, a material with a spiritual, treasures on earth with treasures in heaven, food and clothing with the kingdom and righteousness of God. But beneath and beyond all these there is a contrast more fundamental still. In the end, just as there are only two kinds of piety, the self-centred and the God-centred, so there are only two kinds of ambition: one can be ambitious either for oneself or for God. There is no third alternative.

Ambitions for self may be quite modest (enough to eat, to drink and to wear, as in the Sermon) or they may be grandiose (a bigger house, a faster car, a higher salary, a wider reputation, more power). But whether modest or immodest, these are ambitions for myself—*my* comfort, *my* wealth, *my* status, *my* power.

Ambitions for God, however, if they are to be worthy, can never be modest. There is something inherently inappropriate about cherishing small ambitions for God. How can we ever be content that he should acquire just a little more honour in the world? No. Once we are clear that God is King, then we long to see him crowned with glory and honour, and accorded his true place, which is the supreme place. We become ambitious for the spread of his kingdom and righteousness everywhere.

When this is genuinely our dominant ambition, then not only will *all these things . . . be yours as well* (*i.e.* our material needs will be provided), but there will be no harm in having secondary ambitions, since these will be subservient to our primary ambition and not in competition with it. Indeed, it is then that secondary ambitions become healthy. Christians should be eager to develop their gifts, widen their opportunities, extend their influence and be given promotion in their work—not now to boost their own ego or build their own empire, but rather through everything they do to bring glory to God. Lesser ambitions are safe and right provided that they are not an end in themselves (namely ourselves) but the means to a greater end (the spread of God's kingdom and righteousness) and therefore to the greatest of all ends, namely God's glory. This is the 'Supreme Good' which we are to *seek first*; there is no other.

# Matthew 7:1-12
## A Christian's relationships: to his brothers and his father

Matthew 7 consists of a number of apparently self-contained paragraphs. Their link with each other is not obvious. Nor does the chapter as a whole follow on from the previous chapter with any clear sequence of thought. Many commentators conclude, therefore, that originally these blocks of material belonged to different contexts, that Matthew himself assembled them, and that he perhaps did his 'scissors and paste' work a trifle clumsily. But it is not necessary to reach this conclusion. The connecting thread which runs through the chapter, however loosely, is that of relationships. It would seem quite logical that, having described a Christian's character, influence, righteousness, piety and ambition, Jesus should concentrate finally on his relationships. For the Christian counter-culture is not an individualistic but a community affair, and relations both within the community and between the community and others are of paramount importance. So some account is given in Matthew 7 of the network of relationships into which, as the followers of Jesus, we are drawn. These might be set out as follows:

1. to our brother, in whose eye we may discern a splinter, and whom we have a responsibility to help, not judge (1–5).

2. to a group startlingly designated 'dogs' and 'pigs'. They are people all right, but such is their animal nature that we are told not to share God's gospel with them (6).

3. to our heavenly Father to whom we come in prayer, confident that he will give us nothing but 'good things' (7–11).

4. to everybody in general: the Golden Rule should guide our attitude and behaviour towards them (12).

5. to our fellow pilgrims who walk with us along the narrow way (13, 14).

6. to false prophets, whom we are to recognize and of whom we are to beware (15–20).

7. to Jesus our Lord whose teaching we are committed to heed and obey (21–27).

## 1. Our attitude to our brother (1–5)

*Judge not, that you be not judged.* ²*For with the judgment you pronounce you will be judged, and the measure you give will be the measure you get.* ³*Why do you see the speck that is in your brother's eye, but do not notice the log that is in your own eye?* ⁴*Or how can you say to your brother, 'Let me take the speck out of your eye,' when there is the log in your own eye?* ⁵*You hypocrite, first take the log out of your own eye, and then you will see clearly to take the speck out of your brother's eye.*

Jesus does not anticipate that the Christian community will be perfect. On the contrary, he assumes both that there will be misdemeanours and that these will give rise to tensions, to problems of relationships. In particular, how should a Christian behave towards a fellow member who has misbehaved? Has Jesus any instructions about discipline within his community? Yes, in such a situation he forbids two alternatives, and then commends a third, a better, a more 'Christian' way.

### a. The Christian is not to be a judge (1, 2)

Jesus' words *Judge not, that you be not judged* are well known but much misunderstood. To begin with, we must reject Tolstoy's belief, based on this verse, that 'Christ totally forbids the human institution of any law court', and that he 'could mean nothing else by those words'.[1] But Jesus' prohibition cannot possibly mean the one thing Tolstoy says it must mean, for the context does not refer to judges in courts of law but rather to the responsibility of individuals to one another.

Next, our Lord's injunction to 'judge not' cannot be understood as a command to suspend our critical faculties in relation to other people, to turn a blind eye to their faults (pretending not to notice them), to eschew all criticism and to refuse to discern between truth and error, goodness and evil. How can we be sure

[1] P. 331.

that Jesus was not referring to these things? Partly because it would not be honest to behave like this, but hypocritical, and we know from this and other passages his love of integrity and hatred of hypocrisy. Partly because it would contradict the nature of man whose creation in God's image includes the ability to make value-judgments. Partly also because much of Christ's teaching in the Sermon on the Mount is based on the assumption that we will (indeed should) use our critical powers. For example, we have repeatedly heard his call to be different from the world around us, in that we are to develop a righteousness which exceeds that of the Pharisees, to do 'more than others' in the standard of love we adopt, not to be like the hypocrites in our piety or like the heathen in our ambition. But how can we possibly obey all this teaching unless we first evaluate the performance of others and then ensure that ours is different from and higher than theirs? Similarly, in Matthew 7, this very command not to 'judge' others is followed almost immediately by two further commands: to avoid giving 'what is holy' to dogs or pearls to pigs (6), and to beware of false prophets (15). It would be impossible to obey either of these commands without using our critical judgment. For in order to determine our behaviour towards 'dogs', 'pigs' and 'false prophets' we must first be able to recognize them, and in order to do that we must exercise some critical discernment.

If, then, Jesus was neither abolishing law courts nor forbidding criticism, what did he mean by *Judge not*? In a word, 'censoriousness'. The follower of Jesus is still a 'critic' in the sense of using his powers of discernment, but not a 'judge' in the sense of being censorious. Censoriousness is a compound sin consisting of several unpleasant ingredients. It does not mean to assess people critically, but to judge them harshly. The censorious critic is a fault-finder who is negative and destructive towards other people and enjoys actively seeking out their failings. He puts the worst possible construction on their motives, pours cold water on their schemes and is ungenerous towards their mistakes.

Worse than that, to be censorious is to set oneself up as a censor, and so to claim the competence and authority to sit in judgment upon one's fellow men. But if I do this, I am casting both myself and my fellows in the wrong role. Since when have they been my servants, responsible to me? And since when have I been their lord and judge? As Paul wrote to the Romans, applying the truth of Matthew 7:1 to their situation: 'Who are you to pass judgment on the servant of another? It is before his own master that he stands or falls' (14:4). Paul also applied the same truth to himself when he found himself surrounded by hostile detractors: 'It is the Lord who judges me. Therefore do not pronounce judgment before the time, before the Lord comes, who will bring to light the things now hidden in darkness and will disclose the purposes of the heart.'[1] The simple but vital point which Paul is making in these verses is that man is not God. No human being is qualified to be the judge of his fellow humans, for we cannot read each other's hearts or assess each other's motives. To be censorious is to presume arrogantly to anticipate the day of judgment, to usurp the prerogative of the divine Judge, in fact to try to play God.

Not only are we not the judge, but we are among the judged, and shall be judged with the greater strictness ourselves if we dare to judge others. *Judge not, that you be not judged. For with the judgment you pronounce you will be judged, and the measure you give will be the measure you get.* The rationale should be clear. If we pose as judges, we cannot plead ignorance of the law we claim to be able to administer. If we enjoy occupying the bench, we must not be surprised to find ourselves in the dock. As Paul put it, 'Therefore, you have no excuse, O man, whoever you are, when you judge another; for in passing judgment upon him you condemn yourself, because you the judge are doing the very same things.'[2]

To sum up, the command to *judge not* is not a requirement to be blind, but rather a plea to be generous. Jesus does not tell us to cease to be men (by suspending our critical powers which help to distinguish us from animals) but to renounce the presumptuous ambition to be God (by setting ourselves up as judges).

### b. The Christian is not to be a hypocrite (3, 4)

*Why do you see the speck that is in your brother's eye, but do not notice the log that is in your own eye?* [4]*Or how can you say to your brother, 'Let me take the speck out of your eye,' when there is the log in your own eye?*

Jesus now tells his famous little parable about 'foreign bodies' in people's eyes, specks of dust on the one hand and logs or beams on the other. James Moffatt referred to them as the 'splinter' and

[1] 1 Cor. 4:4, 5.
[2] Rom. 2:1; *cf.* Jas. 3:1.

the 'plank'. Earlier Jesus exposed our hypocrisy in relation to God, namely practising our piety before men to be seen by them; now he exposes our hypocrisy in relation to others, namely meddling with their peccadilloes, while failing to deal with our own more serious faults. Here is another reason why we are unfit to be judges: not only because we are fallible humans (and not God), but also because we are fallen humans. The fall has made all of us sinners. So we are in no position to stand in judgment on our fellow sinners; we are disqualified from the bench.

The picture of somebody struggling with the delicate operation of removing a speck of dirt from a friend's eye, while a vast plank in his own eye entirely obscures his vision, is ludicrous in the extreme. Yet when the caricature is transferred to ourselves and our ridiculous fault-finding, we do not always appreciate the joke. We have a fatal tendency to exaggerate the faults of others and minimize the gravity of our own. We seem to find it impossible, when comparing ourselves with others, to be strictly objective and impartial. On the contrary, we have a rosy view of ourselves and a jaundiced view of others. Indeed, what we are often doing is seeing our own faults in others and judging them vicariously. That way, we experience the pleasure of self-righteousness without the pain of penitence. So *you hypocrite* (5) is a key expression here. Moreover, this kind of hypocrisy is the more unpleasant because an apparent act of kindness (taking a speck of dirt from somebody's eye) is made the means of inflating our own ego. Censoriousness, writes A. B. Bruce, is a 'Pharisaic vice, that of exalting ourselves by disparaging others, a very cheap way of attaining moral superiority'.[1] The parable of the Pharisee and the publican was our Lord's own commentary on this perversity. He told it 'to some who trusted in themselves that they were righteous and despised others'.[2] The Pharisee made an odious and inaccurate comparison, magnifying both his own virtue and the publican's vice.

What, instead, we should do is to apply to ourselves at least as strict and critical a standard as we apply to others. 'If we judged ourselves truly', wrote Paul, 'we should not be judged.'[3] We would not only escape the judgment of God; we would also be in a position humbly and gently to help an erring brother. Having

[1] P. 128.
[2] Lk. 18:9.
[3] 1 Cor. 11:31.

first removed the log from our own eye, we would see clearly to take the speck from his.

*c. The Christian is rather to be a brother (5)*
*You hypocrite, first take the log out of your own eye, and then you will see clearly to take the speck out of your brother's eye.*

Some people suppose that in the parable of the foreign bodies Jesus was forbidding us to act as moral or spiritual oculists and meddle with other people's eyes, and telling us instead to mind our own business. This is not so. The fact that censoriousness and hypocrisy are forbidden us does not relieve us of brotherly responsibility towards one another. On the contrary, Jesus was later to teach that if our brother sins against us, our first duty (though usually neglected) is 'go and tell him his fault between you and him alone'.[1] The same obligation is laid upon us here. To be sure, in certain circumstances we are forbidden to interfere, namely when there is an even bigger foreign body in our own eye which we have not removed. But in other circumstances Jesus actually commands us to reprove and correct our brother. Once we have dealt with our own eye trouble, then we shall see clearly to deal with his. A bit of dirt in his eye is, after all, rightly called a 'foreign' body. It doesn't belong there. It is always alien, usually painful and sometimes dangerous. To leave it there, and make no attempt to remove it, would hardly be consistent with brotherly love.

Our Christian duty, then, is not to *see the speck* in our brother's eye while at the same time we *do not notice the log* in our own (3); still less to *say* to our brother '*Let me take the speck out of your eye*' while we have not yet taken the log from our own (4); but rather this, *first* to *take the log* out of our own eye, so that then with the resulting clarity of vision we shall be able to *take the speck* out of our brother's eye (5). Again, it is evident that Jesus is not condemning criticism as such, but rather the criticism of others when we exercise no comparable self-criticism; nor correction as such, but rather the correction of others when we have not first corrected ourselves.

The standard of Jesus for relationships in the Christian counter-culture is high and healthy. In all our attitudes and behaviour towards others we are to play neither the judge

[1] Mt. 18:15.

(becoming harsh, censorious and condemning), nor the hypocrite (blaming others while excusing ourselves), but the brother, caring for others so much that we first blame and correct ourselves and then seek to be constructive in the help we give them. 'Correct him,' said Chrysostom, alluding to someone who has sinned, 'but not as a foe, nor as an adversary exacting a penalty, but as a physician providing medicines,'[1] yes, and—even more—as a loving brother anxious to rescue and to restore. We need to be as critical of ourselves as we often are of others, and as generous to others as we always are to ourselves. Then we shall anticipate the Golden Rule to which Jesus brings us in verse 12 and act towards others as we would like them to act towards us.

## 2. Our attitude to 'dogs' and 'pigs' (6)

*Do not give dogs what is holy; and do not throw your pearls before swine, lest they trample them under foot and turn to attack you.*

At first sight and hearing this is startling language from the lips of Jesus, especially in the Sermon on the Mount, and indeed immediately after his appeal for constructive brotherly behaviour. But Jesus always called a spade a spade. His outspokenness led him to call Herod Antipas 'that fox' and hypocritical scribes and Pharisees 'whitewashed tombs' and a 'brood of vipers'.[2] Here he affirms that there are certain human beings who act like animals and may therefore be accurately designated 'dogs' and 'pigs'.

The context provides a healthy balance. If we are not to 'judge' others, finding fault with them in a censorious, condemning or hypocritical way, we are not to ignore their faults either and pretend that everybody is the same. Both extremes are to be avoided. The saints are not judges, but 'saints are not simpletons' either.[3] If we first remove the log from our eye and thus see clearly to take a speck from our brother's eye, he (if he is a true brother in the Lord) will appreciate our solicitude. But not everyone is grateful for criticism and correction. According to the book of Proverbs, this is one of the obvious distinctions between a wise

[1] P. 345.
[2] Lk. 13:32; Mt. 23:27, 33.
[3] Spurgeon, p. 42.

man and a fool: 'Do not reprove a scoffer, or he will hate you; reprove a wise man, and he will love you.'[1]

Who then are these 'dogs' and 'pigs'? By giving them these names Jesus is indicating not only that they are more animals than humans, but that they are animals with dirty habits as well. The dogs he had in mind were not the well-behaved lapdogs of an elegant home but the wild pariah dogs, vagabonds and mongrels, which scavenged in the city's rubbish dumps. And pigs were unclean animals to the Jew, not to mention their love for mud. The apostle Peter was later to refer to them by bringing together two proverbs: 'The dog turns back to his own vomit,' and 'The sow is washed only to wallow in the mire.'[2] The reference is at least to the fact that unbelievers, whose nature has never been renewed, possess physical or animal life, but not spiritual or eternal life. We remember also that Jews called Gentile outsiders 'dogs'.[3] But Christians certainly do not regard non-Christians in this contemptuous way. So we have to penetrate more deeply into Jesus' meaning.

His command is that we should *not give dogs what is holy* and *not throw* our *pearls before swine*. The picture is plain. A Jew would never hand 'holy' food (perhaps food previously offered in sacrifice) to unclean dogs. Nor would he ever dream of throwing pearls to pigs. Not only were they also unclean, but they would probably mistake the pearls for nuts or peas, try to eat them and then—finding them inedible—trample on them and even assault the giver. But if the picture or parable is clear, what is its meaning? What is the 'holy' thing, and what are the 'pearls'? Some of the early fathers thought the reference was to the Lord's Supper or Eucharist, and argued from it that unbelieving, unbaptized people should not be admitted to Communion.[4] While they were no doubt right in this teaching, it is extremely doubtful whether Jesus had this question in mind at all. It is better to find a link with the 'pearl of great value' in his parable, which refers to the kingdom of God[5] or salvation, and by extension to the gospel.

[1] Pr. 9:8.

[2] 2 Pet. 2:22.

[3] *Cf.* Mt. 15:26, 27; Phil. 3:2; Rev. 22:15.

[4] For example, chapter IX of the *Didache*, probably an early second-century document, includes this instruction: 'Let no one eat or drink of your Eucharist, but they who have been baptized into the name of the Lord; for concerning this also the Lord has said, "Give not that which is holy to the dogs." '

[5] Mt. 13:46.

We cannot possibly deduce from this, however, that Jesus was forbidding us to preach the gospel to unbelievers. To suppose this would stand the whole New Testament on its head and contradict the Great Commission (with which Matthew's Gospel ends) to 'go and make disciples of all nations'. Extreme Calvinists cannot use it as an argument against evangelism, for Calvin himself urged that it is our duty 'to present the doctrine of salvation indiscriminately to all'.[1]

So then the 'dogs' and 'pigs' with whom we are forbidden to share the gospel pearl are not just unbelievers. They must rather be those who have had ample opportunity to hear and receive the good news, but have decisively—even defiantly—rejected it. 'It ought to be understood', Calvin wisely continued, 'that *dogs* and *swine* are names given not to every kind of debauched men, or to those who are destitute of the fear of God and of true godliness, but to those who, by clear evidences, have manifested a hardened contempt of God, so that their disease appears to be incurable.'[2] Chrysostom uses a similar expression, for he identifies the 'dogs' as people 'living in incurable ungodliness',[3] and in our day Professor Jeremias has defined them as 'those who have wholly abandoned themselves to vicious courses'.[4]

The fact is that to persist beyond a certain point in offering the gospel to such people is to invite its rejection with contempt and even blasphemy. Jesus applied the same principle to the ministry of the twelve when he gave them his charge before sending them out on their first mission. He warned them that in every town and house they entered, although some people would be receptive or 'worthy', others would be unreceptive or 'unworthy'. 'If anyone will not receive you or listen to your words,' he went on, 'shake off the dust from your feet as you leave that house or town.'[5]

The apostle Paul also followed this principle in his mission work. On his first expedition he and Barnabas said to the Jews who 'contradicted' their preaching in Pisidian Antioch: 'It was necessary that the word of God should be spoken first to you. Since you thrust it from you, and judge yourselves unworthy of

[1] P. 349.
[2] P. 349.
[3] P. 348.
[4] *Jesus' promise to the nations* (1953: SCM, 1958), p. 20.
[5] Mt. 10:14 = Lk. 10:10, 11.

eternal life, behold, we turn to the Gentiles.' And when the Jews
incited the city leaders to drive them out, 'they shook off the dust
from their feet against them' and went on to Iconium.[1] Much the
same happened in Corinth on the second missionary journey.
When the Jews opposed and reviled him, Paul 'shook out his
garments' and said to them: 'Your blood be upon your own
heads! I am innocent. From now on I will go to the Gentiles.'[2]
For the third time Paul reacted in the same way when in Rome the
Jewish leaders rejected the gospel. 'Let it be known to you then',
he said, 'that this salvation of God has been sent to the Gentiles;
they will listen.'[3]

Our Christian witness and evangelistic preaching are not to be
entirely indiscriminate, therefore. If people have had plenty of
opportunity to hear the truth but do not respond to it, if they
stubbornly turn their backs on Christ, if (in other words) they cast
themselves in the role of 'dogs' and 'pigs', we are not to go on
and on with them, for then we cheapen God's gospel by letting
them trample it under foot. Can anything be more depraved
than to mistake God's precious pearl for a thing of no worth and
actually to tread it into the mud? At the same time to give people
up is a very serious step to take. I can think of only one or two
occasions in my experience when I have felt it was right. This
teaching of Jesus is for exceptional situations only; our normal
Christian duty is to be patient and persevere with others, as God
has patiently persevered with us.

## 3. Our attitude to our heavenly Father (7–11)

*Ask, and it will be given you; seek, and you will find; knock, and it will
be opened to you.* [8]*For every one who asks receives, and he who seeks finds,
and to him who knocks it will be opened.* [9]*Or what man of you, if his son
asks him for bread, will give him a stone?* [10]*Or if he asks for a fish, will
give him a serpent?* [11]*If you then, who are evil, know how to give good gifts
to your children, how much more will your Father who is in heaven give
good things to those who ask him?*

It seems natural that Jesus should move on from our relationship
with our fellow men to our relationship with our heavenly

[1] Acts 13:44-51.
[2] Acts 18:5, 6.
[3] Acts 28:17-28.

Father, the more so because our Christian duty of discrimination (not judging others, not casting pearls before pigs, and being helpful without being hypocritical) is much too difficult for us without divine grace.

### a. The promises Jesus makes

This passage is not the first instruction on prayer in the Sermon on the Mount. Jesus has already warned us against pharisaic hypocrisy and pagan formalism, and has given us his own model prayer. Now, however, he actively encourages us to pray by giving us some very gracious promises. For 'nothing is better adapted to excite us to prayer than a full conviction that we shall be heard'.[1] Or again, 'He knows that we are timid and shy, that we feel unworthy and unfit to present our needs to God . . . We think that God is so great and we are so tiny that we do not dare to pray . . . That is why Christ wants to lure us away from such timid thoughts, to remove our doubts, and to have us go ahead confidently and boldly.'[2]

Jesus seeks to imprint his promises on our mind and memory by the hammer-blows of repetition. First, his promises are attached to direct commands: *Ask . . . seek . . . knock . . .* (7). These may deliberately be in an ascending scale of urgency. Richard Glover suggests that a child, if his mother is near and visible, asks; if she is neither, he seeks; while if she is inaccessible in her room, he knocks.[3] Be that as it may, all three verbs are present imperatives and indicate the persistence with which we should make our requests known to God. Secondly, the promises are expressed in universal statements: *for every one who asks receives, and he who seeks finds, and to him who knocks it will be opened* (8).

Thirdly, Jesus illustrates his promises by a homely parable (9–11). He envisages a situation with which all his hearers will have been daily familiar, namely a child coming to his father with a request. If he asks for bread, will he be given something which looks a bit like it but is in fact disastrously different, *e.g.* a stone instead of a loaf, or a snake instead of a fish? That is, if the child asks for something wholesome to eat (bread or fish), will he receive instead something unwholesome, either inedible (a stone) or positively harmful (a poisonous snake)? Of course not!

[1] Calvin, p. 351.
[2] Luther, p. 234.
[3] P. 70.

Parents, even though they are *evil*, *i.e.* selfish by nature, still love their children and give them only *good gifts*. Notice that Jesus here assumes, even asserts, the inherent sinfulness of human nature. At the same time, he does not deny that bad men are capable of doing good. On the contrary, *evil* parents give *good* gifts to their children, for 'God drops into their hearts a portion of his goodness'.[1] What Jesus is saying is that even when they are doing good, following the noble instincts of parenthood and caring for their children, even then they do not escape the designation 'evil', for that is what human beings are.

So the force of the parable lies rather in a contrast than in a comparison between God and men. It is another *a fortiori* or 'how much more' argument: if human parents (although evil) know how to give good gifts to their children, how much more will our heavenly Father (who is not evil but wholly good) *give good things to those who ask him?* (11). 'For what would he not now give to sons when they ask, when he has already granted this very thing, namely, that they might be sons?'[2] There is no doubt that our prayers are transformed when we remember that the God we are coming to is 'Abba, Father', and infinitely good and kind.

Professor Jeremias has demonstrated the novelty of this teaching of Jesus. He writes that, with the help of his assistants, he has carefully examined 'the prayer literature of ancient Judah—a large, rich literature, all too little explored', but that 'in no place in this immense literature is this invocation of God as *Abba* to be found . . . *Abba* was an everyday word, a homely family word. No Jew would have dared to address God in this manner. Jesus did it always . . . and authorizes his disciples to repeat the word *Abba* after him.'[3] What could be simpler than this concept of prayer? If we belong to Christ, God is our Father, we are his children, and prayer is coming to him with our requests. The trouble is that for many of us it seems too simple, even simplistic. In our sophistication we say we cannot believe it, and in any case it does not altogether tally with our experience. So we turn from Christ's prayer-promises to our prayer-problems.

[1] Calvin, p. 353.
[2] Augustine, 11:16.
[3] Joachim Jeremias, *The prayers of Jesus* (SCM, 1967), pp. 96, 97.

## b. *The problems men raise*

Confronted by the straightforward promises of Jesus, *Ask, and it will be given you; seek, and you will find,* people raise several objections which we need now to consider.

1. *Prayer is unseemly.* 'This encouragement to pray presents a false picture of God. It implies that he needs either to be told what we lack or to be bullied into giving it, whereas Jesus himself said earlier that our heavenly Father knows it and cares for us anyway. Besides, he surely cannot be bothered with our petty affairs. Why should we suppose that his gifts are dependent on our asking? Do human parents wait before supplying their children's needs until they ask for them?'

To this we reply that the reason why God's giving depends on our asking is neither because he is ignorant until we inform him nor because he is reluctant until we persuade him. The reason has to do with us, not with him; the question is not whether he is ready to give, but whether we are ready to receive. So in prayer we do not 'prevail on' God, but rather prevail on ourselves to submit to God. True, the language of 'prevailing on God' is often used in regard to prayer, but it is an accommodation to human weakness. Even when Jacob 'prevailed on God', what really happened is that God prevailed over him, bringing him to the point of surrender when he was able to receive the blessing which God had all the time been longing to give him.

The truth is that the heavenly Father never spoils his children. He does not shower us with gifts whether we want them or not, whether we are ready for them or not. Instead he waits until we recognize our need and turn to him in humility. This is why he says *Ask, and it will be given you,* and why James added, 'You do not have because you do not ask.'[1] Prayer, then, is not 'unseemly'; it is the very way God himself has chosen for us to express our conscious need of him and our humble dependence on him.

2. *Prayer is unnecessary.* This second objection arises more from experience than from theology. Thoughtful Christians look round them and see lots of people getting on fine without prayer. Indeed they seem to receive without prayer the very same things that we receive with it. They get what they need by working for

[1] Jas. 4:2.

it, not by praying for it. The farmer gets a good crop by labour, not prayer. The mother gets her baby by medical skill, not prayer. The family balances its budget by the wage-earning of dad and perhaps others, not by prayer. 'Surely,' we may be tempted to say, 'this proves that prayer doesn't make an ounce of difference; it's so much wasted breath.'

But wait a minute! In thinking about this question, we need to distinguish between the gifts of God as Creator and his gifts as Father, or between his creation-gifts and his redemption-gifts. It is perfectly true that he gives certain gifts (harvest, babies, food, life) whether people pray or not, whether they believe or not. He gives to all life and breath. He sends rain from heaven and fruitful seasons to all. He makes his sun rise on the evil and the good alike.[1] He 'visits' a mother when she conceives and later gives birth. None of these gifts is dependent on whether people acknowledge their Creator or pray to him.

But God's redemption-gifts are different. God does not bestow salvation on all alike, but 'bestows his riches upon all who call on him. For, "every one who calls upon the name of the Lord will be saved." '[2] The same applies to post-salvation blessings, the 'good things' which Jesus says the Father gives his children. It is not material blessings that he is referring to here, but spiritual blessings—daily forgiveness, deliverance from evil, peace, the increase of faith, hope and love, in fact the indwelling work of 'the Holy Spirit' as the comprehensive blessing of God, which is how Luke renders 'good things'.[3] For these gifts we must certainly pray.

The Lord's Prayer, which Jesus taught earlier in the Sermon, brings together both kinds of gift, for 'daily bread' is a creation-gift, whereas 'forgiveness' and 'deliverance' are redemption-gifts. How is it, then, that they can be combined in the same prayer? Probably the answer is this. We pray for daily bread not because we fear we will starve otherwise (since millions get their daily bread without ever praying for it or saying grace before meals) but because we know that ultimately it comes from God and because as his children it is appropriate regularly to acknowledge our physical dependence on him. We pray for forgiveness and deliverance, however, because these gifts are given only in

[1] Mt. 5:45.
[2] Rom. 10:12, 13.
[3] Mt. 7:11 = Lk. 11:13.

answer to prayer, and because without them we would be lost. So prayer is not unnecessary.

3. *Prayer is unproductive.* The third problem is the obvious corollary to the second. People argue that prayer is *unnecessary* because God gives to many who do not ask, and that it is *unproductive* because he fails to give to many who do. 'I prayed to pass an exam, but failed it. I prayed to be healed of an illness, and it got worse. I prayed for peace, but the world is filled with the noise of war. Prayer doesn't work!'—This is the familiar problem of unanswered prayer.

The best way to approach this problem is to remember that the promises of Jesus in the Sermon on the Mount are not unconditional. A moment's thought will convince us of this. It is absurd to suppose that the promise 'Ask, and it shall be given you' is an absolute pledge with no strings attached; that 'Knock, and it will be opened to you' is an 'Open, Sesame' to every closed door without exception; and that by the waving of a prayer wand any wish will be granted and every dream will come true. The idea is ridiculous. It would turn prayer into magic, the person who prays into a magician like Aladdin, and God into our servant who appears instantly to do our bidding like Aladdin's genie every time we rub our little prayer lamp. In addition, this concept of prayer would place an impossible strain on every sensitive Christian if he knew that he was certain to get everything he asked. 'If it were the case', writes Alec Motyer, 'that whatever we ask, God was pledged to give, then I for one would never pray again, because I would not have sufficient confidence in my own wisdom to ask God for anything; and I think if you consider it you will agree. It would impose an intolerable burden on frail human wisdom if by his prayer-promises God was pledged to give whatever we ask, when we ask it, and in exactly the terms we ask. How could we bear the burden?'[1]

Perhaps we could put the matter in this way: being *good*, our heavenly Father gives only good gifts to his children; being *wise* as well, he knows which gifts are good and which are not. We have already heard Jesus say that human parents would never give a stone or snake to their children who ask for bread or fish. But what if the children (through ignorance or folly) were

[1] Alec Motyer, *Studies in the Epistle of James* (New Mildmay Press, 1968), p. 88.

actually to ask for a stone or a snake? What then? Doubtless an extremely irresponsible parent might grant the child's request, but the great majority of parents would be too wise and loving. Certainly our heavenly Father would never give us something harmful, even if we asked for it urgently and repeatedly, for the simple reason that he gives his children only 'good gifts'. So then if we ask for good things, he grants them; if we ask for things which are not good (either not good in themselves, or not good for us or for others, directly or indirectly, immediately or ultimately) he denies them; and only he knows the difference. We can thank God that the granting of our needs is conditional—not only on our asking, seeking and knocking, but also on whether what we desire by asking, seeking and knocking is good. Thank God he answers prayer. Thank God he also sometimes denies our requests. 'I thank God', writes Dr Lloyd-Jones 'that He is not prepared to do anything that I may chance to ask Him . . . I am profoundly grateful to God that He did not grant me certain things for which I asked, and that He shut certain doors in my face.'[1]

*c. The lessons we learn*

Prayer sounds very simple when Jesus teaches about it. Just *Ask* . . . , *seek* . . . , *knock* . . . , and in each case you will be answered. This is a deceptive simplicity, however; much lies behind it. First, prayer presupposes knowledge. Since God gives gifts only if they accord with his will, we have to take pains to discover his will—by Scripture meditation and by the exercise of a Christian mind schooled by Scripture meditation. Secondly, prayer presupposes faith. It is one thing to know God's will; it is another to humble ourselves before him and express our confidence that he is able to cause his will to be done. Thirdly, prayer presupposes desire. We may know God's will and believe he can perform it, and still not desire it. Prayer is the chief means God has ordained by which to express our deepest desires.[2] This is the reason why the 'ask—seek—knock' commands are in the present imperative and in an ascending scale to challenge our perseverance.

Thus, before we ask, we must know what to ask for and whether it accords with God's will; we must believe God can grant it; and

[1] P. 513.
[2] *Cf.* Rom. 10:1.

we must genuinely want to receive. Then the gracious promises of Jesus will come true.

## 4. Our attitude to all men (12)

*So whatever you wish that men would do to you, do so to them; for this is the law and the prophets.*

The logic of the 'so' or 'therefore' (*oun*) with which this verse begins is not plain. It may look back to the previous verse and imply that if God is good to all who seek him in prayer, his children must be good to all likewise. Or it may refer further back to the *Judge not* command, and take up the underlying argument against censoriousness and hypocrisy. In any case it seems that Jesus uttered this principle at different times and in different contexts, for in Luke's version of the Sermon it comes immediately after the three little cameos which illustrate the command to love our enemies.[1] Certainly such love is beyond us apart from the grace of God. It is, in fact, his own love and is one of the 'good things' he gives us through his Holy Spirit in answer to our prayers.[2]

Much has been made by various commentators of the fact that the Golden Rule is found in a similar—but always negative—form elsewhere. Confucius, for example, is credited with having said, 'Do not to others what you would not wish done to yourself;' and the Stoics had an almost identical maxim. In the Old Testament Apocrypha we find: 'Do not do to anyone what you yourself would hate,'[3] and this, it seems, is what the famous Rabbi Hillel quoted in *c.* 20 BC when asked by a would-be proselyte to teach him the whole law while standing on one leg. His rival Rabbi Shammai had been unable or unwilling to answer, and had driven the enquirer away, but Rabbi Hillel said: 'What is hateful to you, do not do to anyone else. This is the whole law; all the rest is only commentary.'[4]

Because this is the best-known example of the supposed parallelism between the Jewish Talmud and the Sermon on the Mount, a further comment may be in place. Some have gone so

[1] Lk. 6:31.
[2] Verse 11 = Lk. 11:13.
[3] Tobit 4:15, NEB.
[4] Recorded in the Talmud: Shabbath 31a.

far as to claim that *everything* in the Sermon is also in the Talmud, plus a great deal more. Professor Jeremias reacts in this way: 'That is exactly the case: that in the Talmud "a great deal more" is to be found, and that one must seek the grain among a great deal of chaff, the scanty golden grain that may be compared with the words of the Sermon on the Mount.'[1] Alfred Edersheim, writing towards the end of the last century, was even more outspoken. He agrees that there is 'wit and logic, quickness and readiness, earnestness and zeal' in the Talmud, but at the same time there is a real 'contrariety in spirit and substance' between it and the New Testament. Indeed, 'taken as a whole, it is not only utterly unspiritual, but anti-spiritual'.[2]

Returning to the Golden Rule, there is really an enormous difference between the negative and rather grudging maxim of Hillel ('Do not do to others what is hateful to you') and the positive initiative contained in the instruction of Jesus ('Do to others what you wish they would do to you'). Even then it may sound a rather low standard, like 'Love your neighbour as yourself'. Actually, however, it is a high standard because self-love is a powerful force in our lives. Edersheim called such neighbour-love 'the nearest approach to absolute love of which human nature is capable'.[3] Also it is a remarkably flexible ethical principle. Self-advantage often guides us in our own affairs; now we must also let it guide us in our behaviour to others. All we have to do is use our imagination, put ourselves in the other person's shoes, and ask, 'How would I like to be treated in that situation?' As Bishop Ryle wrote, 'It settles a hundred difficult points . . . It prevents the necessity of laying down endless little rules for our conduct in specific cases.'[4] Indeed, it is a principle of such wide application that Jesus could add, *for this is the law and the prophets.* That is, whoever directs his conduct towards others according to how he would like others to direct theirs towards him has fulfilled the law and the prophets, at least in the matter of neighbour-love.[5]

[1] P. 10.
[2] Alfred Edersheim, *The life and times of Jesus the Messiah,* I (Longmans, 1883), pp. 525 f.
[3] P. 535.
[4] P. 66.
[5] *Cf.* 5:17; Rom. 13:8–10.

We noted at the opening of this chapter that the Christian counter-culture is not just an individual value-system and life-style, but a community affair. It involves relationships. And the Christian community is in essence a family, God's family. Probably the two strongest elements in our Christian consciousness are an awareness of God as our Father and of our fellow-Christians as our brothers and sisters through Christ, although at the same time we can never forget our responsibility to those outside the family whom we long to see brought in.

So in Matthew 7:1–12 Jesus has introduced us to these basic relationships. At their centre is our heavenly Father God to whom we come, on whom we depend and who never gives his children other than good gifts. Next, there are our fellow believers. And the anomaly of a censorious spirit (which judges) and of a hypocritical spirit (which sees the splinter in spite of the plank) is that it is incompatible with Christian brotherliness. If our fellow Christians are truly our brothers and sisters in the Lord, it is inconceivable that we shall be anything other than caring and constructive in our attitude towards them.

As for those outside the family, there is the extreme case of the 'dogs' and 'pigs', but they are not typical. They are an exceptional group of stubborn people who are 'dogged' and even 'pig-headed', one might accurately say, in their decisive rejection of Jesus Christ. Reluctantly we have to drop them. But if verse 6 is the exception, verse 12 is the rule, the Golden Rule. It transforms our actions. If we put ourselves sensitively into the place of the other person, and wish for him what we would wish for ourselves, we would be never mean, always generous; never harsh, always understanding; never cruel, always kind.

# Matthew 7:13-20
## A Christian's relationships: to false prophets

A number of commentators suggest that the main body of Jesus' Sermon (or teaching) is now over, and that with verse 13 the application or conclusion begins. Certainly he emphasizes here even more strongly than before the necessity of choice. *Enter by the narrow gate*, he begins. That is, the contrast between the two kinds of righteousness and of devotion, the two treasures, the two masters and the two ambitions has been faithfully portrayed; now the time for decision has come. Is it to be the kingdom of Satan or the kingdom of God, the prevailing culture or the Christian counter-culture? Jesus continues with his presentation of the alternative as he describes the two ways (broad and narrow), the two teachers (false and true), the two pleas (words and deeds) and finally the two foundations (sand and rock).

### 1. The inescapable choice (13, 14)

*Enter by the narrow gate; for the gate is wide and the way is easy, that leads to destruction, and those who enter by it are many.* 14 *For the gate is narrow and the way is hard, that leads to life, and those who find it are few.*

What is immediately striking about these verses is the absolute nature of the choice before us. We would all prefer to be given many more choices than only one, or better still to fuse them all into a conglomerate religion, thus eliminating the need for any choice. But Jesus cuts across our easy-going syncretism. He will not allow us the comfortable solutions we propose. Instead he insists that ultimately there is only one choice, because there are only two possibilities to choose from.

First, there are two ways. This concept is found already in the Old Testament. Psalm 1, for example, contrasts 'the way of the righteous' who delight in God's law, bear fruit and prosper, with 'the way of the wicked' who are driven like chaff before the wind and perish. Now Jesus elaborates the picture. One way is easy. The word means 'broad, spacious, roomy' (AG), and some manuscripts combine these images and call this way 'wide and easy'. There is plenty of room on it for diversity of opinions and laxity of morals. It is the road of tolerance and permissiveness. It has no curbs, no boundaries of either thought or conduct. Travellers on this road follow their own inclinations, that is, the desires of the human heart in its fallenness. Superficiality, self-love, hypocrisy, mechanical religion, false ambition, censorious-ness—these things do not have to be learnt or cultivated. Effort is needed to resist them. No effort is required to practise them. That is why the broad road is easy.

The *hard* way, on the other hand, is narrow. Its boundaries are clearly marked. Its narrowness is due to something called 'divine revelation', which restricts pilgrims to the confines of what God has revealed in Scripture to be true and good. C. S. Lewis described in his autobiography how as a schoolboy of thirteen he began to 'broaden his mind'.' I was soon (in the famous words) altering "I believe" to "one does feel". And oh, the relief of it! . . . From the tyrannous noon of revelation I passed into the cool evening twilight of Higher Thought, where there was nothing to be obeyed, and nothing to be believed except what was either comforting or exciting.'[1]

It is a fact that revealed truth imposes a limitation on what Christians may believe, and revealed goodness on how we may behave. And in a sense this is 'hard'. Yet in another sense, as Chrysostom pointed out centuries ago, Christ's hard and narrow way is also to be welcomed as his 'easy yoke' and 'light burden'.[2]

Secondly, there are two gates. The gate leading to the easy way is *wide*, for it is a simple matter to get on to the easy road. There is evidently no limit to the luggage we can take with us. We need leave nothing behind, not even our sins, self-righteousness or pride. The gate leading to the hard way, on the other hand, is *narrow*. One has to look for it to find it. It is easy to miss. As Jesus said in another connection, it is as narrow as a needle's eye.

[1] *Surprised by joy* (Bles, 1955), p. 63.
[2] Mt. 11:30.

Further, in order to enter it we must leave everything behind—sin, selfish ambition, covetousness, even if necessary family and friends. For no-one can follow Christ who has not first denied himself. The entry is also a turnpike gate: it has to be entered one by one. How can we find it? It is Jesus Christ himself. 'I am the door,' he said, 'if any one enters by me, he will be saved.'[1]

Thirdly, there are two destinations. We have already seen this foreshadowed in Psalm 1, where 'prospering' and 'perishing' are the alternatives. Moses made it clearer still: 'See, I have set before you this day life and good, death and evil . . ., blessing and curse; therefore choose life.'[2] Similarly, Jesus taught that the easy way, entered by the wide gate, leads to *destruction*. He did not define what he meant by this, and presumably the precise nature of hell is as much beyond our finite understanding as the precise nature of heaven. But the terrible word 'destruction' (terrible because God is properly the Creator, not the Destroyer, and because man was created to live, not to die) seems at least to give us liberty to say that everything good will be destroyed in hell—love and loveliness, beauty and truth, joy, peace and hope—and that for ever. It is a prospect too awful to contemplate without tears. For the broad road is suicide road.

By contrast, the hard way, entered by the narrow gate, leads to *life*, even to that 'eternal life' which Jesus explained in terms of fellowship with God, beginning here but perfected hereafter, in which we see and share his glory, and find perfect fulfilment as human beings in the selfless service of him and of our fellows.

Fourthly, there are two crowds. Entering by the wide gate and travelling along the easy road to destruction are *many*. The broad and easy road is a busy thoroughfare, thronged by pedestrians of every kind. The narrow and hard way which leads to life, however, seems to be comparatively deserted. *Those who find it are few.* Jesus seems to have anticipated that his followers would be (or at least would appear to be and feel themselves to be) a despised minority movement. He saw multitudes on the broad road, laughing and carefree with apparently no thought for the dreadful end to which they are heading, while on the narrow road there is just a 'happy band of pilgrims', hand in hand, backs turned upon sin and faces set towards the Celestial City, 'singing songs of expectation, marching to the promised land'.

[1] Jn. 10:9.
[2] Dt. 30:15, 19; *cf*. Je. 21:8.

I do not think we can build on this contrast between the *few* and the *many* any speculation that the final number of God's redeemed will be small. If we compare Scripture with Scripture (as we always must), we shall want to put alongside this teaching of Jesus the vision of John that the redeemed before God's throne will be 'a great multitude which no man could number'.[1] How to reconcile these two concepts I do not know. Nor am I clear how this passage relates to the perplexing problem of those who have never heard the gospel. For one word which is common to both crowds, the 'few' and the 'many', is the verb 'enter'. It is because the many 'enter' by the wide gate that Jesus urges his hearers to 'enter by the narrow gate'. This implies that neither crowd is ignorant of the issues; each has been presented with a choice and has deliberately 'entered' one or other way. The whole picture seems to relate only to those who have had the opportunity of decision for or against Christ; it simply leaves out of view those who have never heard. We shall be wise, therefore, not to preoccupy our minds with such speculative questions, as on another occasion Jesus himself implied. Somebody asked him: 'Lord, will those who are saved be few?' But he declined to satisfy their curiosity. Instead he replied: 'Strive to enter by the narrow door.'[2]

To recapitulate, there are according to Jesus only two ways, hard and easy (there is no middle way), entered by two gates, broad and narrow (there is no other gate), trodden by two crowds, large and small (there is no neutral group), ending in two destinations, destruction and life (there is no third alternative). It is hardly necessary to comment that such talk is extremely unfashionable today. People like to be uncommitted. Every opinion poll allows not only for a 'yes' or 'no' answer, but for a convenient 'don't know'. Men are lovers of Aristotle and of his golden mean. The most popular path is the *via media*. To deviate from the middle way is to risk being dubbed an 'extremist' or a 'fanatic'. Everybody resents being faced with the necessity of a choice. But Jesus will not allow us to escape it.

[1] Rev. 7:9.
[2] Lk. 13:23, 24.

## 2. The peril of false teachers (15–20)

*Beware of false prophets, who come to you in sheep's clothing but inwardly are ravenous wolves.* [16] *You will know them by their fruits. Are grapes gathered from thorns, or figs from thistles?* [17] *So, every sound tree bears good fruit, but the bad tree bears evil fruit.* [18] *A sound tree cannot bear evil fruit, nor can a bad tree bear good fruit.* [19] *Every tree that does not bear good fruit is cut down and thrown into the fire.* [20] *Thus you will know them by their fruits.*

### a. Assumptions

In telling people to *beware of false prophets*, Jesus obviously assumed that there were such. There is no sense in putting on your garden gate the notice 'Beware of the dog' if all you have at home is a couple of cats and a budgerigar! No. Jesus warned his followers of false prophets because they already existed. We come across them on numerous occasions in the Old Testament, and Jesus seems to have regarded the Pharisees and the Sadducees in the same light. 'Blind leaders of the blind', he called them. He also implied that they would increase, and that the period preceding the end would be characterized not only by the world-wide spread of the gospel but also by the rise of false teachers who would lead many astray.[1] We hear of them in nearly every New Testament letter. They are called either 'pseudo-prophets' as here ('prophets' presumably because they claimed divine inspiration), or 'pseudo-apostles' (because they claimed apostolic authority[2]) or 'pseudo-teachers'[3] or even 'pseudo-Christs' (because they made messianic pretensions or denied that Jesus was the Christ come in the flesh[4]). But each was 'pseudo', and *pseudos* is the Greek word for a lie. The history of the Christian church has been a long and dreary story of controversy with false teachers. Their value, in the overruling providence of God, is that they have presented the church with a challenge to think out and define the truth, but they have caused much damage. I fear there are still many in today's church.

In telling us to beware of false prophets Jesus made another assumption, namely that there is such a thing as an objective standard of truth from which the falsehood of the false prophets

[1] Mt. 24:11–14.
[2] 2 Cor. 11:13.
[3] 2 Pet. 2:1.
[4] Mt. 24:24; Mk. 13:22; *cf.* 1 Jn. 2:18, 22.

is to be distinguished. The very notion of 'false' prophets is meaningless otherwise. In biblical days a true prophet was one who taught the truth by divine inspiration, and a false prophet one who claimed the same divine inspiration but actually propagated untruth. Jeremiah contrasted them in these terms: false prophets 'speak visions of their own minds', while true prophets 'stand in the council of the Lord', 'hear his word', 'proclaim it to the people' and 'speak from the mouth of the Lord'.[1] Again, 'let the prophet who has a dream tell the dream; but let him who has my word speak my word faithfully. What has straw in common with wheat?'[2] So in referring to certain teachers as 'false prophets' it is clear that Jesus was no syncretist, teaching that contradictory opinions were in reality complementary insights into the same truth. No. He held that truth and falsehood excluded one another, and that those who propagate lies in God's name are false prophets, of whom his followers must beware.

### b. Warnings

After noting these assumptions of Jesus (that there are false prophets, and that there is a truth from which they deviate) we must now consider his warning more precisely: *Beware of false prophets, who come to you in sheep's clothing but inwardly are ravenous wolves* (15). We learn from this metaphor that pseudo-prophets are both dangerous and deceptive.

Their danger is that in reality they are *wolves*. Now in first-century Palestine the wolf was the natural enemy of sheep, which were entirely defenceless against it. Hence a good shepherd, as Jesus was to teach later, was always on the look-out for wolves in order to protect his sheep, whereas the hired labourer (who, not being the sheep-owner, did not care about them) would abandon them at the sight of a wolf and run away, leaving it to attack and scatter the flock.[3] Just so Christ's flock is at the mercy of either good shepherds or paid labourers or wolves. The good pastor feeds the flock with truth, the false teacher like a wolf divides it by error, while the time-serving professional does nothing to protect it but abandons it to false teachers. 'I know', said Paul to the Ephesian elders, 'that after my departure fierce wolves will come in among you, not sparing the flock; and from

[1] 23:16, 18, 22.
[2] 23:28.
[3] Jn. 10:11-13.

among your own selves will arise men speaking perverse things to draw away the disciples after them. Therefore be alert . . .'[1]

What are these 'perverse things' which are a disturbance and a danger to the church? One of the major characteristics of false prophets in the Old Testament was their amoral optimism, their denial that God was the God of judgment as well as of steadfast love and mercy. They were guilty, Jeremiah said to the people, of 'filling you with vain hopes . . . They say continually to those who despise the word of the Lord, "It shall be well with you"; and to everyone who stubbornly follows his own heart they say, "No evil shall come upon you." '[2] Similarly, God complains: 'They have healed the wound of my people lightly, saying, "Peace, peace," when there is no peace.'[3] Such talk was, to say the least, a grave disservice to the people of God. It gave them a false sense of security. It lulled them to sleep in their sins. It failed to warn them of the impending judgment of God or tell them how to escape it.

It is surely not an accident, therefore, that Jesus' warning about false prophets in the Sermon on the Mount immediately follows his teaching about the two gates, ways, crowds and destinations. For false prophets are adept at blurring the issue of salvation. Some so muddle or distort the gospel that they make it hard for seekers to find the narrow gate. Others try to make out that the narrow way is in reality much broader than Jesus implied, and that to walk it requires little if any restriction on one's belief or behaviour. Yet others, perhaps the most pernicious of all, dare to contradict Jesus and to assert that the broad road does not lead to destruction, but that as a matter of fact all roads lead to God, and that even the broad and the narrow roads, although they lead off in opposite directions, ultimately both end in life. No wonder Jesus likened such false teachers to *ravenous wolves*, not so much because they are greedy for gain, prestige or power (though they often are), but because they are 'ferocious' (NIV), that is, extremely dangerous. They are responsible for leading some people to the very destruction which they say does not exist.

They are more than dangerous; they are also deceptive. The 'dogs' and the 'pigs' of verse 6, because of their dirty habits, are

[1] Acts 20:29, 30.
[2] 23:16, 17.
[3] 8:11.

easy to recognize. But not the 'wolves', for they sneak into the flock in the disguise of sheep. As a result, the unwary actually mistake them for sheep and give them an unsuspecting welcome. Their true character is not discovered until too late and the damage has been done.

In other words, a false teacher does not announce and advertise himself as a purveyor of lies; on the contrary he claims to be a teacher of the truth. 'Knowing that Christians are credulous people, he conceals his dark purpose beneath the cloak of Christian piety, hoping that his innocuous disguise will avert detection.'[1] Not only does he feign piety, but he often uses the language of historic orthodoxy, in order to win acceptance from the gullible, while meaning by it something quite different, something destructive of the very truth he pretends to hold. He also hides behind the cover of high-sounding titles and impressive academic degrees.

So, 'Beware!' Jesus warns. We must be on our guard, pray for discernment, use our critical faculties and never relax our vigilance. We must not be dazzled by a person's outward clothing —his charm, learning, doctorates and ecclesiastical honours. We must not be so naive as to suppose that because he is a PhD or a DD or a professor or a bishop he *must* be a true and orthodox ambassador of Christ. We must look beneath the appearance to the reality. What lives under the fleece: a sheep or a wolf?

*c. Tests*

Having noted the assumptions Jesus made and the warnings he gave, we are now ready to look at the test or tests he told us to apply. He changed his metaphor from sheep and wolves to trees and their fruit, from the sheep's clothing which a wolf may wear to the fruit which a tree must bear. In so doing he moved from the risk of non-recognition to the means of recognition. Although you may indeed sometimes mistake a wolf for a sheep, he seems to say, you cannot make the same mistake with a tree. No tree can hide its identity for long. Sooner or later it betrays itself—by its fruit. A wolf may disguise itself; a tree cannot. Noxious weeds like thorns and thistles simply cannot produce edible fruit like grapes and figs. Not only is the character of the fruit determined by the tree (a fig tree bearing figs and a vine grapes), but its condition too (*every sound tree bears good fruit, but the bad tree*

[1] Bonhoeffer, p. 171.

*bears evil fruit*, 17). Indeed, *a sound tree cannot bear evil fruit, nor can a bad tree bear good fruit* (18). And the day of judgment will finalize the difference, as when non-fruitbearing trees are cut down and burnt (19). Therefore (for this is the conclusion which Jesus emphasizes twice) *you will know them by their fruits* (16, 20). What are these fruits?

The first kind of 'fruit' by which false prophets reveal their true identity is in the realm of character and conduct. In Jesus' own allegory of the vine fruitfulness evidently means Christlikeness, in fact what Paul later termed 'the fruit of the Spirit'. This being so, whenever we see in a teacher the meekness and gentleness of Christ, his love, patience, kindness, goodness and self-control, we have reason to believe him to be true, not false. On the other hand, whenever these qualities are missing, and 'the works of the flesh' are more apparent than 'the fruit of the Spirit' —especially enmity, impurity, jealousy and self-indulgence—we are justified in suspecting that the prophet is an impostor, however pretentious his claims and specious his teaching.

But a prophet's 'fruits' are not only his character and manner of life. Indeed, interpreters 'who confine them to the life are, in my opinion, mistaken' wrote Calvin.[1] A second 'fruit' is the man's actual teaching. This is strongly suggested by the other use Jesus made of the same fruit-tree metaphor: 'The tree is known by its fruit. You brood of vipers! how can you speak good, when you are evil? For out of the abundance of the heart the mouth speaks. The good man out of his good treasure brings forth good, and the evil man out of his evil treasure brings forth evil. I tell you, on the day of judgment men will render account for every careless word they utter; for by your words you will be justified, and by your words you will be condemned.'[2] So then, if a person's heart is revealed in his words, as a tree is known by its fruit, we have a responsibility to test a teacher by his teaching. The apostle John gives us an example of this, for the Asian churches to which he wrote had been invaded by false teachers. Like Jesus he warned them not to be deceived, but rather to 'test the spirits (*i.e.* teachers claiming inspiration) to see whether they are of God'.[3] He encouraged them to look for righteousness and love in their teachers and to reject as spurious both the unrighteous and

[1] P. 364.
[2] Mt. 12:33–37; *cf.* Lk. 6:45.
[3] 1 Jn. 2:26; 4:1.

the unloving. But to these moral tests he added a doctrinal one. In general this was whether the teachers' message was in accord with the original apostolic instruction,[1] and in particular whether it confessed Jesus as the Christ come in the flesh, thus acknowledging his divine-human person.[2]

The sixteenth-century reformers, who were accused by the Church of Rome of being innovators and false teachers, defended themselves by this doctrinal test. They appealed to Scripture and maintained that their teaching was not the introduction of something new but the recovery of something old, namely the original gospel of Christ and his apostles. It was rather the medieval Catholics who had departed from the faith into error. 'Cling to the pure Word of God,' cried Luther, for then you will be able to 'recognize the judge' who is right.[3] Calvin made the same emphasis: 'All doctrines must be brought to the Word of God as the standard,' for 'in judging of false prophets the rule of faith (*i.e.* Scripture) holds the chief place'.[4] He also went a step further than this in drawing attention to the motives of false teachers in addition to the substance of their teaching: 'Under the *fruits* the *manner of teaching* is itself included . . ., for Christ proves that he was sent by God from this consideration, that "he seeketh not his own glory, but the glory of the Father who sent him" (John 7:18)'.[5]

In examining a teacher's credentials, then, we have to examine both his character and his message. Bishop Ryle summed it up well: 'Sound doctrine and holy living are the marks of true prophets.'[6] Then I think there is a third test which we must apply to teachers, and this concerns their influence. We have to ask ourselves what effect their teaching has on their followers. Sometimes the falsity of false teaching is not immediately apparent when we look at a teacher's behaviour and system, but becomes apparent only in its disastrous results. This is what Paul meant when he wrote of error's tendency to 'eat its way like gangrene'.[7] Its gangrenous progress is seen when it upsets people's faith,[8]

[1] *E.g.* 1 Jn. 2:24; 4:6.
[2] 1 Jn. 2:22, 23; 4:2, 3;2: Jn. 7–9.
[3] P. 263.
[4] P. 365.
[5] Pp. 364 f.
[6] P. 68.
[7] 2 Tim. 2:17.
[8] 2 Tim. 2:18.

promotes ungodliness[1] and causes bitter divisions.[2] Sound teaching, by contrast, produces faith, love and godliness.[3]

Of course the application of the 'fruit' test is not altogether simple or straightforward. For fruit takes time to grow and ripen. We have to wait for it patiently. We also need an opportunity to examine it closely, for it is not always possible to recognize a tree and its fruit from a distance. Indeed, even at close quarters we may at first miss the symptoms of disease in the tree or the presence of a maggot in the fruit. To apply this to a teacher, what is needed is not a superficial estimate of his standing in the church, but a close and critical scrutiny of his character, conduct, message, motives and influence.

This warning of Jesus gives us no encouragement, however, either to become suspicious of everybody or to take up as our hobby the disreputable sport known as 'heresy-hunting'. Rather it is a solemn reminder that there are false teachers in the church and that we are to be on our guard. Truth matters. For it is God's truth and it builds up God's church, whereas error is devilish and destructive. If we care for God's truth and for God's church, we must take Christ's warning seriously. He and his apostles place the responsibility for the church's doctrinal purity partly upon the shoulders of Christian leaders (whether bishops or other chief pastors), but also and especially upon each congregation. The local church has more power than it often realizes or uses in deciding which teachers it will listen to. Jesus Christ's 'Beware of false prophets' is addressed to us all. If the church had heeded his warning and applied his tests, it would not be in the parlous state of theological and moral confusion in which it finds itself today.

With this paragraph Jesus concludes his delineation of a Christian's relationships. As we now look back and bring them together, we see how rich and varied they are. As a brother the Christian hates hypocrisy, criticizes himself and seeks to give constructive moral support to others. As an evangelist he prizes the gospel pearl so highly that he refuses to expose it to scornful rejection by hardened sinners. As a lover of all men, he is resolved to behave towards them as he would like them to behave towards him. As a child he looks humbly and trustfully to his heavenly

[1] 2 Tim. 2:16.
[2] E.g. 1 Tim. 6:4, 5; 2 Tim. 2:23; Tit. 1:11; 3:9.
[3] E.g. 1 Tim. 1:4, 5; 4:7; 6:3; 2 Tim. 3:16, 17; Tit. 1:1.

Father to give him all the good gifts he needs. As a traveller on the hard and narrow way, he enjoys fellowship with his fellow pilgrims and keeps his eye on the goal of life. As a champion of God's revealed truth, he heeds Christ's warning to be watchful for false teachers who would pervert it and so ravage Christ's flock.

# Matthew 7:21-27
# A Christian's commitment:
# the radical choice

Whether or not we were right in thinking that Jesus began his conclusion with verse 13, he certainly comes to it now. At this point he is not concerned to add further instruction, but rather to ensure a proper response to the instruction he has already given. 'The Lord Jesus winds up the Sermon on the Mount', writes J. C. Ryle, 'by a passage of heart-piercing application. He turns from false prophets to false professors, from unsound teachers to unsound hearers.'[1] R. V. G. Tasker's comment is similar: 'It is not only false teachers who make the narrow way difficult to find and still harder to tread. A man may also be grievously self-deceived.'[2]

So Jesus confronts us with himself, sets before us the radical choice between obedience and disobedience, and calls us to an unconditional commitment of mind, will and life to his teaching. The way he does it is to warn us of two unacceptable alternatives, first a merely verbal profession (21-23) and secondly a merely intellectual knowledge (24-27). Neither can be a substitute for obedience; indeed each may be a camouflage for disobedience. Jesus emphasizes with great solemnity that on a thoroughgoing obedience our eternal destiny depends.

In this respect the two final paragraphs of the Sermon are very similar. Both contrast the wrong and the right responses to Christ's teaching. Both show that neutrality is impossible and that a definite decision has to be made. Both stress that nothing can take the place of an active, practical obedience. And both teach that the issue of life and death on the day of judgment will

[1] Pp. 69, 70.
[2] P. 83.

be determined by our moral response to Christ and his teaching in this life. The only difference between the paragraphs is that in the first people offer a profession of their lips as an alternative to obedience, and in the second a hearing with their ears.

## 1. The danger of a merely verbal profession (21–23)

*Not every one who says to me, 'Lord, Lord,' shall enter the kingdom of heaven, but he who does the will of my Father who is in heaven.* <sup>22</sup> *On that day many will say to me, 'Lord, Lord, did we not prophesy in your name, and cast out demons in your name, and do many mighty works in your name?'* <sup>23</sup>*And then will I declare to them, 'I never knew you; depart from me, you evildoers.'*

The people Jesus is describing here are relying for salvation on a credal affirmation, on what they 'say' to or about Christ. 'Not every one who *says* to me' (21). 'On that day many will *say* to me' (22). But our final destiny will be settled, Jesus insists, neither by what we are saying to him today, nor by what we shall say to him on the last day, but by whether we do what we say, whether our verbal profession is accompanied by moral obedience.

Now a verbal profession of Christ is indispensable. In order to be saved, wrote Paul, we have to confess with our lips and believe in our hearts.[1] And a true profession of Jesus as Lord is impossible without the Holy Spirit.[2] Moreover, the kind of Christian profession Jesus describes at the end of the Sermon appears—at least on the surface—to be wholly admirable. To begin with, it is polite. It addresses him as 'Lord', just as today the most respectful and courteous way of referring to Jesus is still to say 'our Lord'. Next, the profession is orthodox. Although to call Jesus 'Lord' may mean no more than 'Sir', the present context contains allusions both to God as his Father and to himself as the Judge, and therefore seems to imply more. Certainly after his death and resurrection the early Christians knew what they were doing when they called him 'Lord'. It was a divine title, a rendering in the Greek Old Testament of the Hebrew for 'Jehovah'. So from our later perspective we may say that this is an accurate, an orthodox confession of Jesus Christ. Thirdly, it is fervent, for it is not a cold or formal 'Lord' but an enthusiastic

[1] Rom. 10:9, 10.
[2] 1 Cor. 12:3.

'Lord, Lord', as if the speaker wishes to draw attention to the strength and zeal of his devotion.

The fourth point is that it is a public confession. This is no private and personal protestation of allegiance to Jesus. Some have even 'prophesied' in Christ's name, daring to claim as they preach on some public occasion the authority and the inspiration of Jesus himself. More than this, the profession is even at times spectacular. In order to make his point, Jesus cites the most extreme examples of verbal profession, namely the exercise of a supernatural ministry involving prophecy, exorcism and miracles. What these people stress as they speak to Christ on judgment day is the name in which they have ministered. Three times they use it, and each time they put it first for emphasis. They claim that in the name of Christ, openly and publicly confessed, they have prophesied, cast out demons and done many mighty works. And there is no need to doubt the truth of their claim, for 'great signs and wonders' will be performed even by false Christs and false prophets.[1]

What better Christian profession could be given? Here are people who call Jesus 'Lord' with courtesy, orthodoxy and enthusiasm, in private devotion and in public ministry. What can be wrong with this? In itself nothing. And yet everything is wrong because it is talk without truth, profession without reality. It will not save them on the day of judgment. So Jesus moves on from what they are saying and will say to him to what he will say to them. He too will make a solemn profession. The word used in verse 23 is *homologēsō*, 'I will confess'. Christ's confession to them will be like theirs in being public, but unlike theirs in being true. He will address to them the terrible words: *I never knew you; depart from me, you evildoers.* For although they had used his name freely, their name was unknown to him.

The reason for their rejection by him is that their profession was verbal, not moral. It concerned their lips only, and not their life. They called Jesus 'Lord, Lord', but never submitted to his lordship, or obeyed the will of his heavenly Father. Luke's version of this saying is if anything stronger still: 'Why do you call me "Lord, Lord", and not do what I tell you?'[2] The vital difference is between 'saying' and 'doing'. The reason Christ the Judge will banish them from him is that they are *evildoers.* They

[1] Mt. 24:24; 2 Thes. 2:9, 10.
[2] Lk. 6:46.

may claim to do *mighty works* in their ministry; but in their every-day behaviour the works they do are not good, but evil. Of what value is it for such people to take Christ's name on their lips? As Paul expressed it some years later: 'Let every one who names the name of the Lord depart from iniquity'.[1]

We who claim to be Christians in our day have made a pro-fession of faith in Jesus privately in conversion and publicly in baptism and/or confirmation. We appear to honour Jesus by referring to him as 'the Lord' or 'our Lord'. We recite the creed in church, and sing hymns expressive of devotion to Christ. We even exercise a variety of ministries in his name. But he is not impressed by our pious and orthodox words. He still asks for evidence of our sincerity in good works of obedience.

### 2. The danger of a merely intellectual knowledge (24-27)

*Every one then who hears these words of mine and does them will be like a wise man who built his house upon the rock;* [25] *and the rain fell, and the floods came, and the winds blew and beat upon that house, but it did not fall, because it had been founded on the rock.* [26] *And every one who hears these words of mine and does not do them will be like a foolish man who built his house upon the sand;* [27] *and the rain fell, and the floods came, and the winds blew and beat against that house, and it fell; and great was the fall of it.*

Whereas the contrast in the previous paragraph was between 'saying' and 'doing', the contrast now is between 'hearing' and 'doing'. On the one hand, Jesus says, there is the person who *hears these words of mine and does them* (24), and on the other the person who *hears these words of mine and does not do them* (26). He then illustrates the contrast between his obedient and disobedient hearers by his well-known parable of the two builders, the wise man who 'dug deep'[2] and constructed his house on rock, and the fool who could not be bothered with foundations and was content to build on sand. As both got on with their building, a casual observer would not have noticed any difference between them. For the difference was in the foundations, and foundations are not seen. Only when a storm broke, and battered both houses with great ferocity—'rain on roof, river on foundation, wind on

[1] 2 Tim. 2:19.
[2] Lk. 6:48.

walls'[1]—was the fundamental and fatal difference revealed. For the house on the rock withstood the gale, while the house on the sand collapsed in irreparable ruin.

In the same way professing Christians (both the genuine and the spurious) often look alike. You cannot easily tell which is which. Both appear to be building Christian lives. For Jesus is not contrasting professing Christians with non-Christians who make no profession. On the contrary, what is common to both spiritual housebuilders is that they *hear these words of mine*. So both are members of the visible Christian community. Both read the Bible, go to church, listen to sermons and buy Christian literature. The reason you often cannot tell the difference between them is that the deep foundations of their lives are hidden from view. The real question is not whether they *hear* Christ's teaching (nor even whether they respect or believe it), but whether they *do* what they hear. Only a storm will reveal the truth. Sometimes a storm of crisis or calamity betrays what manner of person we are, for 'true piety is not fully distinguished from its counterfeit till it comes to the trial'.[2] If not, the storm of the day of judgment will certainly do so.

The truth on which Jesus is insisting in these final two paragraphs of the Sermon is that neither an intellectual knowledge of him nor a verbal profession, though both are essential in themselves, can ever be a substitute for obedience. The question is not whether we *say* nice, polite, orthodox, enthusiastic things to or about Jesus; nor whether we *hear* his words, listening, studying, pondering and memorizing until our minds are stuffed with his teaching, but whether we *do* what we say and *do* what we know, in other words whether the lordship of Jesus which we profess is one of our life's major realities.

This is not, of course, to teach that the way of salvation, or the way to *enter the kingdom of heaven* (21), is by good works of obedience, for the whole New Testament offers salvation only by the sheer grace of God through faith. What Jesus is stressing, however, is that those who truly hear the gospel and profess faith will always obey him, expressing their faith in their works. The apostles of Jesus never forgot this teaching. It is prominent in their letters. The first letter of John, for example, is full of the perils of a verbal profession: 'If we say we have fellowship with

[1] Bruce, p. 135.
[2] Calvin, p. 370.

him while we walk in darkness, we lie . . . He who says "I know him" but disobeys his commandments is a liar.'[1] The letter of James, on the other hand, is full of the perils of an intellectual knowledge. An arid orthodoxy cannot save, he writes, but only a faith which issues in good works; so we have to be 'doers of the word, and not hearers only'.[2]

In applying this teaching to ourselves, we need to consider that the Bible is a dangerous book to read, and that the church is a dangerous society to join. For in reading the Bible we hear the words of Christ, and in joining the church we say we believe in Christ. As a result, we belong to the company described by Jesus as both hearing his teaching and calling him Lord. Our membership therefore lays upon us the serious responsibility of ensuring that what we know and what we say is translated into what we do.

Thus the Sermon ends on the same note of radical choice of which we have been aware throughout. Jesus does not set before his followers a string of easy ethical rules, so much as a set of values and ideals which is entirely distinctive from the way of the world. He summons us to renounce the prevailing secular culture in favour of the Christian counter-culture. Repeatedly during our study we have heard his call to his people to be different from everybody else. The first time this became clear was in his commission to us to be both 'the salt of the earth' and 'the light of the world'. For these metaphors set the Christian and non-Christian communities over against each other as recognizably, indeed fundamentally, distinct. The world is like rotting food, full of the bacteria which cause its disintegration; Jesus' followers are to be its salt, arresting its decay. The world is a dark and dismal place, lacking sunshine, living in shadow; Jesus' followers are to be its light, dispelling its darkness and its gloom.

From then on the opposing standards are graphically described, and the way of Jesus commended. Our righteousness is to be deeper because it reaches even our hearts, and our love broader because it embraces even our enemies. In piety we are to avoid the ostentation of hypocrites and in prayer the verbosity of pagans. Instead our giving, praying and fasting are to be real,

[1] 1 Jn. 1:6; 2:4.
[2] Jas. 1:22–25; 2:14–20.

with no compromise of our Christian integrity. For our treasure we are to choose what endures through eternity, not what disintegrates on earth, and for our master God, not money or possessions. As for our ambition (what preoccupies our mind) this must not be our own material security, but the spread of God's rule and righteousness in the world.

Instead of conforming to this world—whether in the form of religious Pharisees or of irreligious pagans—we are called by Jesus to imitate our heavenly Father. He is a peacemaker. And he loves even the ungrateful and selfish. So we must copy him, not men. Only then shall we show that we are truly his sons and daughters (5:9, 44-48). Here then is the alternative, either to follow the crowd or to follow our Father in heaven, either to be a reed swayed by the winds of public opinion or to be ruled by God's word, the revelation of his character and will. And the overriding purpose of the Sermon on the Mount is to present us with this alternative, and so to face us with the indispensable necessity of choice.

That is why the Sermon's conclusion is so appropriate, as Jesus sketches the two ways (narrow and broad) and the two buildings (on rock and sand). It would be impossible to exaggerate the importance of the choice between them, since one way leads to life while the other ends in destruction, and one building is secure while the other is overwhelmed with disaster. Far more momentous than the choice even of a life-work or of a life-partner is the choice about life itself. Which road are we going to travel? On which foundation are we going to build?

# Matthew: 7:28, 29
# Conclusion: who is this preacher?

Many people—including adherents of other religions and of none—tell us that they are prepared to accept the Sermon on the Mount as containing self-evident truth. They know that it includes such sayings as 'Blessed are the merciful, for they shall obtain mercy,' 'Love your enemies,' 'No one can serve two masters,' 'Judge not, that you be not judged' and 'Whatever you wish that men would do to you, do so to them.' Beautiful! Here, they say, is Jesus of Nazareth the moral teacher at his simplest and best. Here is the core of his message before it became encrusted with the worthless additions of his interpreters. Here is the 'original Jesus', with plain ethics and no dogmas, an unsophisticated prophet of righteousness, claiming to be no more than a human teacher, and telling us to do good and to love one another. 'The Jesus of dogma I do not understand,' a Hindu professor once said to Stanley Jones, 'but the Jesus of the Sermon on the Mount and the cross I love and am drawn to.' Similarly, a Muslim Sufi teacher told him that 'when he read the Sermon on the Mount he could not keep back the tears'.[1]

But this popular explanation of the Sermon cannot stand up to serious examination. It is mistaken on two counts—first in its view of the teacher and secondly in its presentation of his teaching. For when we look more closely at both, something very different emerges. We considered in the last chapter the distinctiveness of his teaching, his sketch of the Christian counter-culture and his summons to radical discipleship. It remains for us now to consider the uniqueness of the teacher himself.

What we shall find is that it is impossible to drive a wedge

[1] Stanley Jones, *Christ at the round table* (Abingdon, 1928), pp. 38, 60.

between the Jesus of the Sermon on the Mount and the Jesus of the rest of the New Testament. Instead, the preacher of the Sermon on the Mount is the same supernatural, dogmatic, divine Jesus who is to be found everywhere else. So the main question the Sermon forces upon us is not so much 'What do you make of this teaching?' as 'Who on earth is this teacher?' This was certainly the reaction of those who heard the Sermon preached.

*And when Jesus finished these sayings, the crowds were astonished at his teaching, 29 for he taught them as one who had authority, and not as their scribes.*

What struck the first hearers of the Sermon (*the crowds*, as well as *his disciples*, 5:1) was the preacher's extraordinary authority. He did not hum and haw, or hesitate. He was neither tentative nor apologetic. Nor again, on the other hand, was he ever bombastic or flamboyant. Instead, with quiet and unassuming assurance he laid down the law for the citizens of God's kingdom. And *the crowds were astonished*, even—for the Greek verb is a strong one—'dumbfounded'.[1] 'After nineteen hundred years,' comments A. M. Hunter, 'we are astonished too.'[2]

It should be profitable, then, to try to analyse this 'authority' of Jesus, as displayed in the Sermon. On what was it grounded? What was his own self-awareness which led him to speak in this way? What clues does the Sermon itself give of how he understood his identity and his mission? We do not have far to seek in order to find answers to these questions.

## 1. Jesus' authority as the teacher

The crowds were astonished at his *teaching*, for he *taught* them with authority. Yes, he presented himself first and foremost as a teacher, and he amazed his listeners by the substance, the quality and the manner of his instruction. But of course there had been thousands of other teachers in Jewry and elsewhere. Many were his contemporaries. What then was so special about him?

He somehow assumed the right to teach absolute truth. He was a Jew, but his message was not Jewish. He was interpreting

[1] Lenski, p. 314.
[2] P. 96.

Moses' law, but in such a way as to show that it was God's. What he had to say was not culturally conditioned in the sense that it was limited to a particular people (Jews) or a particular place (Palestine). Being absolute, it was universal. So he spoke as one who knew what he was talking about. 'We speak of what we know,' he said in another context.[1] He knew who would be great in God's kingdom and who least, who was 'blessed' in God's sight and who was not, which way led to life and which to destruction. With complete self-confidence he declared who would inherit the kingdom of heaven, who would inherit the earth, who would obtain mercy, see God and be fit to be called God's children. How could he be so sure?

Commentators have searched for language adequate to describe this peculiar flavour of Jesus' teaching. I have collected some of their attempts. They have tended to depict Jesus as either a king or a law-maker. 'He spoke royally,' wrote Spurgeon,[2] with 'royal assurance'[3] or with 'sovereignty'.[4] Gresham Machen's expression was that 'he claimed the right to legislate for the kingdom of God',[5] while James Denney combined the pictures of king and law-maker in writing both of his 'practical sovereignty over man's conscience, will and affections' and of his 'supreme moral authority, legislating without misgiving, and demanding implicit obedience'.[6] And Calvin said the crowds were astonished 'because a strange, indescribable and unwonted majesty drew to him the minds of men'.[7]

His hearers naturally compared and contrasted him with the many other teachers with whom they were familiar, especially the scribes. What struck them most was that he taught them *as one who had authority* and not at all *as their scribes*. For the scribes claimed no authority of their own. They conceived their duty in terms of faithfulness to the tradition they had received. So they were antiquarians, delving into commentaries, searching for precedents, claiming the support of famous names among the rabbis. Their only authority lay in the authorities they were constantly quoting. Jesus, on the other hand, had not received a

[1] Jn. 3:11.
[2] P. 46.
[3] Plummer, p. 117.
[4] Stonehouse, p. 199.
[5] *Christianity and liberalism* (1923; Eerdmans, n.d.), p. 36.
[6] *Studies in theology* (lectures delivered in 1894: Hodder, 1906), pp. 31, 42.
[7] P. 371.

scribal education,[1] scandalized the establishment by sweeping away the traditions of the elders, had no particular reverence for social conventions, and spoke with a freshness of his own which captivated some and infuriated others. A. B. Bruce summed up the difference by saying that the scribes spoke '*by* authority', while Jesus spoke '*with* authority'.[2]

If he did not teach like the scribes, he did not teach like the Old Testament prophets either. They did not share the scribes' addiction to the past. They lived in the present. For they claimed to be speaking in the name of Jehovah, so that the living voice of the living God was heard through their lips. Jesus also insisted that his words were God's words: 'My teaching is not mine, but his who sent me.'[3] Yet there was a difference. The commonest formula with which the prophets introduced their oracles, namely 'Thus says the Lord', is one Jesus never used. Instead, he would begin 'Truly, truly I say to you', thus daring to speak in his own name and with his own authority, which he knew to be identical with the Father's.[4] This 'Truly, I say to you' (*amēn legō humin*) or 'I tell you' (*legō humin*) occurs six times in the Sermon on the Mount (5:18; 6:2, 5, 16, 25, 29). On six more occasions, namely in the six antitheses of chapter 5, we find the even stronger assertion with its emphatic *egō*, 'But *I* say to you' (*egō de legō humin*). Not that he was contradicting Moses, as we have seen, but rather the scribal corruptions of Moses. Yet in doing this he was challenging the inherited tradition of the centuries and claiming to replace it with his own accurate and authoritative interpretation of God's law. He thus 'stood forth as a legislator, not as a commentator, and commanded and prohibited, and repealed, and promised, on his own bare word'.[5]

So certain was he of the truth and validity of his teaching that he said human wisdom and human folly were to be assessed by people's reaction to it. The only wise people there are, he implied, are those who build their lives on his words by obeying them. All others by rejecting his teaching are fools. He may even have been applying to himself those words of personified wisdom which occur in Proverbs 1:33, 'He who listens to me will dwell secure.' It is by paying heed to him who is the wisdom of God that man learns to be wise.

[1] *Cf.* Jn. 7:15.
[2] P. 136.
[3] Jn. 7:16.
[4] *Cf.* Jn. 14:8–11.
[5] Plummer, p. 118.

## 2. Jesus' authority as the Christ

There is evidence in the Sermon on the Mount, as in many other parts of his teaching, that Jesus knew he had come into the world on a mission. 'I have come,' he could say,[1] just as elsewhere in Matthew's Gospel he referred to himself as having been 'sent'.[2] In particular, he had not come, he insisted, 'to abolish the law and the prophets', but he had come 'to fulfil (*plērōsai*) them'.

The claim sounds innocent enough until one reflects on its implications. What he is asserting is that all the adumbrations and predictions of both law and prophets found their fulfilment in him, and that therefore all the lines of the Old Testament witness converged on himself. He did not think of himself as another prophet or even as the greatest of the prophets, but rather as the fulfilment of all prophecy. This belief that the days of expectation were now over and that he had ushered in the time of fulfilment was deeply imbedded in the consciousness of Jesus. The first recorded words of his public ministry were: 'The time is fulfilled (*peplērōtai*), and the kingdom of God is at hand.'[3] In the Sermon on the Mount there are five direct references to God's kingdom.[4] They imply—though with varying degrees of clarity—that he himself had inaugurated it, and that he had authority to admit people into it and to bestow on them its blessings. All this means, in a word, that Jesus knew himself to be the Christ, God's Messiah of Old Testament expectation.

## 3. Jesus' authority as the Lord

We have already had occasion to observe that the ascription to Jesus of the title 'Lord' does not necessarily imply a recognition of him as the divine Lord. As N. B. Stonehouse put it: 'The flexibility of the Greek word "Lord" must indeed be recognized: not every instance of its use implies a consciousness of divine authority. Not everyone who addressed Jesus as Lord clearly chose this name as the equivalent of deity; it could as a polite form of address mean little more than our "sir".'[5] Nevertheless, in some contexts Jesus seems deliberately to have accepted the

[1] 5:17; cf. 9:13; 10:34; 11:3, 19; 20:28.
[2] 10:40; 15:24; 21:37.
[3] Mk. 1:15; cf. Mt. 4:17.
[4] 5:3, 10; 6:10, 33; 7:21.
[5] P. 254.

fullest implications the title could bear, as when he associated it with his other and favourite title 'Son of man', who in Daniel's vision would receive universal dominion,[1] and with David's 'lord' who would sit at God's right hand.[2]

Only the context can help us to judge how much dominion and deity may rightly be included in the word 'Lord'. Take as an example the section in the Sermon on the Mount in which Jesus referred to people who addressed him as 'Lord, Lord'.[3] He was not complaining that they chose this title, for he accepted it as appropriate. His point was rather that they were using it glibly and were not investing it with its true meaning. He was not just 'Sir' to be respected; he was 'Lord' to be obeyed. The Lucan equivalent makes this plain, as we saw: 'Why do you call me "Lord, Lord", and not do what I tell you?'[4] Thus Jesus saw himself as more than a teacher, giving advice which people might or might not heed at their discretion; he was their master, issuing commandments, expecting obedience and warning them that their eternal welfare was at stake. Clearly, in all this Jesus was no ordinary rabbi. A Jewish rabbi's pupils sat at his feet to study Torah. Jesus was also in one sense a rabbi, since he taught his disciples the true meaning of Torah. But his expectation was not just that they would absorb his teaching; it was that they would be devoted to him personally. This, no doubt, is why he was not content with the title 'Rabbi' on its own, for in fact he was their 'Teacher and Lord'.[5] This too is why they in their turn did not just become 'rabbis', guarding and handing on the tradition of his teaching; they were also, and even more, 'witnesses' to him.

## 4. Jesus' authority as the Saviour

It is plain in the Sermon that Jesus knew the way of salvation and taught it. He was able to declare who was blessed and who was not. He could point to the narrow gate which led on to the hard way which ended in life. And he was quite clear which kind of house would survive the storms of judgment, and which would founder.

[1] Dn. 7:14; Mt. 24:39, 42, 'your Lord'.
[2] Mk. 12:35–37.
[3] Mt. 7:21–23.
[4] Lk. 6:46.
[5] Jn. 13:13.

But if we penetrate more deeply into his message, we find that he not only taught salvation; he actually bestowed it. Even in the beatitudes he appears in the role of one who virtually himself distributes blessedness and gives the kingdom. Professor Jeremias thus quotes with approval J. Schniewind's insistence 'that the beatitudes are concealed testimonies by Jesus to himself as the saviour of the poor, the sorrowing etc.'.[1]

Or consider how Jesus appointed his hearers, that little group of peasants, 'the salt of the earth' and 'the light of the world'. How could they possibly have a restraining and enlightening influence in the world? Only because they followed Jesus. It is because he himself was not 'evil' as he described the rest of mankind[2] that he could impart to them some of his goodness and make them 'salt'. It is because he did not share in the universal darkness but was himself 'the light of the world'[3] that he could impart light to them and make them shine.

It is further significant that in Matthew's Gospel the Sermon on the Mount (chapters 5–7), representative of Jesus' words, is followed by an account of his practical ministry (chapters 8 and 9), representative of his works. For here we see him claiming authority to forgive sins and actually bestowing forgiveness on a paralysed man (9:2–6), and then likening himself as the saviour of sinners to a physician of the sick (9:12).

## 5. Jesus' authority as the Judge

The whole Sermon on the Mount was preached against the sombre background of the coming day of judgment. Jesus knew it was a reality and desired it to be a reality in the minds and lives of his followers. So he declared the conditions of salvation and warned of the causes of destruction, especially in his graphic portrayal of the two ways and their two destinations.

Much more striking than this emphasis on the certainty of future judgment was his claim that he himself would be the Judge.[4] The self-centredness of the scene he described is quite extraordinary. Three times he used the personal pronouns 'I' and 'me'. First, he would himself be the Judge, hearing the evidence

[1] Jeremias, p. 24.
[2] 7:11.
[3] Jn. 8:12.
[4] 7:22, 23.

and passing the sentence. For on that solemn day, he said, 'many will say to *me* "Lord, Lord" . . . and then *I* will declare to them . . .' Thus the accused will address their case to him, and he will be the one to answer them. No-one but he will decide and declare their destiny. Secondly, he will be himself the criterion of the judgment. People will bring forward as evidence their use of his name in their ministry, but this will be inadmissible as evidence. '*I* never knew you,' he will say to them. The destiny of human beings will depend not on their knowledge and use of his name, but on their knowledge of him personally. Not service for Christ, but relationship to Christ will be the issue. Thirdly, the sentence he pronounces will be concerned with him also: 'Depart from *me*, you evildoers.' The terribleness of the 'destruction'[1] and of the 'ruin'[2] which he predicted is that it will involve banishment from his presence. No worse fate could be envisaged, he implied, than eternal separation from himself.

Thus did the carpenter of Nazareth make himself the central figure of the judgment day. He will himself assume the role of Judge (and later in Matthew's Gospel he describes in greater detail how he will 'sit on his glorious throne' to judge mankind[3]). Further, the basis of the judgment will be people's attitude to him, and the nature of the judgment will be exclusion from his presence. It would be hard to exaggerate the staggering egocentricity of these claims.

### d. Jesus' authority as the Son of God

In the Sermon on the Mount Jesus gives us a comprehensive doctrine of God. He is the Creator, the living God of the natural order, who gives sunshine and rain, and supplies birds with food, flowers with clothing and human beings with the necessities of life. He is also the King, whose righteous and saving rule has irrupted into human lives through Jesus. But above all—again through Jesus—he is our Father. Addressing his disciples, Jesus constantly referred to him as 'your Father in heaven', whose children they were, whose mercy they must copy, whose loving providence they must trust and to whom they must come con-

---

[1] Mt. 7:13.
[2] Mt. 7:27.
[3] 25:31 ff.

fidingly in prayer, knowing that he will never give them anything but 'good gifts'.

In all these sayings Jesus called God 'your Father'. Then once he referred to 'the will of *my* Father'.[1] Never, however, did he include himself with his disciples and speak of God as 'our Father'. Of course he taught *them* to pray 'Our Father',[2] but he was not associating himself with them. Indeed, he could not. For although he gave his followers the privilege of addressing God by the same intimate title which he himself used ('Abba, Father'), yet still he was deeply conscious that God was his Father in a sense altogether different, indeed unique. This he was later to express in a saying which Matthew also records: 'All things have been delivered to me by my Father; and no one knows the Son except the Father, and no one knows the Father except the Son and anyone to whom the Son chooses to reveal him.'[3] This exclusive Sonship Jesus did not explicitly claim or state in the Sermon on the Mount, but it is already implicit in his precise use of the personal possessives 'my Father', 'our Father', 'your Father'.

## 7. The authority of Jesus as God

I realize that, whenever we venture to enquire into the divine self-consciousness of Jesus, we are trying to take soundings in water too deep for us to fathom. That he knew God as 'my Father' is clear, and also that he knew his own Sonship to be unique. But now we can take a further hesitating step. For there is evidence that he thought of himself as being on a par with God, even one with God. It is not that he ever said this in so many words in the Sermon, but that his claim to exercise divine prerogatives and his ways of speaking of himself imply it. Three examples may be given.

The first concerns the final beatitude. It will be remembered that eight beatitudes are generalizations in the third person ('Blessed are the meek, the merciful, the peacemakers,' *etc.*), while a ninth changes to the second person as Jesus addresses his disciples: 'Blessed are you when men revile you and persecute you and utter all kinds of evil against you falsely on my account.

[1] Mt. 7:21.
[2] Mt. 6:9.
[3] Mt. 11:27.

Rejoice and be glad, for your reward is great in heaven, for so men persecuted the prophets who were before you.'[1] It is this analogy with the prophets which is arresting. The logic seems to be this: Jesus expects his followers to have to suffer for his sake ('on my account'), and then likens their persecution to that of the Old Testament prophets. Now those prophets suffered for their faithfulness to God, while the disciples of Jesus were to suffer for their faithfulness to him. The implication is unavoidable. If he is likening his disciples to God's prophets (and he did later 'send' them out as the prophets had been 'sent'[2]), he is likening himself to God. As Chrysostom put it at the end of the fourth century, 'He here ... covertly signifies his own dignity, and his equality in honour with him who begat him.'[3]

A similar equivalent is implied in the two other examples. When he warned them that a person who merely addressed him as 'Lord, Lord' would not enter the kingdom of heaven, one would have expected him to go on 'but he who submits to my lordship' or 'but he who obeys me as Lord'. And this is, in fact, what we find in Luke's version of the Sermon, where calling him 'Lord, Lord' is contrasted with doing what he says. But according to Matthew 7:21 he continued, 'but he who does the will of my Father who is in heaven'. If, then, Jesus regarded obeying him as Lord and doing the Father's will as equivalents, he was putting himself on a level with God. It is all the more impressive because Jesus was not going out of his way to make an assertion about himself. Such was not his purpose in the context. This token of his divine self-consciousness slipped out when he was speaking about something quite different, namely the meaning of true discipleship.

The same is true in the third example. It comes in the following verses which are about the day of judgment and have already been mentioned. Everybody knew that God was the Judge. So did Jesus. He did not here advance a direct and specific claim that God had committed the judgment of the world to him. He just knew that on the last day people would appeal to him and that he would have the responsibility to pass sentence on them. And in saying so, he again equated himself with God.

Here, then, is your 'original Jesus', your 'simple, harmless

[1] Mt. 5:11, 12.
[2] *Cf.* Mt. 10:1 ff.
[3] Pp. 207 f.

teacher of righteousness', whose Sermon on the Mount contains 'plain ethics and no dogmas'! He teaches with the authority of God and lays down the law of God. He expects people to build the house of their lives on his words, and adds that only those who do so are wise and will be safe. He says he has come to fulfil the law and the prophets. He is both the Lord to be obeyed and the Saviour to bestow blessing. He casts himself in the central role of the judgment-day drama. He speaks of God as his Father in a unique sense, and finally implies that what he does God does and that what people do to him they are doing to God.

We cannot escape the implication of all this. The claims of Jesus were indeed put forward so naturally, modestly and indirectly that many people never even notice them. But they are there; we cannot ignore them and still retain our integrity. Either they are true, or Jesus was suffering from what C. S. Lewis called a 'rampant megalomania'. Can it be seriously maintained, however, that the lofty ethics of the Sermon on the Mount are the product of a deranged mind? It requires a high degree of cynicism to reach that conclusion.

The only alternative is to take Jesus at his word, and his claims at their face value. In this case, we must respond to his Sermon on the Mount with deadly seriousness. For here is his picture of God's alternative society. These are the standards, the values and the priorities of the kingdom of God. Too often the church has turned away from this challenge and sunk into a bourgeois, conformist respectability. At such times it is almost indistinguishable from the world, it has lost its saltness, its light is extinguished and it repels all idealists. For it gives no evidence that it is God's new society which is tasting already the joys and powers of the age to come. Only when the Christian community lives by Christ's manifesto will the world be attracted and God be glorified. So when Jesus calls us to himself, it is to this that he calls us. For he is the Lord of the counter-culture.

# The Message of
# the Sermon on the Mount

# Study guide

# STUDY GUIDE

It's all too easy just to skim through a book like this without letting its truth take root in our lives. The purpose of this study guide is to help you genuinely to grapple with the message of the Sermon on the Mount and think about how its teaching is relevant to you today.

Although designed primarily for Bible study groups to use over a seven-week period, this series of studies is also suitable for private use. When used by a group with limited time, the leader should decide beforehand which questions to discuss during the meeting and which should be left for group members to work on by themselves during the following week.

To get the most out of the group meetings, each member of the group should read through the part of the Sermon on the Mount to be looked at in each study, together with the relevant pages of this book. As you begin each session, pray that the Holy Spirit will bring this ancient sermon to life and speak to you through it.

# SESSION ONE
## *Matthew 5:1-16 (pages 15-68)*

1   Read 5:1–16

The author begins by discussing the 'counter-culture' of the younger generation. What evidence of this is there where you live? How do you react to it? How do you think Jesus would have reacted?

2   For the author, the key text in this Sermon is Mt. 6:8: 'Do not be like them' (p. 18). Most people outside the church

think of Christians as being different from others. But what do *they* tend to think of as the distinctive marks of a Christian? Why do you think this is so?

3 You might like to discuss the question of whether or not the Sermon as reproduced by Matthew is authentic. What reasons can you think of on either side? What do you make of the author's conclusion (p. 23)?

4 Matthew (5:3) has 'Blessed are the poor in spirit', while Luke (6:20) has simply 'Blessed are you poor'. What are the suggested answers to this discrepancy (pp. 31f.)? Which do you find the most persuasive, and why?

5 Is it possible to put the demands of the Sermon into practice or is it hopelessly impracticable? A number of suggestions have been made to deal with the problem of its being an apparently unattainable ideal (pp. 26ff.):

a How would you answer someone who said that the Sermon on the Mount was intended only for super-saints and that ordinary Christians do not have to worry about its high standards?

b How would you answer someone who said that the Sermon is a 'thinly Christianized form of the Old Testament law ...' (p. 35), implying that, as Christians saved by grace alone, we can safely ignore it?

c How would you answer someone who said that the Sermon represents a future heavenly ideal rather than something to be aimed at now?

6 What does the author see as the twofold purpose of this Sermon (pp. 36ff.)? In what ways does it have these effects on you?

## STUDY GUIDE

7  What does it mean to be 'blessed'? In what ways have you experienced something of the blessings described here? Is Jesus referring to a benefit we receive now or to some sort of future reward? Or is there an element of both?

It is suggested that you study the Beatitudes (5:3–12) on your own after the group meeting and perhaps spend some time discussing your answers at your next session together. Questions 8–11 are to get you going. Groups should move now to question 12.

8  How does the author classify the Beatitudes (pp. 38ff.)? What do you find helpful in this sequence of ideas?

9  Rewrite the Beatitudes by inserting specific situations in your life – e.g. 'Blessed are the peacemakers' could be written as 'Blessed is the one who helps John and Mary to talk to each other again'. How might you put them into practice more than you do now?

10  In view of all these qualities, why is persecution inevitable (pp. 52ff.)? In what ways are you persecuted? How do you respond? What does Jesus say your reaction should be?

11  'The ways of the God of Scripture appear topsy-turvy to men' (p. 56). In what ways has this been true in your experience recently?

12  Make a list of some of the qualities people normally associate with power and influence. Now look back at 5:3-12 and note down the qualities which Jesus lists. How do you explain the difference?

13  In what ways do you, both as individuals and as members

of the Christian community, behave as the 'salt of the earth' (5:13)? What things make Christians less 'salty'? Think of practical ways in which you could have a greater effect on society.

14 In what ways are you, both as individuals and as members of the Christian community, the 'light of the world' (5:14)? What things prevent the light from being seen? Think of practical ways in which you could 'shine' more brightly.

15 Resolve to act on your answers to questions 13 and 14 during the coming week. Pray for one another as you begin to do this. You might like to discuss how you get on next time you meet.

# SESSION TWO

## Matthew 5:17-30 (pages 69-91)

You might like to begin by discussing your answers to the last session's questions (8-11) on 5:3-12.

1 Read 5:17-20
   a Why should anyone have thought that Jesus had come 'to abolish the law and the prophets'?

   b What three kinds of teaching are there in the Old Testament (pp. 71f.)? In what sense does Jesus 'fulfil' each of these?

   c What two things does Jesus say his disciples should do with the Old Testament (p. 74)? How do you match up to his standards in this area?

    **d** Given the enthusiasm of the scribes and Pharisees for keeping the law, how can the Christian's righteousness *exceed* theirs (pp. 74ff.)?

    **e** Jesus goes on to illustrate what he means with six examples of what the scribes and Pharisees were teaching, set against his own interpretation of the law's requirements. What evidence is there to support this way of viewing 5:21-48 (pp. 76ff.)?

**2** **Read 5:21-26**
    **a** Some people suggest that here Jesus is forbidding killing of any sort. What do you think, and why?

    **b** The author suggests that Jesus is making a rather different point here, and that he means not simply murder but even apparently rather less serious things like anger and insults (p. 83). Why are these 'tantamount to murder in God's sight' (p. 85)?

    **c** What practical instruction does Jesus give (5:23-26)? Can you think of ways in which this would restore any broken relationships in your own experience? Is there anything that you should now do in the light of this?

**3** **Read 5:27-30**
    **a** In what ways does the author suggest the scribes and Pharisees were distorting the commandment against adultery (pp. 87f.)?

    **b** What instructions does Jesus give to enable his disciples to maintain sexual purity? How does 'moral sentry-duty' (p. 90) work out in practice for you?

# SESSION THREE

## Matthew 5:31-48 (pages 92-124)

1   Read 5:31-32, together with Matthew 19:3-9
  a What distinguishes Jesus' teaching from that of the scribes and Pharisees (pp. 93ff.)?

  b You might like to discuss the arguments for and against the authenticity of the 'exceptive clause' in 5:32 and 19:9 (pp. 96f.). Which do you find the most persuasive?

  c How does the author approach the question of divorce (pp. 98f.)? In what ways does this accord with biblical teaching?

2  Read 5:33-37, together with Matthew 23:16-22
  a How were the scribes and Pharisees distorting the commandment against the breaking of oaths (pp. 99f.)?

  b What does Jesus tell his disciples to do to avoid this distortion? How does this apply to you?

  c How is what Jesus says here to be reconciled with the fact that God himself uses oaths in Scripture? And does it prohibit Christians from, for example, giving evidence on oath in a court of law (pp. 101f.)?

3   Read 5:38-42
  a The law of Moses does indeed lay down the penalty of 'eye for eye, and tooth for tooth' (Ex. 21:24). But the scribes and Pharisees were evidently distorting this commandment (p. 104). How?

  **b** Jesus clearly forbids personal revenge. But how would you answer someone who went further and claimed that, on the basis of this passage, a Christian should never use force against anyone (pp. 105ff.)?

4 Read 5:43-48
  **a** How have the scribes and Pharisees distorted the law in this instance (p. 115)?

  **b** 'Since the God of the Old Testament obviously hates his enemies, why shouldn't we hate ours?' How would you answer this question (pp. 116f.)?

5 Read 5:44 and Luke 6:27-28
  **a** In what three specific ways are we to 'love our enemies' (p. 118)? Are you conscious of particular 'enemies' towards whom you need to take this sort of action?

  **b** 'It is not enough for Christians to *resemble* non-Christians; our calling is to outstrip them ... God's people must imitate God rather than men ...' (p. 121). How is this possible for us as manifestly imperfect human beings?

  **c** 'Jesus *does* expect of his followers the very things which others think cannot reasonably be expected of anybody' (p. 123). How do you react to this? Pray together as you consider its implications for the way you live.

# *SESSION FOUR*

*Matthew 6:1-18 (pages 125-152)*

1 Read 6:1-4

a Having spoken about true *moral* righteousness in chapter 5, Jesus turns now to the righteousness his disciples are to display in their *religious* activity. What do you make of the apparent contradiction between 6:1 and 5:16 (p. 127)?

b The idea of 'reward' comes several times in this passage. How would you answer someone who suggests that this is an unworthy motive for Christian discipleship (pp. 131ff.)?

c What is the great danger involved in religious duties like giving alms (pp. 128ff.)? How does Jesus instruct his disciples to avoid this? How does this apply to you?

2 Read 6:5-6
Why does the hypocrite pray? How does Jesus instruct his disciples to avoid falling into the same trap (pp. 132ff.)? How does this apply in your own private prayer?

3 Read 6:16-18
a Fasting is not a popular pastime these days! What reasons does the author give for commending the practice (pp. 135ff.)?

b 'To do anything in order to be seen by men is bound to degrade it, while to do it to be seen by God is equally bound to ennoble it' (p. 140). Think about your religious activities in the light of this statement. Does anything need to be changed?

4 Read 6:7-15
a Can you think of ways in which you 'heap up empty phrases' when you pray? What does Jesus give as the main reason why his disciples should not do this (p. 144)?

## STUDY GUIDE

**b** If God 'knows what you need before you ask him' (6:8), why do we need to pray at all (p. 145)?

**c** The distinctive thing about Christian prayer is the nature of the God we address. What does the Lord's Prayer tell us about God? How are these aspects reflected in your own prayers?

**d** This model prayer begins by focusing attention on God – on *his* name, *his* kingdom and *his* will – rather than our own reputation, influence and desires. How much of a priority is this in your own prayers?

**e** What do you understand by 'bread' in 6:11 (pp. 148f.)? Why does Jesus specify '*daily* bread'?

**f** Why is God's forgiveness of us dependent on our forgiving those who have wronged us (pp. 149f.)? Can you think of anyone against whom you harbour resentment or bitterness? How do you think God views this?

**g** What problems does the request 'lead us not into temptation' give rise to? How does the author answer these (p. 150)? What do you think?

**h** 'In the Lord's Prayer Christians are obsessed with God …' (p. 151). How does this attitude differ from the prayers of a. The Pharisees, and b. the Gentile pagans?

# SESSION FIVE
## Matthew 6:19-34 (pages 153-173)

In the first half of chapter 6, Jesus has called his disciples to renounce religious hypocrisy and live as children of their heavenly Father. He turns now to the subject of material needs and ambitions. Again the call is the same: be different!

1 Read 6:19-21

   a This is the first of four choices which Jesus lays before us. Do these verses mean that Christians should, for example, have no savings (pp. 154f.)? If not, what is Jesus getting at here?

   b What do you think Jesus means by 'treasures in heaven' (p. 156)? What distinguishes them from 'treasures on earth'?

2 Read 6:22-23

Bearing in mind the previous verses, what is the 'eye' a picture of here (pp. 157f.)? What sort of things distort your vision? What can you do to make your eye 'sound'?

3 Read 6:24

What would count as 'mammon' in your life (p. 158)? How would you answer someone who said that Jesus is mistaken and that it *is* possible to serve (literally, 'be a slave to') God and mammon?

4 Read 6:25-34

   a What is the significance of the 'Therefore' at the beginning of 6:25 (pp. 159f.)?

   b Jesus contrasts the ambitions of the Gentiles (6:32) with

what his disciples should seek after (6:33). What are your ambitions in life? How do these verses relate to them?

c List the reasons Jesus gives for *not* being preoccupied with food and clothing (pp. 161ff.). How much does concern for material things influence your life? What do these verses suggest you can do to lessen your anxiety about these things?

d The author mentions three wrong deductions which some people make on the basis of these verses (pp. 165ff.). What are they and how would you answer them?

e In contrast to the inappropriate and unworthy ambitions of the heathen, Jesus gives altogether higher goals for the Christian to seek. What does it mean to 'seek first the kingdom of God' (pp. 170f.)? How does this apply to you? In what ways will tomorrow need to be different if you take this seriously?

f Do you agree with the author's interpretation of what it means to 'seek first God's righteousness' (pp. 171f.)? If not, how would you explain it? Either way, what changes do you need to make to your life in the light of this command?

g 'Lesser ambitions are safe and right provided that they are not an end in themselves (namely ourselves) but the means to a greater end (the spread of God's kingdom and righteousness)' (p. 173). Spend some time thinking and praying about your goals in life in the light of this statement.

# *SESSION SIX*

## *Matthew 7:1-12 (pages 174-192)*

From looking at the way Christians are to live as individuals, Jesus turns now to our relationships, beginning with our attitude to our fellow believers.

1  Read 7:1-5
   a  We begin with the command 'Judge not ...'. Why was Tolstoy wrong to say that 'Christ totally forbids the human institution of any law court' (p. 175)? Why is it wrong to say that Christ is here telling his disciples to refrain from making value-judgments (p. 176)? What then *does* Jesus mean here?

   b  'To be censorious is ... to try to play God' (p. 177). Can you think of instances when you have done this? What does Jesus warn about the consequences?

   c  What is the picture of the speck and the log intended to illustrate (pp. 177f.)? Can you think of ways in which this applies to you? What is the solution?

   d  'Jesus actually commands us to reprove and correct our brother' (p. 179). But what precautions should we take before doing so? Are there any situations known to you which require your action on this point?

2  Read 7:6
   a  What does the author suggest is meant by 'dogs' and 'pigs' (pp. 180ff.)? Do you know anyone who would come into this category? Why is it so important to obey this prohibition?

3 Read 7:7-11
   a Jesus turns now to our relationship with our heavenly
   Father and continues his teaching on prayer. On what
   basis does he encourage his disciples to pray (pp. 184f.)?

   b How would you answer someone who said that prayer is
   unseemly because it implies that God is ignorant or
   needs to be bullied into giving us what we need (p.
   186)?

   c How would you answer someone who said that prayer is
   unnecessary because most people get what they need
   without it (pp. 186f.)?

   d How would you answer someone who said that prayer is
   unproductive and doesn't always work (p. 188f.)?

   e 'Prayer presupposes knowledge ... faith... desire' (p.
   189). How can we grow in each of these three qualities?

4 Read 7:12
   'Such love is beyond us apart from the grace of God' (p.
   190). Think of situations where you have failed to live up
   to this high standard and pray together for the grace to
   love as God loves.

# SESSION SEVEN

*Matthew 7:13-29 (pages 193-222)*

1 Read 7:13-14
   a Jesus describes two ways. What are the four
   characteristics of each (pp. 193ff.)? To what extent have

you found what Jesus says here to be true in your own experience?

b 'There is no third alternative' (p. 196). What are the implications for us if we believe this?

2   Read 7:15-20
a Why are false prophets so dangerous (pp. 198f.)?

b In what way are false prophets deceptive (pp. 199f.)? How does Jesus instruct his disciples to tell the difference between the true and the false (pp. 200ff.)? How is this aspect of Jesus' teaching to be applied in your own situation?

3   Read 7:21-23
Jesus comes now to his conclusion. What positive features can you identify in those whom Jesus calls 'evildoers' (pp. 206ff.)? What is the crucial thing they lack?

4   Read 7:24-27
a Ultimately, there are only two possible responses to this Sermon (pp. 208f.). What are they?

b Can you think of ways in which you have heard the words of Jesus without putting them into practice? What are the dangers of doing this?

c 'The Bible is a dangerous book to read ... the church is a dangerous society to join' (p. 210). Why?

5   Read 7:28-29
a How would you answer someone who said that the Sermon on the Mount is a plain account of Jesus' ethical teaching without the unnecessary supernatural dogma

about Jesus which Christianity has acquired since (pp. 212f.)?

b  What was the reaction to Jesus' teaching (pp. 213f.)? How did he differ from the scribes? What was this due to?

c  The author goes on to suggest that the Sermon supports fundamental Christian claims about Jesus and his authority (pp. 213ff.). What evidence is there that Jesus is the Christ? The Lord? The Saviour? The Judge? The Son of God? God himself?

d  'Only when the Christian community lives by Christ's manifesto will the world be attracted and God be glorified' (p. 222). What steps do you need to take in order to align your life more closely with Jesus' teaching in this Sermon? Pray for one another as you put these into practice.